VIKING
Published by the Penguin Group
Penguin Books USA Inc., 375 Hudson Street,
New York, New York 10014, U.S.A.
Penguin Books Ltd, 27 Wrights Lane, London W8 5TZ, England
Penguin Books Australia Ltd, Ringwood, Victoria, Australia
Penguin Books Canada Ltd, 10 Alcorn Avenue,
Toronto, Ontario, Canada M4V 3B2
Penguin Books (N.Z.) Ltd, 182–190 Wairau Road,
Auckland 10, New Zealand

Penguin Books Ltd, Registered Offices:
Harmondsworth, Middlesex, England

First published in 1995 by Viking Penguin,
a division of Penguin Books USA Inc.

1   3   5   7   9   10   8   6   4   2

ISBN 0-670-86236-3

CIP DATA AVAILABLE

This book is printed on acid-free paper
∞

Printed in the United States of America
Set in Adobe Minion
Designed by Kathryn Parise

To Rosie

ACKNOWLEDGMENTS

Dr. Howard Frost did some wonderful work tracking down sources who did not want to talk and others who wanted to tell their story. His training as an analyst at the Central Intelligence Agency honed a sharp mind that was never satisfied with one account but always searched for the checks and balances that sifted rumor from fact and fact from fiction. I am truly grateful for all his hard work.

Lia Macko helped with the early research. Her enthusiasm, hard work, and tenacious nature will prove a real asset for any law firm that finally gets the benefit of her talents after she obtains her degree.

Jaimie Seaton, my assistant, put up with the additional pressure of producing this book under very tight deadlines. She is not only very resourceful but also is remarkably tolerant of the tension that arises during the production of a book.

A large number of people took the trouble to speak to me and to review the manuscript. I am grateful to them all for their time and their insights into the Ames case and the workings of the intelligence community.

It is common for authors to curse their publishers for their incompetence and inefficiency. I have found Jane von Mehren, my editor, Tamar Mendelson, her assistant, and all the other staff at Viking Penguin to be consummate professionals. On the production team: Teddy Rosenbaum, Kathie Parise, Amy Hill, Neil Stuart, Roni Axelrod, Alix Mac-Gowan, and Cindy Achar. And on the sales and marketing team: Cathy Hemming, Mary Ellen Curley, Paul Slovak, Matthew Bradley, Dave Nelson, and Mike Geoghegan. This book was produced under very tough deadlines, and each time they got tougher, Jane and her colleagues rose to the challenge. I could not have asked for a better team.

Finally, I am truly fortunate to be one of those writers who can work from home. This blessing means that I can spend time with my wife and children and actually have a life. It also means that my wife, René, has to be very understanding of the creative process, which she sees in all its highs and lows. She is a wonderful woman and it is her love that makes all this both possible and worthwhile.

CONTENTS

SELLOUT

ONE

"Think. Think. Think."

For Les Wiser, Presidents' Day, Monday, February 21, 1994, was going to be a very good day. For more than two years, he had been tracking a man he had come to both admire and despise, a man who had done more damage to national security than any other individual in American history; a man so clever that he had fooled every security check for more than ten years, and yet a man so stupid that he had practically sent an open invitation to Wiser to come and get him.

This had been the toughest of all his cases in his seven years in the Counter Intelligence Division of the FBI's Washington office. Nothing, not the occasional Russian spy, not the routine surveillance at the Russian Embassy at Sixteenth and M streets, four blocks from the White House, had prepared him for this. Aldrich Ames would be the highest-profile case of his career, the one that would make or break him and the one that would teach the T-Bars—Those Bastards Across the River, at Langley—a serious lesson about life in the real world of spies.

Well, that Monday was the day. Wiser and his FBI team had decided to move in because the next day Ames believed he was due to fly to Ankara and Moscow on an assignment for the CIA. Such a trip was both routine and dangerous, a possible opportunity for Wiser's target to defect to the people who had been paying his bills for so many years. For months now, the FBI, in concert with the CIA, had maintained the fiction that their target was a legitimate employee with legitimate work. There had been assignments to Rome and New York. There had been movement within the Agency, and now there was the supposed trip to Moscow, a final piece of reassurance designed to lull their target into a sense of false security just before the trap was sprung. And all the time Wiser and his men had been watching, photographing, taping, and copying. Now the net had closed, Operation Nightmover was in its final phase, and Rick Ames was about to be snared.[1]

Mark Hulkower, the assistant U.S. attorney in charge of the prosecution of the Ames case, had met up with Wiser early that morning to get the arrest warrants for Ames and his wife, Rosario, from Judge Barry Poretz in the Alexandria District Court in Virginia. It was a public holiday and both men were wearing jeans and open-necked shirts, projecting a casual image that belied the seriousness of the case. Hulkower, described by his boss as "one of the best prosecutors in America," made a perfect partner for Wiser. The prosecutor is in his late thirties and is a keen basketball fan who is fond of tossing a ball at visitors to his office. He has a ready sense of humor, something that endeared him to Wiser, who looked and occasionally acted like a young Groucho Marx. The vital pieces of paper in hand, they walked across the parking lot and got into the unmarked FBI car that awaited them. Caught up in the excitement of the moment, the Bureau driver turned on the siren and headed for the Ames house, a journey of about fifteen minutes. As the car left the parking lot, Wiser was already on the phone to his team, telling them that the operation was a Go.[2]

For Rick Ames, this day was the beginning of another exciting stage in his career—not his apparently successful career at the CIA but his covert career as the Russian master spy who for many years had managed to make a mockery of America's counter intelligence efforts. He was looking forward to tomorrow's trip. It would be an opportunity to see his masters in Moscow and a chance to arrange for more money to help pay for the apparently endless purchases that his forty-two-year-old wife, Rosario, seemed to need to keep her happy. It would also be an opportunity to set up a new communications network; Rosario had become convinced that people had been snooping around and she was worried that the Agency might have started the long-feared investigation. He had tried to reassure her, but she was getting increasingly paranoid. This trip would set her fears to rest.

When the telephone rang, it was the office calling him to an early-morning meeting to discuss the final details of his trip to Moscow the next day. He was disappointed, because he had been looking forward to spending the holiday at home with his family. But there was no time to waste. He swiftly put on his coat and left the house. As he walked the short distance to his car, there was no sign of the FBI agents who were now surrounding him. There were about twenty of them that morning, some on foot, others in unmarked vehicles that were parked in sight of the house with still more just around the corner.

He got into his maroon Jaguar XJ6 and backed out of the driveway of his house at 2512 North Randolph Street in the leafy suburb of Arlington, Virginia. He made a right turn onto Quebec, which is a short street leading to Nellie Custis Drive. The FBI had two cars waiting at the junction, one with a right-turn signal blinking, and one apparently turning left. As the unsuspecting fifty-two-year-old Ames pulled up behind them, two other cars came around the corner with their red lights flashing.

"He looked in his rearview mirror and, seeing the red light, pulled to the side so that they could pass, so that they could go about doing what they were going to do. Except that they were there for him," recalled Wiser.[3]

The whole operation took about forty-five seconds, and suddenly Ames realized that the moment of reckoning had come. He was politely asked to step out of the car and place his hands on the roof of the Jaguar. Then he was frisked before being handcuffed and placed in the back of one of the FBI vehicles for the short drive to their base in the nearby office and shopping complex at Tysons Corner.

At first Ames protested. "What's this about?" he shouted at the FBI agents. "You've got the wrong guy."

When he realized the protests were making no difference, he settled into the car, apparently already resigned to his fate. There were no more anguished protests, no look of fear at what might lie ahead. Instead, he hunched in the backseat, muttering to himself over and over again, "Think. Think. Think."[4]

The first words he spoke in the car when he was told that he was about to be charged with spying were: "Espionage? You've got to be kidding." It was a mantra he would repeat again and again during the short journey, as if merely uttering the words would convince his captors of his innocence.

Back at the house, Rosario was in the upstairs bathroom putting on her makeup before taking her son, Paul, to school. Her mother, Cecilia, who had arrived a few days earlier from Colombia, was still asleep in the guest bedroom. Rosario made the school run to nearby Alexandria every morning in her 1989 Honda four-door, and as usual, she was late. The bell rang, and as the housekeeper went to answer the bell, Rosario moved from the bathroom to look down the stairs at the front door. A young man and a heavily pregnant woman were standing on the doorstep. She knew immediately and instinctively what the couple wanted. It was the fear she had lived with for more than eighteen months since discovering that her husband was a traitor. Back then, she had hoped that Rick might be able to remain undiscovered until he retired in eight years' time. It had always been a forlorn hope. But Rosario had convinced herself that everything would be all right, that the Agency would never discover what her husband had been doing. She told herself that he was doing nothing important, and so they would never bother with him. She could not have been more wrong.

The FBI agent at the door asked Rosario to step outside the house, out of earshot of her son, and explained that she would have to come with them. She was allowed inside the house for a final hug and a kiss with Paul and an embrace from her mother. She took off some of the gold jewelry she was wearing, packed some clothes, and then moved unresisting toward the car. It was only when she was seated in the back of the car that the handcuffs were placed around her wrists—an unusual courtesy, because the cuffs are usually put on at the moment of arrest. But the FBI wanted Rosario on their side. From the beginning they wanted her to feel that this was as uncomfortable for them as it obviously was for her. They wanted her to tell them what she knew and to turn against her husband.

These subtleties were largely lost on Rosario. As the car pulled away, she could only think of two things: the enormity of her husband's betrayal—not of his country but of herself and her family—and the damage it would do to her son. Over the previous months it had been Paul, and not Rick, who had sustained her. Although essentially a selfish and vain woman, she genuinely loved her son. She glanced back over her shoulder to see Paul staring at her from the living-room window. It was a sight she would recall many times in the dark months that lay ahead.

In the car carrying Rick to the FBI office, news of Rosario's arrest came over the radio, along with a report that FBI agents had secured the house and were beginning a search of the premises. This information seemed finally to bring home to Rick that his life had taken a dramatic turn for the worse. As the message ended, he bowed his head deep into his chest and said: "Oh, fuck."[5]

There was no immediate announcement of the arrests to the media, and the comfortable middle-class area was rife with gossip all that day. William Rhoads, one of the Ameses' neighbors, watched with his wife as five official cars drew up to the house "with people in them, just waiting for something to happen."[6]

The Rhoadses watched as the agents went up to the house, waited at the door, and then disappeared inside. With the curiosity of a retired man with time on his hands, Rhoads got his binoculars from a back room and peered through them at the scene that unfolded before him. He was certain that the Feds—he noted that all the cars had District of Columbia license plates, so this had to be a federal action—were running a drug bust, given the lavish lifestyle of his neighbors and Rosario's Colombian origins.

A short time later, Nancy Everly, Rick's sister, arrived at the house. The FBI had offered Rosario the option of having her mother and Paul stay in a hotel for the night or having Rick's sister come to take care of the child. Rosario had always gotten on well with Nancy, and, more important, Paul liked his aunt, and so the FBI had summoned her to the house. It was to fall to Nancy, the most loyal sister a traitor could have, to hold the family together over the next few months as the magnitude of her brother's betrayal began to surface.

Later that afternoon, FBI agents went from house to house on the quiet street to ask some standard questions about the Ameses. Just how well had the neighbors known them? Had they ever noticed anything suspicious about the family? The answers were uniformly bland. Rick and Rosario had kept to themselves, and only occasionally had neighbors seen little Paul playing on the perfectly manicured lawn that ran down to the street. The FBI men, understanding the storm that was about to be unleashed, told each resident that he or she could speak to the press. Rhoads asked the agents what the Ameses had done and was told: "Well, all we can tell you is that it's not drugs and you're going to have to wait."

Rick and Rosario arrived at the FBI office at Tysons Corner a few minutes apart. In one room a fake operations center had been set up that was specifically designed to deal a devastating psychological blow to the couple. The walls were lined with enormous blown-up photographs of the Ames house. There were pictures of all the dead drops the couple had used over the past two years, along with transcripts of telephone conversations and logs of the surveillance teams. To add to the "lived-in" look, the tables had the coffee stains, the piles of old newspapers, and the candy wrappers that are common to all such offices. Separately, Rick Ames and then Rosario were led into this room, the agents telling them that they needed a few moments to organize the paperwork before processing them.

In the ten-minute journey from Arlington to Tysons Corner, Rick had been trying to convince himself that once again he could talk himself out of trouble. Clearly, the Bureau thought they had evidence or they wouldn't have arrested him. But perhaps it would not be enough. After all, they had made mistakes in the past with Felix Bloch and Edward Lee Howard, and maybe the investigators had been forced to move too early. But as his eyes took in the room and the clear evidence that every move he had made over the past few months—every covert meeting, every private conversation, every stroke on his computer keyboard—had been watched and recorded by the FBI, he knew his career as a spy was over. As he saw the wealth of evidence in the room, his shoulders hunched and his head sank into his chest. It was just the admission of defeat that the FBI wanted to see.

"If the FBI is arresting me, then I'm sure they have a good case," he said.

Good case or not, Ames was experienced enough to know that if you are arrested, the first rule is to say nothing. To the chagrin of the Bureau agents he followed his training and refused to answer their questions. Instead, he asked for a lawyer.

Rosario, too, was taken into the fake office, but she either didn't understand the full extent of what she was being shown or else she was made of sterner stuff, because she continued to deny any involvement in spying. The pair were taken to separate rooms to be read their rights and to be photographed and fingerprinted. When Rosario was led to the interview room, she broke down, alternately sobbing and protesting her innocence to anyone who was prepared to listen.

"During the whole time, she was pretty upset and distraught and completely denied her husband had been spying and that she had been assisting him," said Hulkower.

Wiser then controlled what turned out to be a three-hour-long interrogation. He produced document after document, which he carefully laid down in front of her. There were transcripts of telephone conversations that made it clear that Rosario not only knew about Rick's spying but had actually participated in some of it. There were the records of surveillance operations that showed Rick meeting his Soviet and Russian controllers. There were the hundreds of thousands of dollars that Rick had paid into bank accounts in Virginia, Switzerland, and Colombia. But a crying, sometimes screaming Rosario continued to deny everything.

Both Wiser and Hulkower had obviously seen all the evidence and been outraged at the role Rick had been playing. They had little sympathy for Rosario. According to the evidence the FBI had produced, she had freely spent much of Rick's ill-gotten gains. They determined to squeeze her until they could hear the pips squeak.

"Mrs. Ames knew she was riding on a Russian gravy train, and when she learned of it, she jumped in with both feet," Hulkower said. "She did it for the same reason as the evidence establishes Mr. Ames did it—money."[7]

The FBI had decided on a strategy of keeping the couple apart after the arrests. While confident about their case, they wanted Ames to sweat while they worked on Rosario. They knew from the months of surveillance that she was an intelligent but volatile woman, prone to bouts of savage temper and periods of depression and instability. In the ruthless game they were playing, these were weaknesses they could comfortably exploit.

The two agents who had arrested Rosario, including the pregnant Spanish-speaking woman, conducted the immediate interrogation.

"The case is clear against Rick," they explained to Rosario. "There is no doubt of his guilt, so you might as well confess to everything and do what you can to help our case. We are not interested in you." The agents then proceeded to dazzle her with the extent of their knowledge about her life with Rick and the spying Ames had masterminded over the previous nine years.

"They had far more information about me and Rick than I ever knew," she said.[8]

The experience was devastating. She had expected a recitation of petty crimes, the passing of pieces of intelligence that Rick had told her the Soviets knew anyway. Instead, she was hammered with one fact after another. Rick had been a master spy, they said, one of the best. He had not just betrayed his country; he had betrayed the Agency that had employed the Ames family for most of this century. Worst of all, he was directly responsible for the deaths of at least ten American agents working in the Soviet Union. Rick Ames was a mass murderer.

She found it impossible to accept that the man she thought she knew so well, whom she had once loved so much, could have betrayed her so cunningly and so successfully. Above all, she had to come to terms with the fact that Rick was a killer, that the father of her child was little better than the gangsters who nightly engaged in drug-related killings in downtown Washington. She turned to the one anchor that remained in her life and asked the FBI agents if she could call her son to see if he was all right. They agreed, and while she was on the phone with Nancy Everly and her mother, they heard her saying: "I'll tell them what I know; I've got to take care of myself."

She hung up the phone, turned to the agents, and said: "Okay, I've been lying." It was an admission of defeat, a recognition that she had nowhere to turn and that a confession was perhaps her only chance of surviving the onslaught that had been unleashed against herself and her husband. What followed was to be one of the rare occasions when Rosario would be honest with herself and with her interrogators, a time when her defenses were so far down that the real Rosario emerged as a terrified and defenseless ingenue. Now Hulkower came into the room to confront Rosario.

"I told him what I knew, which wasn't much," she said.

She admitted that Rick had been a spy for years, and at first said she had known about it since 1991, but then changed her story to say that she had discovered his other life the following year. As Hulkower pressed for details, she said she knew nothing of substance, that she had taken no part in his spying, although she had been aware of Rick's trips to South America to meet with the Russians. To the disbelief of the interrogators, she insisted that the lavish lifestyle she had enjoyed since her marriage to Rick had been entirely supported by some wise investments that her husband had made while at the University of Chicago thirty years earlier.

As Hulkower unpeeled layer after layer of the evidence—tape recordings, accounts of meetings with foreign agents, secret bank deposits, the years of deception and lying—Rosario's story gradually changed. Yes, she knew about Rick's spying, and she acknowledged that she participated in discussions with him during which she offered encouragement and advice. She also admitted accompanying him on at least one trip when he signaled his Russian handlers, and commented on the many "structured" deposits Ames had made in his local accounts.[9]

Despite her cooperation, Rosario was not allowed to return home and was not to see her son again.

The pretrial hearing took place the next day. The court documents were unusually detailed, running to thirty-nine pages of single-spaced type. They made for sorry reading, spelling out in exhaustive detail just how much damage Ames had achieved in nearly a decade of spying for the Soviets.

The prosecution claimed that Ames was an agent of the Russian foreign intelligence service, the SVR, which was the heir of the now defunct KGB. Since 1985, Ames had been paid $2.7 million for the information he supplied to the Russians, money that he had laundered through a number of bank accounts both in America and abroad. In return for that money, Ames had handed over a wealth of intelligence data to his masters. Exactly what he had done was not spelled out in the court documents, but it was to prove the most devastating list of betrayals ever seen in the history of American intelligence.

At the time of his arrest, Ames's spying was downplayed by officials, who described it as a serious case but gave no hint of the levels at which he had operated. In fact, as a former chief of the Counter Intelligence

Division in the CIA, Ames was the highest source ever recruited by the KGB. He was in a position to know most of the darkest secrets of the Agency, from personnel to tradecraft, from sources to methods. And he was easily able to obtain any information he did not have, and to pass it on to his masters in Moscow.

Over the nine years he had been spying for the U.S.S.R., Ames had betrayed almost every member of the Operations Directorate of the CIA, the men and women who go into the field to recruit sources, run agents, and gather intelligence. He had handed over personnel records, photographs, and details of individual agents' personal and professional characteristics that were to prove priceless for the Russians in countering the work of the CIA in the final years of the Cold War and into the current era. In addition, he passed over thousands—no one knows how many thousands—of pages of CIA documents, most of them marked top secret, which he would simply run through the photocopier or transfer to a floppy disk and take home to hand over to his controllers at a later date.

He managed to track down and identify all the CIA's major sources in the Soviet Union and passed their names to Moscow. At least ten of these agents were killed, including Top Hat, the most valuable source the CIA had ever recruited in the Soviet Union. His betrayals extended beyond the CIA as well: Ames revealed the identity of the most important asset recruited by British intelligence inside the KGB, who narrowly escaped arrest and almost certain death. Dozens of other agents were compromised and operations betrayed.

"Ames was without doubt the most valuable asset the Soviets or the Russians have ever had in Western intelligence in modern times," said one senior Western intelligence official. "He was unique in that he betrayed everybody and everything without any hesitation. His commitment was absolute, and he did it all without any real drive from Moscow. He simply acted as a vacuum cleaner, sweeping everything up that came within range and passing it along."[10]

The result of Ames's treachery was the effective destruction of the CIA's operations against the Soviet Union at the end of the 1980s and the beginning of the 1990s. Of course, technical intelligence—information gathered by satellites and other means—was still a valuable resource. But in intelligence, it is the eyes and ears on the ground that provide the confirmation of decisions taken or plans being made, and without that intelligence, policymakers are working, if not in the dark, than certainly partially blind. For nearly a decade, at a time when Communism was collapsing and democracy was struggling to find its feet, the world's largest intelligence organization had no operating sources inside the Soviet Union. It is hard to overemphasize this extraordinary lapse, both for the blindness it produced in Western policymakers and for what it tells us about the requirements of intelligence in the post–Cold War world.

Yet, for much of that decade, the CIA refused to accept that Ames was a spy in their midst. They refused to believe that anyone would enter their culture and abuse it so directly and with such terrible consequences. The signs were there for anyone who took the trouble to look closely: Ames was an alcoholic with a long history of substance abuse. His superiors had reported him drunk numerous times, and yet nobody had taken any action. He had divorced his first wife and then married a foreign national, an act in itself grounds for restricting his promotion. He had consistently received poor performance reports, failing at almost every assignment he took on. Each of these failures on its own should have been sufficient to stop his career in its tracks. Yet it was time-card punching and not performance that mattered at the CIA, and so Ames stayed at his desk, serving his time and getting promoted.

And then there was his personal lifestyle. He had paid more than $500,000 in cash for a house as large as the head of the CIA's—and even the director of central intelligence had a mortgage. Ames ran up credit-card bills that were far in excess of those of any other employee at a similar level and were clearly unsustainable with the salary he earned from the Agency. He drove a new Jaguar sports car, and yet none of the apparently intelligent Agency officers thought to ask just how he could afford such a car on a salary that allowed them to buy only Honda Accords. He paid tens of thousands of dollars into his personal bank accounts in Virginia, money that again far exceeded his normal salary.

Even a cursory check of his lifestyle would have revealed that Ames was receiving money from sources outside the Agency. That investigation would in turn have been certain to discover his spying activity and would have shut down the most valuable intelligence operation ever mounted by the Russians against the United States.

But counter espionage at the Agency was hamstrung by the culture at Langley. There was a fundamental belief that one of their own could do no wrong. As later investigations were to reveal, this culture went much deeper than simply the refusal to believe (in defiance of all the known laws of espionage) in the existence of traitors. What existed at Langley was an introspective society in which behavior that would be completely unacceptable in the outside world was treated as normal. Drunkenness, sexual discrimination, and financial abuses were commonplace, and acceptable as part of the price to be paid for working in the "wilderness of mirrors." The FBI had been trying to force the Agency to search for the traitor the Bureau was convinced was hiding at Langley; the CIA's tactics of delay and obstruction not only were frustrating but also created a great deal of bad blood between the two groups. They were supposed to be fighting on the same side against the Russians, but frequently the war was between the two agencies in Washington, a failing that Moscow swiftly exploited.

For Les Wiser and his team of FBI agents the task of discovering the traitor at Langley was a triumph in and of itself. But the Ames story is more than just the tale of the hunt for a traitor. After all, Ames was a dull drunk, a man who in any other walk of life would have been considered a failure, and yet a man who turned out to be a master spy. Once in jail, he seemed to understand perfectly well the success he had finally made of his life. He seemed quiet, peaceful almost, as if all the anxiety of the past few years had been put to rest. He relished the attention from his interrogators and the media, using every opportunity to sarcastically criticize the ineptitude of the people who had seen fit to hire him in the first place. Intelligence, he claimed, was worthless currency, and the CIA was not even producing properly minted banknotes.

In normal times, few would have paid attention to Ames. Like other spies before him, he would have been jailed, tried, and sentenced to serve out the rest of his life in a small cell in a prison that nobody would ever visit. But these were not normal times, and the arrest of Rick Ames was to act as a catalyst for all those who felt that American intelligence had failed to deliver in the Cold War and was failing to adjust to the needs of the post-Communist world. For them, Ames became a symbol of the CIA's indolence and served as a salutary illustration of the need to clean house.

For most of his career, Ames worked in the Soviet/East European Division of the Operations Directorate of the CIA, the single most important area within the Agency, which focused on getting secret intelligence against the Soviet target. The SE Division was supposed to justify all the other branches of the CIA. It was there that the sources deep inside the Kremlin were recruited and run. It was there that the vital pieces of intelligence were gathered and circulated to the president and the joint chiefs of staff to help them make the decision about peace and war. It was there that the Cold War could—literally—have been won or lost.

And yet Ames managed to destroy the operating capability of the SE Division so completely that for years it was producing no useful intelligence at all. That alone should have set alarm bells off across the intelligence community. But, as later investigations were to reveal, such was the culture of obsessive secrecy within both the SE Division and the Directorate of Operations (DO) that nobody was ever told the full extent of the damage that had been done. Even successive directors of central intelligence were not told that their most important asset had essentially stopped functioning.

The fact that such an important area of the CIA was allowed to operate in this way is indicative of just how deeply and destructively the Agency's culture has been ingrained into the officers who work in the covert side of the Agency. It is they and not their masters at Langley or in the White House who know best. It is they who decide who should know what, and when. That arrogance allowed Rick Ames to survive and prosper at enormous cost to America and her allies.

Just how high a price will eventually be paid as a result of Rick Ames's acts is still unclear. As each month goes by, new information appears that makes the damage assessment look bleaker and bleaker. Every covert officer compromised, every piece of tradecraft built up over the years handed over to the Russians, every code at risk, every source betrayed—those are the immediate consequences to the intelligence-gathering capability of the CIA. But there are other problems still to be resolved: the future of the Agency itself, the rebuilding of shattered morale, and the restoration of confidence among America's allies that intelligence shared with Washington is not also shared with Moscow.

As one senior British intelligence officer put it: "When we lost Kim Philby to the Russians, it took us twenty years to recover. It will take the CIA just as long."[11]

The irony is that Ames was a failure who became one of the world's greatest spies. But his real legacy will be that his cumulative acts of treachery have so undermined the American intelligence community that it will be forever changed by his acts. The CIA as we know it today will be radically altered, and many other branches of American intelligence will be changed as well. Rick Ames has turned out to be many things: failed CIA officer, Soviet master spy, and agent of change. This is his story.

TWO

Sowing the Seeds

Rick was born Aldrich Hazen Ames on May 26, 1941, in River Falls, Wisconsin, a small rural community of around six thousand people that was surrounded by rolling hills and lush green meadows. For a man who was later to become such a calculating traitor, his background was one that many less fortunate Americans might envy. His family can trace their roots in America well back into the last century. Theirs was a classic story of Middle America, a solidly prosperous, well-educated family who gave to the community and received a great deal in return. Running through the generations were a love of the arts, a concern for others, and a clear belief in the fundamentals of American life: family, community, and democracy.

In a small town like River Falls, the Ames family were prominent figures. Rick's father, Carleton, taught at River Falls Teachers College, where Rick's grandfather Jesse had a long tenure as president. Located in the west-central part of Wisconsin, between Eau Claire and Minneapolis–St. Paul, the school at River Falls was originally founded in the western part of the state in 1874 by some New Englanders as the River Falls Normal School.[1]

The town in the post–World War II years was a typical "old-time" American community. There was little diversity, and it was a place for people who were strongly committed to teaching (especially to training educators) and who were comfortable working at a minor league college at a low salary.

Jesse Hazen (J.H.) Ames, Rick's grandfather, was born in Maine, Wisconsin, in 1875. His father, George, had moved to the area from the Green Mountains of New Hampshire after being discharged from the Union Army. Jesse's mother's family, the McMains (shortened by some members to "Main") had come from Canada to northeastern Wisconsin when that part of the state was being settled in the 1850s. His father had come to work in the lumber business, and served as foreman with the Sherry Lumber Company, where J.H. worked for a while before deciding that he wanted to teach.[2]

He went to Stevens Point Normal School for his training, then served as principal of a number of schools in Cumberland, Ellsworth, and Stanley, Wisconsin. In 1909, J.H. came to River Falls Normal School to teach social studies, and served as interim president in 1911. He left to join the University Extension Service in Eau Claire, returning to River Falls in 1914 to supervise the training school. After the incumbent president, J. W. Crabtree, resigned in 1917, J.H. was elected president, a position he was to hold for the next twenty-eight years. Such a prestigious post made J.H. a formidable presence in the town and he had a continuing impact on several generations of students. A commentary on President Ames in the 1946 annual, *The Meletean*, notes that he "has directed the institution through nothing short of a revolution," in terms of his overseeing its progression from a normal school to a college and then the recognition of the new stature of the institution by the North Central Association of Colleges and Universities.[3]

Rick's father, Carleton C. Ames, was born on August 5, 1905. He was the 1922 River Falls High School valedictorian, and opted to follow in his father's footsteps, graduating from the River Falls Teachers College in 1925. After he had held four teaching jobs in twelve years in what looked like an uninspiring career, Dad stepped in.[4] In a useful piece of nepotism, Jesse brought his son to River Falls in 1937 to teach sociology and the history of Europe and the Far East.

It is difficult at this distance to establish the relationship between father and son, but it is clear that Jesse was a powerful man and an undoubtedly strong influence on his son. Pictures from the time show a stern figure, and his writings depict time and again a high sense of moral rectitude combined with a sense of mission. Despite his success at school (something Rick was later to emulate), Carleton seems an altogether weaker figure, with little of the ambition that propelled Jesse forward. Perhaps recognizing his son's lack of drive, or perhaps because he wanted him to be close to his own influence, Jesse must have decided to bring Carleton under his own wing at River Falls. Given that Carleton's life later showed such a continuing sense of failure, this closeness must have been both corrupting and stifling.

East Asia was the focus of Carleton's work; he did his dissertation on the role of the British in Burma while he was on leave from River Falls at the University of Wisconsin at Madison, and he received his doctorate there in 1949. Carleton only taught in the history department for the last four or five years of his time at River Falls. Tenure wasn't hard to obtain, provided the teaching was satisfactory, because there was no need to establish a track record of published research, a normal requirement in more prestigious universities.[5] But Carleton never bothered to get tenure, perhaps because his father controlled appointments at the school and he thought there was no need for such a formality. Or it may be that, even in that comparatively relaxed environment, tenure for Carleton would have been impossible because of opposition from his colleagues.

From the beginning, Carleton's appointment sat uneasily with other members of the faculty. As at all schools, there were rivalry and backbiting among the teachers, and Carleton was seen as a favorite son who had gotten his job not on merit but through his father's influence. Today, the memory of his presence and his performance as a mediocre teacher still rankles.

"Ninety percent of the faculty regarded Carleton as a first-class case of nepotism," said Bennie Kettelkamp, the former chairman of the River Falls biology department. "Many of us felt Carleton had no business being on the faculty."[6]

Two years after he arrived in River Falls, Carleton married Rachel Aldrich, an attractive, innocent woman who came to River Falls from New Richmond. She was born on May 27, 1918, and graduated

from New Richmond High School, about twenty miles north of River
Falls, in 1936. In a classic teacher-meets-student love story, Rachel attended one of Carleton's classes, they fell in love, and they were married
in 1939. From the outset, it was clear to family and friends that this was
an old-fashioned marriage, in which the husband was the dominant
partner and the obviously highly intelligent wife was content to subordi-
nate her ambitions to her spouse's career.

"Within the family, and to his friends, Carleton was called King, apparently because he had once played a king in a college production. And
no one called his wife Rachel. In the family," said Nancy Everly, "it was
King and Rae."[7]

Rachel completed her B.S. in secondary education as an English major
in 1940, a year before Rick was born. The births of Nancy and Alison followed in 1942 and 1945. Despite the clear talents she showed later in life,
Rachel was content to bring up her children and did not work for much
of the time they stayed in River Falls.[8] Rachel was a good mother, and
friends say that she seemed to give her children all the love they might
have wanted. Rachel confided to Helen Wyman, the wife of Walker
Wyman, a former history professor at River Falls and a family friend,
that another friend had suggested that children be named after relatives.
So she gave Rick her family name (Aldrich) and Jesse's middle name
(Hazen).[9]

The Ameses first lived in the Spring Street area—at 423 East Cascade
Avenue. By all accounts, Rick's was a normal childhood, or as normal as
any child's can be when seen through the eyes of other children. Accounts from contemporaries paint a picture of a happy boy, a member of
the Cub Scouts who was cheerful in class and enthusiastic at both work
and play, dressing up in Halloween costumes for the annual parade
down Main Street and skinny-dipping in Pete's Creek behind Ted Pe-
dersen's dilapidated barn.

"I was one of the older kids and he was just a little boy," said Shirley
Bouvin, who lived across the street, describing Rick as a child. "I babysat
at the Ameses' during the day sometimes. It was an older house, bedrooms upstairs, beautiful woodwork, open porch in front, two-story, the
traditional kind of house.

"His father wasn't that friendly. His mom wasn't the greatest housekeeper. I think he had a little two-man tent he used on the side of the house in an empty lot. But he was just a small boy with dark hair."[10]

At the East Cascade Avenue house, the Ameses lived just across the alley from the Enstads, and Rick used to play with Bob Enstad, who was three years older than he. Today, Bob is a night editor at the *Chicago Tribune* and recalls Rick as a friendly, if reserved, kid with whom he would share adventures in the local playground and climb trees. After Rick's arrest, Enstad published his account of his childhood memories and this provoked a number of letters from people who had known Carleton at River Falls. It was the memory of the father and not the son that drove the correspondence, and even after all those years, the memory of Carleton apparently still rankled. All the letters were uncomplimentary, with one of them describing Rick's father as a "total bore."[11]

Bob and Rick attended the Campus School, which was attached to the university, for their elementary training. Rick went to the school through fifth grade. Analu Jurgens, who was younger than Rick and also attended the Campus School, described Rick as a "cute kid, nice, playful, outgoing, and pretty popular at school with quite a few friends." Rick would play with her older brother, Ernie, and she would play with his sister, Nancy. The boys would play marbles, football, kickball, and softball, and the girls would play Monopoly and dolls.[12]

Mark Wyman, now a historian and professor at Illinois State University in Normal, remembers running around with Rick as a child, climbing trees, splashing in the spring puddles and winter snowmelt. Charles A. (Chuck) Wall was perhaps Rick's closest boyhood friend and recalls him as "probably the first person I remember outside my family." Rick and Chuck competed for the affection of a classmate at the Campus School, a pretty little girl named Sara. At a memorable picnic, said Mark Wyman, "Rick and Chuck were wrestling over who was going to have the right to kiss Sara. She was so tiny."[13]

"Rick was not a Boy Scout," said his sister Nancy. "He did not do any sports then, he was interested in chess; he was an intellectual kid. He wore glasses as a boy of ten. Rick always had terrible eyesight. He kept to himself. Rick was a very private person."[14]

The relationship between Rick and his father appears to have been a supportive one, at least while Rick was a young boy. Carleton had an interest in poetry and a talent for theater, enthusiasms that he would pass on to Rick; he would often read poetry to his son when Rick was a little boy.

For the town gossips, the Ames family was a constant source of rich material. There were the artistic adventures, the relationship between Jesse and Carleton, and finally, the constant rumors about Carleton's drinking. According to Maruca Jurgens, a family friend, Carleton had friends fetch him whiskey lest his own entry into local taverns embarrass his strict and religious father.[15] There were weekend binges when he would vanish, only to return bleary-eyed and hungover, and there were the tantrums at home. But this was a close-knit family that had no mechanism for dealing with such emotional trauma or the sickness of alcoholism. Instead, the family simply had to conceal the harsh reality and present a united front to the world. That, too, produced its own pain, which was passed on to Rick.

"Emotions were to be repressed, not shared," Nancy remembers. "The family placed emphasis on good manners; it was partly the era, of course, but we were expected to be polite in our dealings with each other, and with parents and other adults. . . . In our family you never probed or pried, never asked, 'What are you thinking? How do you feel?' "[16]

In 1950, after thirteen years under the watchful eye of his father, Carleton had clearly had enough, and he cast around for some escape from the drudgery of life in River Falls. Coincidentally, the Central Intelligence Agency was also looking for recruits who could fill a series of gaps in their operations in the Far East. It is a measure of just how desperate the Agency was that they had to go as far as River Falls to find people. But Carleton had the skills they wanted: a knowledge of the history of South Asia, some knowledge of the languages, and, best of all, a desire to find a new challenge.

This was a turbulent time for American foreign policy. It was the early 1950s and Communism was on the march. A bloody civil war in China had just come to an end with a Communist government in power in Beijing since 1949; the Korean War began in 1950 and the Indochina war was occupying the French. It was the CIA, building on its experience in the Far East during World War II, that saw itself fighting on the front line to keep the Communist hordes at bay. The Agency had been an early supporter of Chiang Kai-shek's forces in their fight against the Communists in China and, even when that battle was lost, the CIA kept on funding and arming the defeated forces, who continued the struggle from their new headquarters in Taiwan.[17]

One of the most important covert operations at the time, called Project Paper, was supposed to produce an invasion of China by Nationalist forces based in Burma. The Agency chose as its surrogate a Nationalist general named Li Mi who had escaped from China with a force of 2,250 men in 1950. His ranks swelled to around 4,000 soldiers as other troops trickled over the border, and the Agency decided this force was an ideal nucleus on which to build an invasion. Civil Air Transport, the airline owned by the CIA, delivered tons of arms to the rebels, and Agency personnel helped in their training. Two efforts to cross the border in 1951 were easily repulsed by Chinese troops, and it appeared that Li Mi was going to be of little real value to the Agency. However, the CIA's commitment to the region remained total. There were 200 CIA men in neighboring Thailand, 600 in Taiwan, and more than 100 in Burma.

It was into this ferment of intrigue that Carleton was recruited. He was approached at the beginning of 1952 by a recruiter from Langley who offered him employment and a chance to travel to Rangoon as a first assignment. Carleton appears to have jumped at the opportunity, as he wrote to Eugene Kleinpell, the president of River Falls College, on March 17, 1952:

> This letter is to ask you to transmit to the Board of Regents my request for leave of absence without pay for one year, beginning next September 1. . . . I have been requested to spend some time in the service of the United States Government. This is in the intelligence service, probably in the Far East. Presumably, my services are expected to be of some value in the present situation.
>
> Further, since my field of study and teaching is in modern history and in Far Eastern history, it would seem that the experience which I would get through such work would be at least as valuable to me and to the institution when I return as additional graduate study. Therefore, I think, the granting of leave might very well be justified.

The request was granted by the board on the assumption that Carleton would return to River Falls within a year. The family moved to Washington, D.C., and rented an apartment at 4941 North Capitol Street. Carleton commuted to work at Langley via bus and streetcar. What was supposed to be a one-year leave swiftly extended as the training provided by the Agency stretched from weeks into months. Ames wrote to Kleinpell on August 3, 1952, to say simply that he was enjoying life but "I can tell you little or nothing of what I am doing. The work so far is extremely interesting. Right now I am in training with no definite information as to the next move."

The reason Carleton was not in Burma already was that the Agency's involvement with Li Mi had been exposed, causing a furor in both America and Burma. The Chinese Communists had first aired the allegation that America was involved in funding and arming guerrillas based in Burma in December 1951. This was robustly denied both by the State Department and by Dean Acheson, the secretary of state. But in February of the following year, *The New York Times* reported that Li Mi's troops had been seen carrying new American weapons. Further information on Operation Paper continued to trickle out during 1952, forcing the CIA to put many of its operations in the area on hold.

To add to its problems, the man created by the Agency was turning into a monster. Li Mi had begun an involvement in the opium business that was later to create the Golden Triangle, which continues to be one of the world's principal sources of heroin. At the same time, his invasions of China were still unsuccessful, and so he turned his attention to the Burmese government, believing that he stood a better chance of overthrowing it than he did of conquering Beijing. The offensive he launched in the fall of 1952 against the Burmese army proved the final straw for the government, which the following year proposed a resolution at the UN condemning the presence of Chinese Nationalist troops on Burmese territory as an act of aggression. The United States refused to support the motion, and the Burmese government unilaterally terminated all American aid programs in the country. As the CIA had been using aid programs as a cover for most of its operations, this was a quiet but effective way of stopping the CIA's support for Li Mi.

Carleton was an unwitting victim of all this intrigue. Originally re-cruited to go straight to Burma to work for the CIA, but officially em-ployed by the State Department, he ended up cooling his heels in Washington for nearly a year. In February 1953, he wrote to the patient Kleinpell to request an extension of his year's leave of absence for a further year to September 1, 1954. That letter was followed four months later by another when it was clear that his plans had changed radically.

"The morass of red tape that surrounds everything here is unbeliev-able until one has experienced it," he wrote on June 13. "I shall be re-signing shortly from the State Department to accept a grant from a foundation which will finance me for a year's study in Burma. It is a rather generous grant. . . . Not much other news from this front. I could write at length about political questions as seen from this angle, but per-haps I'd better not."

In fact, with the CIA's relations with Burma at an impossibly low level, the Agency had decided that the further deployment of officers to the country was politically unwise. But this did not diminish the Agency's requirements for political intelligence on the country and the groups within it. So Carleton was simply given a different cover. The CIA arranged for him to receive a Fulbright Fellowship, which al-lowed him to travel to Burma as an academic.[18] This was a common cover for CIA officers at the time, and one that allowed them all the latitude they needed to travel in the host country doing "academic" research.

Carleton and his family arrived in Rangoon in December 1953 and settled into a life that still reflected many of the glories of a country that played an important part in the British Empire. They lived in a large house at 84 Park Road in a compound for expatriates, with servants to do the cooking and the washing. The house was spacious, far larger than the Washington apartment and bigger than the house in River Falls. Its architecture was full of Eastern romance, with louvered slats in place of windows and huge fans to stir the stifling summer heat.

Now independent, Burma retained many of the trappings of the Raj and a measure of civilized behavior that Carleton and his family had never experienced before. For Carleton and Rick it was a stimulating experience, and Rick, then aged twelve, got better acquainted with his father, whom he accompanied on trips upcountry to see local political leaders. At the same time, Rick seemed to flourish in the clubby atmosphere of Rangoon. He learned to play tennis and became a competent swimmer, and he gained some good friends among the children of other expatriate Americans in the country.

Jane Wilhelm was in Rangoon with her husband, who was fulfilling a business contract, when she first met the Ameses. She and Rachel Ames became fast friends, and Rachel decided to send her children to the Methodist English School where the Wilhelms' three children were already enrolled.[19] As far as the Wilhelms were concerned, Carleton was in Burma to do a research project on British involvement with the country. "Carleton was a very handsome man, tall, with a beautiful mane of gray hair," said Jane.[20]

She detected no sign of the alcoholism that had now fully taken hold of Carleton, but for his superiors back at Langley, it was beginning to cause a problem. "CIA records reflect Carleton Ames received a particularly negative performance appraisal from this tour and that the elder Ames had a serious alcohol dependency."[21]

Perhaps it was the alcohol, or perhaps it was insecurity engendered by the political situation in Burma, but Carleton was clearly unwilling to sever the umbilical cord that kept him attached to River Falls. He wrote to Kleinpell on February 25, 1954, asking for a further extension of his leave of absence, saying that he intended to return to teaching in September. Although this was granted, Ames sent a telegram to Kleinpell on July 13 saying simply: "Govt says stay Burma not returning Sept—Ames."

This was followed by a letter dated July 1, but presumably posted after the telegram, which blames the confusion on the Burmese government and a mix-up over his visa:

> I am very painfully aware of the problems which this change in my plans is creating for you. It is a poor return for all the favors and consideration you have always shown me. You may be sure I would not be doing this if I had any choice.
>
> Just what I will do at the end of another year, I am not sure. I expect that I will be able to find another job without too much trouble, although I would have preferred to return to River Falls.

In fact, there never seems to have been any likelihood of his returning to his old school. He was in the Agency now, and in the way of the organization, once he was hired on the staff, he was guaranteed a job for life, despite his poor performance. It was a pattern of tolerance not just of incompetence but of routine substance abuse that was to be repeated almost exactly twenty-five years later with Rick.

In late 1955, the family moved back from Rangoon and rented a Cape Cod house on Davidson Road in McLean just across the road from the high school. The school had opened the same year to meet the growing demand of an expanding population in a community that back then was semirural. So new was the school that Joseph Lyons, the assistant principal, was pleased that there wouldn't be football on the grass the first year because he was concerned about the children getting tetanus from the recently vacated pasture.[22]

The Ameses were certainly not the ordinary suburban family. Their experience abroad set them apart and their literary enthusiasm ensured that they would play a prominent part in the creative life of the school. Rachel got a job teaching English there and appears to have been as good a teacher as friends claimed she was a supportive mother.

"Rachel did a great job," said Margaret Mims Hamilton, who was in Rachel's twelfth-grade advanced English literature class. "She really knew and loved her subject and made it challenging for the students. The class dealt much with Shakespeare, which was an area she particularly enjoyed. Once, she even built a replica of the Globe Theatre for the class, and had a Shakespeare dinner for them. The senior class was divided up into a fast and a slow group, but Rachel never approached teaching the slow group as if they couldn't enjoy Shakespeare or other parts of English lit as much as the fast group."[23]

Emily Horne Ray, who was a freshman with Rick, described Rachel as having a glamorous air about her that made her stand out from the other teachers.

"She always had flair," Ray said. "She would wear bangly earrings, some makeup, and sometimes have hennaed hair. She was friendly and extremely intellectual and very well liked by her students. One time, the class which had been studying The Canterbury Tales with her came to her house, stood outside in the front yard, and recited the opening lines from the Chaucer epic. Rachel came out in her shorts to listen."[24]

The school drew children who would otherwise have gone to Fairfax, Herndon, and Falls Church high schools. There were middle- and upper-class kids, as well as children from blue-collar and lower-middle-class backgrounds. The school divided into three groups, the academics and artistic types, the jocks, and the also-rans. While there, Rick was very active in the Thespian Society, served on the newspaper staff, participated for four years on the debate squad, and sat on the student council cabinet one year. He was voted "wittiest" by his classmates during his senior year, and the black-and-white photograph showing this award has Rick hamming it up, clutching his belly with his face screwed up in a huge guffaw. He was also a National Merit Scholarship semifinalist. Although his 1959 yearbook indicates that he intended to go to Dartmouth upon graduation, he never actually enrolled.

From interviews with more than a dozen of his classmates, a common picture emerges of a boy who was quick-witted, funny, and bright. Slightly geeky, with his spectacles and his unathletic style, he was nonetheless popular, as boys who find approval through humor frequently are. But among all that positive approval is a consistent memory of a boy described as "alone" or "different"; "You never knew what was really going on in his mind."[25]

A typical analysis comes from Michael Horwatt, a contemporary of Rick's with a shared interest in student government and acting who later became a Virginia Commonwealth attorney and represented Rick in his divorce. "He didn't come across as Mr. Macho or James Bond or anything like that. He had a certain kind of quality, almost like he could become part of the woodwork." There was a "certain vulnerable and inscrutable part" of Rick Ames, and the impression that "somehow he was so alone. There are certain people, you know what's going on inside them, and others you don't. I never was quite sure what was in there."[26]

Knowledge of his father's alcoholism was common among the children at the school, although it was simply defined as "a drinking problem." With hindsight, one might say it is Rick's relationship with his difficult father—about whom nobody from his school days has a positive word to say—that is critical to what came later. Rick always sought the approval of his father but, except for the years in Rangoon, rarely, if ever, received it, just as Carleton had worked so hard to win the support of his own father and had similarly failed. For children in such a negative environment escape comes through either withdrawal or exhibitionism, and Rick chose the latter, using jokes and his quick mind to overcome the lack of support at home.

The transition from class wit to actor was a short one. The idea of role-playing was simple enough and might have meant little had it not been for what followed later. Clearly, Rick at an early age was able to disguise the reality of an uncomfortable home life by substituting the roles he played onstage, in the school debates, or as the class joker.

The psychiatrists who would later pore over Rick's past and present in order to understand what caused his betrayal would trace it back to these early years and his relationship with his father. Rick, a child starved of approval, grew into a man who sought the regard of a substitute father figure, which was the CIA, the organization most closely associated with his father. When he failed to win the Agency's approval, he looked elsewhere for favor and found it at last with the Soviets, who were only too willing to lavish praise and money on a man who became a prized asset. For the Soviets both commodities came cheap, and by then, blinded by years of alcohol abuse, Rick was unable to see the complete sham his life had become.

All that lay ahead of him, though it was during this period that Rick had his first real contact with the Agency that would be his employer and nemesis in the years to come. At the end of his sophomore year at McLean High School, Rick needed a summer job. Then, as now, the CIA had a policy of encouraging the sons and daughters of its employees to join the organization. It was not exactly a fast-track employment program, but close to it, the theory being that one loyal employee was likely to breed another one. What does not seem to have occurred to the Agency then or later was that a drunken, failed CIA employee might breed a son who was destined to become the image of his father.

The job Rick received that summer was records analyst—marking up classified documents for filing. This was a General Schedule–3 on the federal government salary scale, which placed it two rungs off the bottom and well below the highest level of GS-15. He appears to have enjoyed the work at the CIA, and he returned the following year; by the time he arrived at the University of Chicago at age eighteen in the fall of 1959, he had decided that he wanted to make a career at the Agency.

THREE

Behind the Scenes

Rick started two years of general coursework at the University of Chicago on October 3, 1959, and stayed through the spring of 1961. He had intended to study foreign cultures, with history as an elective, but this seems to have been a sop to his father, who wanted his son to follow in his footsteps, not just into the Agency but in his scholarly interests as well. Once taken by university life, he dropped out to concentrate on what appears to have been his prime passion: acting.

In the 1950s, the University of Chicago didn't have much of a drama department—even now, drama is taught through the English department—so student productions tended to be rough-and-ready affairs. There were three main theater groups at the university—the University Theater, the Court Theater (the summer-stock company), and Blackfriars—the student musical comedy/Hasty-Pudding-like group, which is the one Rick joined.[1]

Students at Chicago were not really politicized in the late 1950s, and the radical counterculture had not yet begun to impact the Midwest as it had the West Coast. Although there was a growing leftist sentiment (there was a sit-in at an administration building, protesting the Vietnam War, in 1962) and some radical right and anarchist groups active at the school, these were very much on the fringe.

There has been speculation that Ames dropped out of the university when he came under the influence of one of these groups for a short while. But there is no evidence to support this. On the contrary, his fellow students and those who worked with him at the time describe an amiable colleague who was devoted to the theater and determined to make a success as an actor. Unfortunately, as with so much in Rick's life, the enthusiasm was not matched by the talent.

Mike Hrinda, a Blackfriars actor and now a Chicago doctor, remembers Ames as "ragged, sloppy, and disorganized," and he recalls that Ames wore a lot of black clothes and a brown tweed jacket.[2]

Another fellow student recalls Rick as "the man with the worst body odor I have ever known."[3] But apart from that single memory that has lingered down the years, most of the other recollections are of an amiable, if distant, young man who tried hard.

James Best, now a political science professor at Kent State University, produced *Silver Bells and Cockle Shells*, a 1960 Blackfriars play in which Rick Ames was involved. Best remembers him as a competent performer with "a passably decent singing voice."[4]

Inevitably in the politics that are generated around any theater, Rick became involved in the fights between different creative forces. And in the summer of 1961 it was Rick who took on the role of theater snitch at the Court, where a new technical director had been hired. He crossed swords with Michael Einisman, one of Rick's fellow undergraduates, who had been hired to help produce some plays. The director tried to force Einisman out of his job by making professional life unpleasant for him and giving several staff members who reported to Einisman the same salaries as Einisman himself. Two of the stooges who helped the director make life unpleasant for Einisman were Robert Strang and Rick Ames, who passed on any unpleasant news. This early piece of spying by Rick was significant not just as an illustration of student life but because it showed the beginnings of a pattern that would emerge much more strongly later. This was a small, closed community of which Rick was a part. He was Einisman's friend, or at least the producer considered him so. And yet Rick was prepared to betray him without any second thoughts.

Eventually, the director's obstructionism became so frustrating that

Einisman had to confront Ames to let him know how upset he was at what Ames and the director were doing.

"He didn't seem to have much understanding for the problems he was contributing to," recalled Einisman. "But when I started crying, he became more sympathetic. He did seemed moved when he finally realized he was hurting someone."

Einisman describes Ames as someone who was "sort of a tough guy, a bit dirty, semishaved, someone who frequently looked as if he had just gotten up. He would wear very dark clothes, [and] generally appeared kind of grubby-looking."

"There was a flatness in his personality," Einisman observed. "He didn't seem any smarter than about fifty percent of the students. His acting ability was also not particularly remarkable. I could see him playing a part of a Bolshevik, or a Nazi, or a typically authoritarian German father," but not much more, he said. "Rick was not a broad-gauged actor," and was "probably in the lower half in ability of the people involved in theater at Chicago. He would not be able to play a ne'er-do-well or light-handed role."[5]

Of the Chicago group of actors and technical workers, perhaps the people who remembered Rick best were Robert and Dorothy Strang, who worked with him in the technical operations of Blackfriars. Strang and Ames dealt with the lighting for the Court Theater. Hanging lights and the pipes for lights on the trees outside was somewhat risky work, as it meant clambering around unsecured to the tree, some thirty feet above a concrete court. Strang was happy to have Ames's company, as Ames was a great climber and a hard worker, enthusiastic and a good conversationalist.

Ames, "although always very nice, was not too outgoing. To get a rise out of him, you'd have to do quite a bit," noted Strang. "Rick was rather limited as an actor. He was a bit 'wooden'—fine as a supernumerary, but not a great acting talent. Those of us who worked on the tech crew would go out drinking at night, and there was a running gag about Rick and the CIA. He would say that his father worked for them and that he would like to work for them too, and we all blew it off, never taking him seriously. Still, he did seem ambitious to share the life that his father had—that was quite clear." Strang added that "Like most students, we had a kind of marginal existence; there were about ten of us in the group, and all of us lived on low incomes. Rick, though, was a bit different, in that you had the impression he could always go back home to his family if finances became too tight."[6]

Rick rose to become an assistant technical director at the university, but this was a meaningless title; he did little more than the man who helped move the scenery and fix the lights. The position was far removed from the glory that Rick really wanted, far removed from the promise he had shown as the "wittiest" in class back at McLean or the boy with the acting talent that his high school teachers so clearly remembered. Any ambitions he might have had to be a professional actor were clearly dashed in Chicago and, lacking a degree, he was left with little choice other than to retreat by taking the line of least resistance back to Washington.

He returned in February 1962 and formally applied for a position at the Agency. On March 23, when he took his first polygraph examination, he admitted that the previous November he and a friend, while drunk, had stolen a delivery bicycle from a local liquor store and later had been arrested by the police. They had been released with a reprimand, and the CIA, noting Ames's frankness, dismissed the action as a fairly typical student prank. The polygraph examiner noted that Ames was "not sparking, but a friendly, direct type" who was generally cooperative throughout the interview.[7] A background investigation (BI) that was completed on May 18, 1962, revealed no negative information from police or credit bureaus. Ames was offered and accepted a job as a GS-4 clerk-typist, doing largely the same kind of work he had performed during his summer vacations.

Rick walked into the Central Intelligence Agency's headquarters for his first day of work in June 1962, some three weeks after his twenty-first birthday. Carved into the white marble of the lobby was a Bible verse, John 8:32, which Ames either never observed or learned to ignore: "And ye shall know the truth, and the truth shall make you free."

He saw his job with the Agency as a stopgap while he completed a university degree, but he was to find the work more enjoyable than he expected. For the next five years he worked his way through the Records Integration Division of the Operations Directorate, rising from a GS-4 to a GS-7, while studying part-time at George Washington University for a bachelor's degree in history. In September 1967, Rick graduated with a B— average. Among the professors who must have taught him, nobody has the slightest recollection of this man, who must already have begun to lose the personality that had thrust him to the fore at McLean and in Chicago.

But already he was starting to develop the first signs of the problems with alcohol that would follow him through the rest of his career. In April 1962, he was arrested for being drunk in Washington, D.C., in 1963 for speeding, and in 1965 for reckless driving. According to Ames, one of the driving offenses was also related to drink. Despite these hiccups, he received good performance appraisals at the Agency and was encouraged to join the Career Trainee Program, which he did in 1967.

At this early stage, there was no attempt to link the incidents of drunkenness to Ames's fitness to be a member of the CIA. In particular, there was no correlation between the performance of Carleton, who, as his CIA records showed clearly, had been an underachiever with alcohol problems, and that of his son. Although it is generally recognized that children of parents with an alcohol dependency stand a better-than-even chance of repeating the addiction, until very recently the Agency considered alcohol abuse as just one of the difficulties that its personnel might encounter in their stressful work. It was not considered grounds for either dismissal or automatic counseling and was frequently not even thought worth mentioning in an employee's annual assessment by his or her supervisor. This remarkable failing in a community where secrecy is a byword and where drunkenness is known to lead to indiscretion is extraordinary.

As part of the routine screening of all applicants accepted into the training program to become operations officers, Ames was given a psychological assessment, which placed him at the low end of the spectrum in terms of the qualities necessary for a successful man in the field. Ames appeared to be "an intellectual and a loner, rather than a gregarious person capable of meeting and recruiting people of diverse backgrounds and cultures."[8]

These were surprising gaps in a person applying to go into field work. For any intelligence officer running or recruiting sources in foreign countries, confidence and an appealing social gregariousness are essential. The controller has to be able to bond with his source so as to provide encouragement and reassurance at critical moments. In fact, Ames had none of the appropriate characteristics for the job, and by ignoring these deficiencies, the Agency was to play to the weaknesses that had haunted Ames during his early life: a lack of affirmation by his peers and low self-esteem. These in turn contributed to his drinking and fading career prospects, and certainly played a part in his eventual decision to begin spying for the Soviets.

Despite the cautious appraisals of the psychological profile, Ames completed the course and was described as a "strong" trainee who was intelligent, mature, enthusiastic, and industrious. It was perhaps the best assessment Rick was to receive during his whole career at the Agency.

While on the training course, Rick had met a fellow CIA trainee, Nancy (Nan) Jane Segebarth, a slender young blonde from upstate New York, the daughter of a banker and university administrator, Robert Segebarth, and his wife, June Robbins. They were married at Fairfax Unitarian Church on May 24, 1969.

That same year, Carleton and Rachel moved to Hickory, North Carolina. There have been suggestions that Carleton may have chosen Hickory in part because of a teaching job at a local community college, but none of the four or five schools in the area has any record of Carleton as a professor. In fact, by the time he retired from the Agency, years of drinking had begun to take their toll and he was able to enjoy the relaxation of a work-free existence for only a few years. He and Rachel built a house out by a lake and lived there until Carleton died of throat cancer on November 8, 1972.[9]

Rachel moved from the lakeshore house to the center of town, into a large two-story house on Fifth Avenue, NE. She immediately began work for Boyd and Hassell, a local real-estate firm, and then transferred to work with Hazel Eckard, a close friend with whom she traveled to Europe and North Africa.[10]

While his parents were going through the trauma of starting a new life, Rick was beginning the serious part of his career at the Agency—though not without some trauma of his own. It is CIA policy that there be no husband-and-wife teams working for the Operations Directorate, so Nan Ames was required to resign from her position when Rick was assigned overseas to Ankara, Turkey, in 1969, a transfer that coincided with his promotion to GS-10. Nan resented the fact that she had been forced to leave the Agency to make way for her husband's career. Although the feminist movement had yet to really develop, Nan was an early victim of exactly the kind of sexual discrimination the feminists wanted to change. She did some freelance work for the CIA in Ankara; however, it was mostly administrative duties and not the exciting action in Operations. People in the Ankara station at the time remember her as being "aggressive" and "pushy," outspoken in her demands for job parity. "Wanted to be called an operations officer," one colleague remembers. "A bigger pain than he was."[11]

Turkey has always been a hotbed of international intrigue, and Ames found himself ideally placed at an exciting time. The country lies just across the Black Sea from the Soviet Union, Romania, and Bulgaria. Since Turkey and the Soviet Union shared a border, Ankara was a prime post for recruiting agents for the United States from the local assortment of Soviet embassy, trade, and press employees.

During his first years in the station, Ames received glowing reports from his supervisors as a "strong" performer. It is unclear just why he was so well supported, because there is no evidence that he ever actually recruited a working source or took much of a hand in running those that already existed. But as he pushed harder to deliver, his performance rating declined to "proficient" in year two. One of Ames's supervisors from that time remembers him as dull and lackadaisical. He "did what he was supposed to do, went where you asked him to, but he wasn't impressive," the supervisor said.[12] Another colleague put it more brutally: "He was on a rubber rung of a career ladder."[13] A supervisor who had Ames as a junior case officer and had signed a highly unflattering report about him recalled that "Ames couldn't recruit his goddamned grandmother—a real loser."[14]

By the end of the third year, the Ankara station chief had concurred with the initial psychological profile completed four years earlier that Rick was "unsuited for field work and should spend the remainder of his career at Headquarters." The performance appraisal report noted that Ames preferred "assignments that do not involve face-to-face situations with relatively unknown personalities who must be manipulated." Such a comment was devastating for an operations officer, and Ames was discouraged enough to consider leaving the Agency.[15]

But he had nowhere to go and clearly judged that despite his past problems the Agency still was some kind of home for him. He and Nan returned to Langley in 1972 and moved to 11614 Vantage Hill Road in the Golf Course Island area of Reston, Virginia. Rick was assigned to work in the rejuvenated Soviet section, and after a period spent in Russian language training he took up the post in 1973. Here he was assigned to select Soviet officials for recruitment. Over the next four years, Rick received four evaluations that rated him as a "strong performer" and one that described him as "proficient." These helped him recover from the debacle in Ankara, but notes in his file also make clear that he had problems about delaying key decisions and an inattention to detail and disregard for regulations. These were to become serious issues later, but for now they were simply notes in the files and of insufficient importance to delay his progress up the Agency ladder.

Despite his clear ability to function better in a home environment, Ames continued to have problems with drink. At a Christmas party in 1973, he became so drunk that he had to be helped home by officers from the CIA's Office of Security. The following Christmas, Ames again became drunk and was discovered by a CIA security officer engaged in sex with another CIA employee. Both incidents were noted in his file with an "eyes only" note from the Office of Security (OS) limiting access to the information. There was no attempt to speak to his supervisors about the incidents, which were put down to festive exuberance rather than a drinking problem.[16]

Nevertheless, Rick's tenure in the Soviet section—more formally known as the Soviet/East European Division, or SE Division—came at a fascinating time, a pause at the end of an era which had seen the Agency's operations in Russia virtually destroyed by the work of James Jesus Angleton, the head of counter intelligence at the CIA. It was the Angleton legacy that was to critically influence the course of counter intelligence at the Agency and to allow Ames to flourish for so long deep inside the Agency's ranks. Recovery from the Angleton period meant a resurgence of old-fashioned CIA spying, but it also brought with it weighty prejudices that were to keep the revitalized CIA from operating effectively. This new era, of which Rick was to be a part, was about to start: the CIA would once again begin to pursue the Soviet target with the kind of aggression the task demanded.

James Jesus Angleton had become head of counter intelligence at the CIA in 1954, a post he held until he was fired twenty years later. His was an extraordinary career that began with the OSS in World War II and continued through many of the twists and turns of the Cold War. As the head of one of the most important branches of the CIA, Angleton could have been a benign influence—or as benign as anyone can be when looking for the enemy within—but he corrupted the very organization he set out to protect.

Angleton's problems began in December 1961, when Anatoli Golitsin, a KGB officer, defected to the Americans in Helsinki. For two years he was debriefed by the SE Division of the CIA, but, both egocentric and exceptionally demanding, he proved a difficult subject, and the Agency was unable to decide whether he was a genuine defector or a plant. In the end, the Soviet Division decided to pass the buck to Angleton in counter intelligence.[17]

It is certain that Golitsin would have known of Angleton's existence. He was already a legend, and the British spy Kim Philby, who was a friend and drinking buddy of Angleton's, had briefed the KGB extensively on the CIA officer. Whether the KGB planted Golitsin with a view to undermining the CIA or whether he was a genuine defector remains unclear. What is certain is that if his defection was not a KGB plot, it turned out to be everything that Moscow Center might have wished.

What Golitsin told Angleton was that in 1959, two thousand senior KGB officers had been summoned to Moscow to be briefed on what became known as the Monster Plot, a deception plan so bold that it would totally undermine the ability of the Main Enemy, the Americans, to develop a coherent and effective foreign policy. Golitsin said that the split between Russia and China was a myth, that the two countries remained close. He added that there were other, major deception operations in the pipeline that would be revealed in due course. Over the next few years, Golitsin would claim that tensions between the Soviet Union and the Warsaw Pact countries were a myth, that the Yugoslav split with the

Soviets and the Romanian split were part of the deception. Even the Prague Spring, which saw the rise of Alexander Dubček's reformist government and ended with the 1968 invasion of Czechoslovakia by Soviet tanks, Golitsin said, was a deception cooked up by the Czech Communists and the Soviets.

Finally, Golitsin claimed that to ensure the success of these deceptions, the KGB had planted a mole deep inside the CIA, someone so well placed that he could affect the thinking and operations of the Agency and ensure that the Soviet deception plan not only went undetected but actually succeeded. Golitsin knew little about the Big Mole, as he came to be known, except that he was code-named "Sasha" and his last name might begin with the letter *K*.

This idea of a mole in the Agency was brilliantly planted by Golitsin. The very year that he came into Angleton's hands, Kim Philby had defected to Moscow in a spy scandal that would show remarkable similarities to the Ames case thirty years later. Philby had been the station chief in Washington for Britain's Secret Intelligence Service, known as SIS or MI6, and he and Angleton had become very close friends. The two had first met in 1944 and had kept in touch over the years. When Philby came to Washington in 1949, the two men would meet once a week for a drink or dinner, and Angleton considered Philby one of his closest friends in the intelligence community. When Philby defected, Angleton was devastated. He simply could not believe, despite all the evidence, that Philby was a traitor and that he had managed to deceive him for so many years. His pride was hurt and his confidence in his own abilities as a spymaster had been dealt a cruel blow.

Then along came Golitsin with his story of a highly placed mole inside the CIA. It was a story that appeared all too believable to Angleton. After all, if Philby could be a traitor, nothing was impossible. And Angleton was damned if he would get caught out a second time. And there began the greatest witch-hunt ever seen in American intelligence.

The conviction that there was a mole within was enhanced when Yuri Nosenko, another KGB officer, defected to the Americans in January 1964. Golitsin had warned that the KGB would send a false defector to discredit him, and he claimed Nosenko was the man. Nosenko had arrived in Washington at a strange time, just two months after President

Kennedy had been shot, and the Warren Commission was in full swing, trying to discover exactly who had done what and why. Lee Harvey Oswald, the assassin, was known to have visited Moscow, and Nosenko claimed to have been part of a small team in the KGB that had been set up after the assassination to learn what links, if any, Soviet intelligence had with Oswald. Nosenko told his American debriefers that there were no such links, that Oswald had simply been interested in the Soviet Union, had traveled there, but had no ties to Soviet intelligence. This was not believed at the CIA, and when Nosenko later claimed that Golitsin himself was a plant, Angleton chose to believe Golitsin, who was pandering to his own prejudices, rather than Nosenko.

If Angleton had accepted what Nosenko said, then much of the work that he had started in the Counter Intelligence Division would have come to nothing; yet again, the great spymaster would have been duped by a Russian plant, Golitsin. Without doubt, his career in the CIA would have been over. Instead, Nosenko was kept in solitary confinement for the next three years while he was the subject of an exceptionally hostile interrogation. This failed to break him and he continued to maintain his innocence and to insist that Golitsin was a plant. Eventually Nosenko was rehabilitated and was later employed by the CIA as an analyst.

Meanwhile, the hunt for the Big Mole was in full swing. Every single one of the thousand or so men and women in the Soviet Division at the CIA was looked at. Most of the personnel and operational files were either shown to Golitsin at Langley or taken to his apartment in New York or his country house near Albany. There, in a total breach of regulations, the files were left for Golitsin to sift through at his leisure. With such a wealth of material, it is hardly surprising that Golitsin was able to come up with an endless list of suspects, particularly as successive world events or the actions of world leaders could be skewed to fit the grand conspiracy theory. As the years passed, Harold Wilson, the British prime minister; Olof Palme, the Swedish premier; Willy Brandt, the West German chancellor; Armand Hammer, the American tycoon; Averell Harriman, the former governor of New York and ambassador to Moscow; Lester Pearson, the Canadian prime minister; and Henry Kissinger, the American national security adviser and secretary of state, were all Soviet agents or assets. In fact, there was no hard evidence to support any of these allegations, most of which were based on Golitsin's uncorroborated testimony.

Inside the SE Division, things were much worse. Over the years, Golitsin fingered officer after officer, claiming that each was a suspect. Angleton would then turn his team loose on the unfortunate victim, and it was frequently impossible to prove a negative, that victim A is not a Soviet spy. Instead, dozens of careers were ruined as suspects were shunted to one side into makeshift jobs and many others resigned. Morale plummeted and the SE Division virtually ceased to function. Toward the end of the 1960s and into the 1970s, there was almost no activity in the SE Division against its principal target, no recruiting of sources and no running of existing agents. The focus was entirely inward as each individual tried to fend off the increasing paranoia of Angleton and his team.

Bob Gates joined the Intelligence Directorate in the mid-1960s and was later to become the director of central intelligence. At the time, he was struck by how little intelligence was coming out of the Directorate of Operations (DO). "Thanks to Angleton, we had no Soviet sources. As an analyst, I got nothing from the clandestine service on Soviet internal things," said Gates.[18]

The second reason why this corruption of the clandestine service is important is for the lessons it provided for the future. It should have been apparent to all involved that one man should never again be allowed to destroy such a vital area of the CIA. Part of the reason why Angleton was allowed to prosper for so long was the culture of silence within the clandestine service. There was a general acceptance that the DO was a world of its own and that its problems were best contained within its elite ranks. This had helped produce a certain esprit de corps, but it has also removed the directorate from the day-to-day reality of work at the Agency. After Angleton, steps should have been taken to make the DO more accountable in terms of internal and external oversight. This was to be attempted on a number of occasions but each time it was frustrated by the stubborn and insular culture of the DO. It would prove a fatal flaw that contributed a great deal to the tragedy that was about to unfold.

Dick Helms, who had been Angleton's strong supporter, resigned as director of central intelligence (DCI) in February 1973 and was replaced by Jim Schlesinger, who brought in William Colby to be the deputy director, operations (DDO). Colby and Angleton were old sparring partners, and Angleton lost no time in incorporating Colby into his conspiracy theory, using as an excuse some of Colby's unreported contacts in Vietnam with a French doctor who later turned out to be a Communist. The allegations of wrongdoing by Colby were completely without foundation, so that when Schlesinger became secretary of defense in July 1973 and Colby moved to the DCI slot, he lost little time in moving against Angleton.

Schlesinger had discovered that Angleton had been running a series of illegal operations inside America against anti–Vietnam War protesters. Colby had learned that despite his mission to recruit sources in the Soviet intelligence organizations, Angleton had failed to develop a single source of any merit. Schlesinger also learned that the SE Division was totally paralyzed, unable to do anything for fear of the action's being construed as some weird new strand of the Angleton conspiracy. On February 20, 1974, Colby fired Angleton, who was an unwilling victim and who spent the next fourteen years issuing dark warnings about the Soviet penetration of the CIA. Ironically, he was to die before his dark warnings were finally proved true in the case of Rick Ames.

Once he realized how deeply the rot had penetrated the SE Division, Colby set about reconstructing the Agency's most important operation. First he fired or reassigned many of the personnel from the Counter Intelligence Division, transferring most of their functions to the Office of Security. Those acts were a clear signal to everyone inside the Agency that never again would a witch-hunt on the scale of that organized by Angleton be tolerated. The changes had an important psychological effect, too. For those who remained in the Agency and those who came in later, the memory of Angleton and his molehunters was extremely painful. They had seen friends whose careers had been destroyed by unfounded allegations, they had seen their mission compromised, and they had been forced to work in an atmosphere of fear and mutual recrimination. There was a determination on the part of everyone at the Agency that this should never, ever happen again.

There was a second side effect that was also to have an important influence on the Ames case. Angleton had ignored many of the conventions that existed between the CIA and the FBI. He had authorized spying operations in the United States, which was traditional FBI territory. He had taken FBI files that the Bureau shared with the CIA, and passed them to Golitsin. And he had chosen to ignore valuable intelligence that had been passed to the Agency by the FBI because it did not suit his conspiracy theories. For all these reasons, the FBI was furious when the extent of Angleton's operations was uncovered. The Bureau was also profoundly disturbed that a man it considered little short of mad could have been tolerated within the Agency for so long. The memory of what the Bureau considered a massive betrayal by the CIA was to linger on, souring relations between the two organizations and impeding the hunt for the real Big Mole.

Rick Ames was to benefit directly from the Angleton heritage. First, the already existing rivalry between the Bureau and the Agency was exacerbated by the Angleton years. The prejudices that suggested the Agency was a bunch of closemouthed wild men more concerned for their own secrets than for national security gained additional currency at the Bureau. At the Agency, the covert operators were convinced that the Bureau was staffed by a bunch of people who might have been proved right once, but were almost as paranoid as Angleton about the threat of penetration by a mole. The sentiment on each side was that the other was a serious threat to be fought with as much vigor as the labyrinthine nature of Washington bureaucratic politics would allow. The Russians and Rick Ames were to exploit this mess to great advantage.

FOUR

The Seeds of Destruction

Sergey Fedorenko is an aerospace engineer who worked in the 1960s for the Soviet State Committee on Science and Technology, normally known as GKNT. He was one of the editors of the classified journal on aviation and space *Voyennaya Aviatsiya i Raketnaya Teknika*. This journal published information from open and semi-open sources in the West, such as journals and research reports from places like RAND and the Hudson Institute. Material from these sources was extracted and provided to higher-level institute people and government specialists at a classified level.[1]

While he was at GKNT, particularly at the Institute of Scientific and Technical Information (run jointly by GKNT and the Soviet Academy of Sciences), he wrote a large analytic survey on the cutting edge of aerospace technology. Because his work was well received by his superiors, he subsequently was invited to work at the Institute for World Economy and International Relations, usually known as IMEMO. Fedorenko worked on projects, partially funded by the KGB, involving quantitative prediction of the likely course of international relations. He was assigned to a long-term study, a situational analysis based on the Delphi technique, which was supervised by Yevgeniy Primakov, now head of the SVR, the organization that replaced the First Chief Directorate of the

KGB. The project was completed by 1979 and was about two thousand pages long. From this study, Fedorenko coauthored a book entitled *Contemporary International Conflict.*

The KGB funded these analyses of international relations because it wanted to see if, using factor or relevance-tree analysis, it could predict how international conflicts would develop. The Delphi technique involves polling experts who work in the field that the survey questions involve. The factor or relevance-tree analysis lays out a branching chain of possible outcomes from specific choices (e.g., choice A leads to choices C or D, but choice B leads to choices E, F, or G; choice C leads to choices H or I, etc.). The various choice paths are assigned probabilities (these probabilities can also be weighted in terms of their desirability as outcomes; hence the term "factored or weighted probabilities"), and computations are done to assess the likelihood of the various final outcomes at the end of the decision tree.

Other models that attracted KGB attention were the PATTERN system developed by Honeywell for forecasting requirements for military hardware in future international conflicts, and the PERT/COST system. PATTERN is a version of relevance-tree analysis that facilitates predictions not only on what sorts of tactical solutions of larger problems there may be (e.g., weapons systems to accomplish a particular objective, or other sorts of tactical decisions), but also helps to assess what strategic goals one could accomplish given certain tactical resources. It is the potential to move from the specific to the general that made PATTERN particularly interesting to the Soviets, since they thought they could use it to predict the likely course of international politics, given the resources and means the various players could bring to bear. PERT/COST uses queue theory to help decide where production bottlenecks might occur and how they might be unblocked. Queue theory could be applied to a McDonald's fast-food restaurant, for example, to match the likely line of customers at any given hour to determine how many cash registers should be working to ensure one person is served every two minutes. The Russians used queue theory to maximize military production, especially the manufacture of intercontinental ballistic missiles.

In the early 1970s, Fedorenko's bosses at IMEMO thought it would be a good idea if he gained some practical international experience by serving some time at the UN. Along with three other IMEMO candidates (and about thirty additional candidates from other Moscow institutes), he was proposed in October 1971 as a Soviet representative to the UN Secretariat. He was selected and moved in May 1972 to New York. Inevitably, before he left Moscow, Fedorenko had been approached by the KGB, whose officers warned him not to keep up his contacts in the American academic community because the KGB was trying to recruit some of the scientists that Fedorenko knew. He was also asked to keep the KGB staff informed of any useful tidbits he might pick up at the UN mission. Fedorenko understood the rules of the game and recognized that he was in New York on sufferance and the length of his stay would, in part, depend on his degree of cooperation with the KGB.

Fedorenko's first assignment was to the Political Affairs Section, headed by John Stoessinger, a friend of Alger Hiss. Fedorenko was to find this assignment, like much of his work at the UN, sterile and boring, with its focus on security affairs and history. Fedorenko moved to the Disarmament Affairs Division in early 1973. This was also a sterile exercise, since UN input into disarmament was minimal; most of the real activity in arms control went on bilaterally, not in fora like the Conference on Disarmament. Fedorenko would travel several times each year to Geneva in connection with this job.

While in New York, Fedorenko decided on a minimalist policy of cooperation with the KGB, whereby he would simply relay to them what he was writing in cables back to Moscow. This tactic worked well until Vladik Enger arrived at the UN in 1973 and insisted on receiving harder intelligence from Fedorenko. Officially, Enger was with the UN Secretariat as a diplomat, but in fact he was a KGB officer charged with gathering intelligence on America and other countries represented at the UN.

Fedorenko first met Ames in early 1973 when he was temporarily assigned to New York and commuting back and forth to Langley. Fedorenko was already on the Agency's books as one of their prime sources. Rick was handed the Fedorenko case by the departing CIA officer, who had a cover job with the Intelligence and Research Department of the State Department. Relationships between case officers and their agents can often be difficult, and this was clearly an area where Rick had failed in the past. But he and Fedorenko hit it off from the start and found that they shared a common view of the world and particularly a shared impression of American-Soviet relations. They both believed that there wasn't any real residual antagonism between Russia and the United States. Both thought it was primarily ill-intentioned individuals in powerful bureaucracies who wanted to keep their jobs alive and their organizations strong who fueled the arms race and U.S.–Soviet tension. Chief among these institutions in the U.S.S.R. were the defense and intelligence sectors. Neither Rick nor Fedorenko saw any real objective reasons for the Cold War and both were determined to do what they could to thaw their small part of it.

This was classic Ames territory, an opportunity to discuss the minutiae of political policy, a throwback to high school debates when he could frame an argument and discuss it on equal terms with a man he clearly respected and liked. Rick and Fedorenko spoke each other's language; they shared the same political philosophy and love of literature. There were none of the tawdry side issues, such as the supply of prostitutes or demands for huge sums of money, that often afflict the relationship of case officer and source. In fact, Ames and Fedorenko became friends and met frequently for lunch and dinner. They would usually meet at the UN in the delegates' lunchroom, or at the cafeteria, or in one of the many bars inside the complex, and since it is such a large place, constantly thronged with people, there was cover in such a busy, central location.

Rick would bring Fedorenko indexes from the National Technical Information Service (NTIS), the Department of Commerce section that produces the Foreign Broadcast Information Service and various unclassified abstracts. Fedorenko would choose which documents he wanted, and Ames would deliver them at their next meeting. This pleased Fedorenko's bosses, who thought the NTIS material was classified (or at least treated it as classified in the U.S.S.R.). In exchange, Fedorenko would share with Rick his insights on Soviet high-level decision-making processes and personalities, and the motivations impelling individuals to pursue different courses of action.

Fedorenko's attempts to satisfy Enger's demands with the intelligence from Ames were not sufficiently successful to allay the questions that had developed about his contacts with American academics. By 1974, Fedorenko believed that he was under suspicion not necessarily of spying but certainly of being overly friendly with the Americans. But by then, the Soviet suspicions were well founded, for Fedorenko had begun spying for the Americans.

It was simple idealism that motivated Fedorenko to betray his country. He believed that there would be less tension between the United States and the U.S.S.R. if the military bureaucracies of the two countries stopped fomenting tension and pushing the arms race. He felt that sharing intelligence on how the Soviets were making foreign affairs decisions would help the United States to avoid policies that might be a provocation to minority hard-liners in Moscow. Like many of those who spied for America, Fedorenko believed he was betraying Communism, not his own country.

Fedorenko was a classic double agent, apparently working for his Soviet masters whereas in reality he was feeding his American controller good intelligence and passing back to the KGB open-source material given to him by Ames. Ames's relationship with Fedorenko is important both because it helped assure his continued promotion up the CIA ladder and because it was to demonstrate the depths to which he would sink while working for his masters in Moscow.

Rick's strong performance at Langley and with Fedorenko in New York made up for the unsuccessful Turkey tour, and in 1976 the Agency decided to promote him to handle operations in New York. He was assigned to FR [Foreign Relations]/New York, the CIA's station in Manhattan. He had two main tasks: running sources at the United Nations and recruiting similar sources from the large Soviet mission there.[2]

While New York offered some possibilities for intelligence officers, it was the United Nations that drew the cream of the world's intelligence agencies. Because the UN tended to attract the best and brightest of the democratic countries and the best-connected and most influential of the totalitarian regimes, it was an ideal recruiting ground. In many ways the UN of the 1970s and 1980s was similar to Vienna before World War II: a hotbed of espionage and intrigue. Fully half of all the Soviet representatives to the UN were believed to be from either the KGB or the GRU, its military equivalent. Aside from them, there were numerous others in the trade mission and Aeroflot who were both targets and active operators in their own right.

For all of them, intelligence was a sophisticated game where everyone knew the unwritten rules: there was no killing and everyone was fair game. For the CIA it was a particularly attractive venue because the Communist representatives were at their most vulnerable in the very heart of decadent capitalism. It was the task of the CIA to target the Soviet or East European diplomat or visiting scientist who drank too much or appeared particularly vulnerable for sexual or financial reasons. Of course, the Russians and their friends were doing exactly the same thing to the Americans and their allies.

In this strange, almost surreal world, the tracking and developing of sources is a lengthy and frustrating business involving hours— sometimes weeks—of fruitless investigation and surveillance. Only very occasionally will an intelligence officer strike gold with a source who is reliable and sane. More often, the patient stalking of a likely target is unsuccessful; he or she is either a plant by the other side or simply has no interest in betraying his or her country.

Ames loved the milieu of the spy. It suited his temperament, which was essentially one of indolence softened by a lavish expense account. For those lazy enough, recruiting sources is the best cover of all. It is possible to spend months talking up worthless contacts as potentially valuable recruits. And when that contact falls away, it is easy to find another drinking and dining companion. In this game of bluff, all CIA supervisors are naturally fairly tolerant of the officer in the field. They have all had the failed contacts, the sources that have gone sour, and so it is difficult to sift the real from the false. In every case, supervisors are dependent on the integrity of the officer working the street. Even if he is as rotten as Ames was, it is very difficult to detect.

During Rick's stay, he and Nan lived in a twenty-story luxury apartment house on East Fifty-fourth Street, at an address that would have been far above his means on his normal Agency salary. But the CIA subsidized the apartments of their officers in New York. So, additionally compensated by a generous entertainment allowance, they were able to enjoy all the benefits of big-city life without any of the uncertainties of living abroad. While in New York, Ames affected the pose of the independently wealthy gentleman spy, which was an effective cover because many people at the Agency had that profile.

While he was in New York, Ames ran another important source, Soviet diplomat Arkady N. Shevchenko, who served as an undersecretary-general at the United Nations. By the time Rick arrived in New York, Shevchenko had already been an agent in place for nearly three years and was providing a stunning catalogue of high-grade political and military intelligence. Shevchenko personally knew senior members of the Politburo and was completely familiar with the inner machinations in Moscow. This was priceless intelligence because it gave insights not just into the raw data but into the thinking that lay behind the decisions. He was also able to recite to his CIA handlers the transcribed contents of cables from Moscow. This allowed the National Security Agency (NSA) to match the transcribed cables with their own coded intercepts and thus to break the Soviet diplomatic codes—a major coup in itself.[3]

When Shevchenko defected to the Americans in April 1978, he was the highest-ranking defector ever to come to the United States. The following month, Vladik Enger was arrested in the New Jersey woods with two other KGB officers, Rudolf P. Chernayev and Vladimir P. Zinyakin, while attempting to pick up a package containing classified documents allegedly dropped off by Lieutenant Commander Arthur E. Lindberg, a U.S. Navy officer. They were arrested near the intersection of Woodbridge Center Road and Highview Road, near Newark, and charged with making contact with an American citizen to collect, on seven or eight occasions, materials involving underwater acoustics, submarine-detection systems, the LAMPS helicopter system for antisubmarine warfare, and other classified Navy systems. Zinyakin was released shortly after detainment because he had diplomatic immunity, but because Enger, thirty-nine, and Chernayev, forty-three, were UN Secretariat employees, they were charged with espionage.[4]

Their case was a bit unusual because they were first released into the custody of Ambassador Anatoliy Dobrynin in exchange for an American businessman with International Harvester, F. Jay Crawford, who had been picked up in early June and was being held in the U.S.S.R. on a currency-violation charge. That October, a jury convicted Enger and Chernayev on three counts of espionage, and the judge sentenced them to fifty years in prison. After six months of negotiations, in late April 1979 the two were allowed to leave the United States in exchange for five dissidents: Aleksandr Ginzburg, a writer and human-rights activist;

Georgiy Vins, a Baptist minister; Eduard Kuznetsov, a Jew seeking to emigrate to Israel; Mark Dymshits, another Jew seeking to emigrate (both Kuznetsov and Dymshits had tried to hijack a Soviet plane in 1970); and Valentin Moroz, a Ukrainian activist. The Russians, who had been living at the Soviet compound in the Riverdale section of the Bronx pending appeal of their sentences, were driven to Kennedy International Airport and boarded at the front ramp of an Ilyushin-62 as the dissidents exited on a rear ramp.[5]

The outcome of these arrests was that the KGB launched two investigations: one into everyone who had contact with Shevchenko and the second to see who had been in touch with Enger. They suspected that Shevchenko might have recruited other traitors from among the Soviets at the UN and they were concerned that Enger might have been set up as a result of information supplied by an American spy working in New York in the Soviet mission. Fedorenko had dealt with both men, and so naturally came under suspicion. There was no hard evidence against him, so he was simply recalled to Moscow, where he found himself the target of an investigation that was to continue intermittently for the next ten years. He had made plans to remain in touch with Ames from Moscow, but these had to be aborted because he considered the friendship too dangerous. As a result, the two lost touch.

Fedorenko had shown Rick that there were people in the enemy camp who thought like him, who understood that among the people (as opposed to the policymakers) there need not necessarily be disagreements on philosophy or politics. On the contrary, Ames had found in Fedorenko a soulmate, somebody with whom he could develop his nascent thinking about breaking down some of the barriers between East and West—"leveling the playing field," as he would later describe it.[6]

By coincidence—and it was a coincidence—while he was running Fedorenko, Rick began meeting every two weeks with Tomas Kolesnichenko, the chief New York correspondent of the Communist Party newspaper *Pravda*. There is no hard evidence that Kolesnichenko was a KGB officer, although it was standard operating procedure for the KGB to send its representatives abroad under cover as *Pravda* or Tass correspondents. Like Fedorenko, Kolesnichenko was a useful foil for Ames. Both men liked to drink and both men had a keen interest in literature (the Russian was a part-time playwright). Over long, liquid lunches, which began with a meeting at Tavern on the Green in Central Park, the two men would talk about relations between the Soviet Union and America, analyzing just why the Cold War had been so costly to both sides. The Russian fed Ames's own perceptions of his failures by reinforcing his own assessment that Americans simply did not have Ames's deep and intuitive understanding of the reality of relations between the two countries. The Russian told him that the leaders in Moscow were convinced that the Americans were determined to destroy them, that the American intelligence community had penetrated every aspect of Soviet life. Given Ames's immature and warped perception of reality, this was a message he could readily understand. If only there were some way he could help convince the Soviets that the Americans were not the all-powerful monsters they imagined, then perhaps the world would be a safer place.

"He didn't directly teach me a lot, but indirectly, I learned an awful lot ... in terms of what the Soviets were all about," Ames said later. "What happened later, frankly, is I got myself in the position where I thought, and still think—call it arrogance if you will—but I'd say: I know what's better. I know what's damaging and I know what's not damaging, and I know what the Soviet Union is really all about, and I know what's best for foreign policy and national security. . . . And I'm going to act on that."[7]

This developing arrogance was to become a hallmark of Ames's betrayal and of his work at the Agency. Yet during his tour in New York, he received the highest performance appraisals of his career. In four out of the five years of the assignment, he was rated as "superior" or "invariably exceeding work standards," and he was regarded by his supervisors as interested, articulate, and capable, so much so that he received several promotions and a bonus. At the end of his tour in 1981, he was ranked near the top 10 percent of all the operations officers at his GS-13 grade, and on the basis of that performance he was promoted to GS-14 in May 1982. However, despite this generally favorable series of evaluations, his supervisors continued to report, as they had done in Turkey and Washington, that he tended to procrastinate, particularly in filing expenses and contact reports.[8]

While he was in New York, there was also the first of a series of security incidents that were to surface only after his arrest. The most significant occurred in 1976 when Ames was on his way to meet a Soviet source and he left his briefcase behind on a New York subway train. It was a stupid but forgivable mistake except that the briefcase was filled with classified documents, some of which clearly identified Fedorenko, that should not have left the CIA station. He realized his error after he had left the station, and alerted the office, which in turn informed the FBI. After a massive hunt, the FBI found the briefcase in the hands of a Polish émigré living in Queens and bought it back. Although the émigré himself appeared innocent, it was unclear whether any of the documents had been compromised. The incident was enough to cause Ames to consider leaving the Agency once again. He felt that on top of his poor performance in Turkey and the bad assessments he had had for failing to file contact reports and expenses, it might prove to be the final career breaker. But he received only a verbal reprimand.

To add to the pressure, his relationship with Nan had been going through a rough patch. He had been offered a number of overseas postings but had turned them all down at her insistence, because she wanted to stay in New York. Rick realized that continuing to reject foreign assignments in an organization that focused its activities abroad was political suicide. The Agency would not continue to offer him assignments indefinitely, and if he wouldn't go outside the continental United States, he was effectively finished at the CIA. So whereas Nan was still determined to stay in New York, he was equally determined to accept the next overseas post that would allow him to stay close to the United States while fulfilling his career obligations to the Agency. If necessary, he thought he could commute back and forth to New York and thus save what was left of his marriage.

The arrogance that was fostered in New York combined perfectly with the seeds of betrayal that had been planted unwittingly by Fedorenko and perhaps with more calculation by Kolesnichenko. Rick came to believe that he really did know better than his peers at the Agency. Subconsciously, too, he came to appreciate that it was talking to Russians and not to his colleagues at the Agency that gave him real satisfaction. *They*—the people he had been taught were the enemy—were the only people who really understood what he was thinking. They gave him the respect he knew that he deserved, the respect he had never received from his father, and that until recently he had not received from the Agency. For now, it was enough that he knew there were people out there who understood. It would take divorce, an expensive new bride, and a career failure in Mexico to translate arrogance and understanding into betrayal.

Already, all the signals were there if only anyone in the CIA had been willing to read them. Ames had become a classic officer at risk: poor performance assessments, problems with drink, clear dissatisfaction with work, and an unhappy marriage. But back then, this was all considered fairly routine in the DO, where the idea that a traitor could upset an excellent security record remained unthinkable. With nobody to counsel or control him, Ames was now set on a course of self-destruction.

FIVE

Courtships

The foreign transfer came in September 1981, and Ames was moved to Mexico City, where he took an apartment in the Zona Rosa—the "Pink Zone"—an upper-class neighborhood. The Zona Rosa, bounded by the Reforma, Insurgentes, Avenida Chapultepec, and Calle Seville, has pretensions of being the capital's equivalent of Montparnasse or Greenwich Village, but lacks the bohemian or cultural life of such neighborhoods. It is, essentially, an area of glitzy shops, expensive restaurants, discotheques, and nightclubs, and is a favorite gathering place for affluent young Mexicans.

The American Embassy is a massive concrete and glass structure that occupies an entire block between Calles Río Sena and Río Danubio. It is situated opposite the Zona Rosa on the other side of the capital's most elegant avenue, the Paseo de la Reforma, with its old stone mansions and sparkling new high-rises. The streets around the embassy are often blocked off for security reasons, and the line of people queuing up to seek visas is frequently blocks long.

For the diplomatic corps from America and Europe, Mexico is an enjoyable assignment—all the comforts of home but sufficiently glamorous to have a touch of the exotic. The diplomats mostly live in the neighboring district of Polanco, with its modern apartment buildings along palm-lined streets, or farther out of the city center in the foothills known as Lomas de Chapultepec, where rambling arabesque homes are set along tranquil shaded avenues.

The diplomatic circuit is a lively one, with nearly every nation having diplomatic representation in the city. Because of the difficulties in getting around the largest city in the world during peak traffic hours in the daytime, formal diplomatic gatherings often consist of working breakfasts or cocktail parties—with a guest list that sometimes includes the president of the republic as well as various ambassadors and diplomats. Informal gatherings tend to be concentrated in diplomatic residences in Polanco or Las Lomas and are sometimes enlivened with the presence of traditional mariachi bands. They are always characterized by the consumption of large quantities of "Cuba"—a rum and Coca-Cola mix—sometimes accompanied by traditional tacos and mole—a spicy dish of chicken in a thick, dark chocolate sauce.

Ames had eagerly sought the transfer, and his job was similar to the one he had left in New York, but this time he was operating outside the reassuring embrace of his own country's borders. It was a prestigious assignment that should have given him the confidence to do his job well. Despite the briefcase incident, he had received plenty of plaudits in New York and all the promotions he might have expected. Although he was not in a management position, Mexico was considered by many in the intelligence community to be one of the great Cold War hot spots. Both the CIA and KGB operated heavily there, because Mexico City was the center for Soviet overseas operations throughout Latin America. With the recent election of President Ronald Reagan, who declared war against the "Evil Empire," the status and intrigue associated with the recruitment of Soviet spies were rising.

But it was a shallow confidence that Rick took with him to Mexico. He still had his drinking problem, and all the insecurities he had felt in Turkey came flooding back once he started work.[1] From the moment he arrived in Mexico City, Rick acted like a man both lacking in self-confidence and seeking the reassurance he seemingly could find only at home in America. Within the first six months he had three torrid and obvious affairs, which were noticed by his colleagues but not entered into his file. Such infidelity was not that unusual among Agency

employees and was generally tolerated. Ames was required to report affairs with foreigners, but neither he nor his colleagues did so.[2] Clearly, he
had made a decision that his marriage was over in everything but name.
At the same time, his drinking got much worse and he gained a justified
reputation for taking long lunches and returning to the office drunk or
not returning at all.

"There was one occasion when I attended a diplomatic reception in
the American Embassy," said Ames. "It was a meeting of the diplomatic
association, a cocktail party. And I had too much to drink and got into a
kind of loud and boisterous discussion, semi-discussion, argument, with
a Cuban—a DGI [intelligence] official. But people noticed that I had
had—that I was drunk. And this caused alarm. But I had already had a
kind of reputation for regularly going out with a group of people and
taking a long lunch and having too much to drink."[3]

On a second occasion, Ames was involved in a traffic accident in Mexico City and was so drunk he could not answer police questions or recognize the U.S. embassy officer sent to help him. Neither incident was
entered in his file.[4]

While Ames was busy in Mexico, back in Washington the FBI and the
CIA had initiated Operation Courtship, the first operation designed to
break down some of the barriers that had grown up between the two
agencies during and since the Angleton era. Its purpose was to target for
recruitment Soviet nationals working either at the embassy in Washington or at various trade missions in the city. The operation was run by the
FBI's Washington field office in Springfield, Virginia. There they sifted
through the CIA's files on embassy and other personnel, consulted with
Agency and Bureau psychologists, and tried to pick likely targets. These
would then be placed under intensive surveillance and at an appropriate
time approached by one of the Courtship squad.[5]

In his excellent book on the Agency, *Inside the CIA*, Ronald Kessler
describes an early attempt to recruit Dimitri Yakushkin, the KGB station
chief in Washington. He was followed by members of the Courtship
squad to the Safeway supermarket in Georgetown (known as the Social
Safeway because so many of the great and the good bump into each

other while doing their shopping). When Yakushkin was separated from his wife, Irina, for a few moments and was left fondling the oranges in the fruit section, the Bureau man approached to make his pitch.

"I am a special agent of the FBI, and I wondered if I could have an opportunity to talk to you," Kessler quotes the FBI agent as saying.

"What is your name?" the Russian asked.

The agent gave a false name, which was immediately apparent when the KGB officer asked to see his identity card.

"I'm sorry. I kind of made that up," the agent said.

"Yeah, I know how it is."

"Would there be a way to arrange an appointment for our SAC [Special Agent in Charge] to speak to you?"

"Sure. Have him come by the embassy anytime," Yakushkin replied, smiling.

"Well, actually, I was hoping for a less formal environment, if that would be okay."

"I don't really think I'd be interested in that."

The agent had been authorized to offer the Russian up to $20 million if he would agree to come over, a high price but worth it if he brought all of Moscow Center's secrets of its operations in America with him. But even that huge sum was not enough to tempt the Russian:

"Young man, I appreciate the offer. If I were twenty years younger, I'd give it serious consideration."

But early in 1982, as Ames was settling in Mexico City, the Courtship team spotted another likely target, Lieutenant Colonel Valeriy Martynov, an officer in the Line X—scientific espionage—section of the KGB station. He had arrived with his wife, Natalya, and two children to take up an official position in the cultural section of the embassy on November 4, 1980. He was spotted at a conference and appeared to the FBI agents to both enjoy American life and want to experience more of it. He was approached by an FBI agent posing as a businessman and the two became friends. The FBI man took Martynov out to dinner and drinks over a period of weeks and was reassured that the KGB officer would be willing to provide information in exchange for cash—$200 per meeting and $1,000 a month paid into an American bank account.

Martynov was able to supply the Americans with a lengthy list of

Soviet priorities for intelligence gathering. At the same time, the Americans were able to feed information to him via a double agent he was supposed to have recruited. Thus, from one source, the Americans were able to get a deep understanding of the strengths and weaknesses of the Soviet military-industrial complex while at the same time feeding the Soviets information that would take their scientists down a series of research-and-development dead ends.

A few months later, Courtship came up with another winner in Major Sergey Motorin, a political affairs specialist at the embassy. He, too, was a KGB officer and was persuaded to help the Americans after he was photographed trading a case of Russian vodka for an American stereo system. Motorin was able to supply the Bureau with insights into the political decision-making in Moscow and into how the Soviets were running different disinformation campaigns. The Soviets, he told the Courtship team, would order their KGB officers in a number of countries to repeat exactly the same anecdote to every American they met. This would filter back to Washington with one source seeming to confirm details supplied by a completely separate source. Thus, the CIA apparently learned that Yuri Andropov, the former head of the KGB and then general secretary of the Communist Party, was a jazz-loving, reformist, "modern" Russian—all of which was a lie.

Both the FBI and the CIA were elated that Courtship had proved itself so magnificently and so soon after it had been established. It was the first time the FBI had achieved such success with staff from the Soviet Union's embassy, and they were understandably proud of their achievement. Although Courtship was supposed to be a cooperative venture, the FBI considered both their recruits from the embassy to be their sources. It was a triumph for the Bureau and proved conclusively to their rivals at Langley that they could find and run sources as well as anyone from the DO. Later, when Ames began his deadly work, these two FBI sources were among the first to be fingered by him. The loss of these two sources was a very personal blow to the FBI and provided a powerful motive for the hunt for the mole that some Bureau agents were to become convinced was lurking somewhere in the CIA.

Mexico, meanwhile, was rapidly turning into a nightmare for Rick. A series of evaluations by his superiors had brought back all the failures of Turkey: the noncompliance with Agency procedures; the late filing of expenses; the lack of contact reports—indeed, the lack of any contacts to report about. Assessment after assessment claimed that Ames was a loser who was heading nowhere fast.

Then a new world opened up for him in the shape of a thirty-year-old Colombian national, Maria del Rosario Casas Dupuy, known as Rosario. She was (and is) a good-looking woman with curly black hair and a clear complexion offset by attractive freckles running over the bridge of her nose to both cheeks. Her face has a strong bone structure but is round enough for the edges to be softened. She has dark and compelling eyes, a clear laugh, and an attractive figure.

Rosario was a tempestuous, insecure single woman who had come to Mexico to escape the confines of home and, perhaps, to find a husband. With her comfortable upper-middle-class background, her clear intelligence, and her beauty, she was an immediate hit on the diplomatic circuit, and invitations to dinners, cultural evenings, and the theater came thick and fast. But Rosario saw herself as more than just a flighty woman on the make, and her background gave her every reason to believe that if she made a match it would be with someone of her own social class and her high intellect. Rick and Rosario hit it off from the first, two outcasts in a foreign country drawn together by their love of literature and especially of T. S. Eliot, who ironically was also James Angleton's favorite poet. Rosario found Rick "cosmopolitan," "cultured," and "traveled."

"What was compelling about him," Rosario explained, "for a person like me who is very nervous and high-strung and passionate about things, he was sort of very stable and very quiet and very calm. Very gentle and sweet . . . He's a hard person to get to know. Little did I know how hard."[6]

In many respects they made an unlikely pair. Rick, the drunken, increasingly withdrawn spy riddled with self-doubt, with a career and a marriage that were coming unglued simultaneously. Rosario, the vivacious intellectual who was attractive and personable, with the opportunity to choose many other, more attractive people, chose Ames, the ultimate geek. But he was eleven years older than she and represented a kind of stability and intellectual challenge she felt her life had been lacking. There is no doubting their love. Even now, after all that has happened, Rosario talks with great fondness of those halcyon days in Mexico when they first met and everything seemed possible in the world they were building together.

"He was terrific, a fascinating person to talk to; very knowledgeable, what we would call in Spanish *puento*, a person who's widely read. That's what fascinates me in a relationship; I have to be able to talk to someone. I need in a man somebody who is at least as smart as I am. I am very widely read, I am extremely intelligent and I cannot deal with a relationship where I am watching football all day or something like that. I have to be on equal terms intellectually and he certainly was—not in philosophy of course, but he never claimed to know any philosophy. He was just a pleasure to talk to, a fascinating person to talk to."[7]

Of course, it may have been Rick's very weakness that Rosario found so appealing. Here was an exotic man from another country, working for the State Department, with the opportunity for more foreign travel in the years ahead. Undoubtedly she was certain she could control his drinking. Today, friends of Rosario who knew the couple say that it was a relationship dominated by the strong-willed woman, and it was Rick who bent to her will.

Not everyone found Rick as fascinating as Rosario did. Professor Ignacio Abello of the University of the Andes says that Rick impressed him as "rather unfriendly" as well as "aloof, cold, and dry."[8] Carlos Gutiérrez, a philosophy professor at the University of the Andes, has a harsher judgment. "They were not the passionate kind. She was very calculating. Rosario was the dominant figure. She led the way and Rick went along. He was not very macho."[9]

Rosario was born in Bogotá, Colombia, on December 19, 1952.[10] Although her family was not wealthy by American standards, they were powerful and well connected.[11] The family also had a good reputation within Colombian society, a reputation for honesty and integrity. Her father, Pablo Casas Santofino, was a prominent Colombian politician, state senator, and businessman.[12] He was also well known as a mathematics professor at the University of the Andes and the National University. At one time later in his career, he also served as dean of the

Foseta del Rosano University, located in Cartagena.[13] Apart from his work at the university, he also worked for the government, and, in fact, he was serving as governor of San Andrés when he died in 1982 from a heart attack.[14]

Rosario's mother, Cecilia Dupuy de Casas, is extroverted and perceptive, her stocky figure belying the fact that she is an outstanding dancer. In addition to her scholarly interests, Cecilia Dupuy de Casas "ran a sort of bohemian salon in her home in Bogotá, a meeting place for students, professors, and musicians with such colorful names as Chocolate Armenteros and Ismael Quintana." Cecilia "had a collection of 5,000 LPs, and she and Rosario would listen for hours to salsa and Cuban music."[15] She was known as "Salcilia" because of her fondness for the salsa and other Latin dances.[16]

She traveled occasionally to Havana, which was one of the centers if not *the* center for salsa and boleros in Latin America. Cecilia has many artistic friends among the Cuban elite, and it was probably through these contacts that she met Fidel Castro on one of her visits. In 1993, the Colombian magazine *Semana* reported that Castro, who was visiting a sick baseball player, dropped in to visit her when she was recuperating from a leg injury in a Havana hospital.[17] Cecilia probably thought of Castro as just another of the high-society friends she had. Greta Wernher, a family friend and professor in the philosophy department at the University of the Andes, saw Cecilia as a romantic figure, interested in Castro because he was a revolutionary who promised a better life for poor people. Cecilia was not very political and would not have been much concerned about Castro's government or ideology.[18]

In her forties, Cecilia returned to the University of the Andes to complete her *licenciatura* (similar to the American B.A., but with a year or two of additional classes and requirements) and graduated from the University of the Andes about the same time as Rosario. She, too, taught at the university—courses on José Martí, the nineteenth-century Cuban poet and patriot; on twentieth-century Hispanic-American literature; and on the general history of literature in the Americas. She also taught courses on Caribbean music, given her strong interest and background in that area. Cecilia was well liked and respected, both by students and by other members of her department. It was unusual for a mother and a daughter to have finished their *licenciaturas* at approximately the same time and to be teaching in similar fields at the same university, but Rosario and Cecilia are an unusual pair. The two are quite close and their mutual academic interests make the bond even closer.[19]

Rosario has a brother, Pablo, and a sister, Claudia. Pablo is an anthropologist who did his undergraduate work at the University of the Andes and is now working for the government as the governor of Gorgona ("Serpent") Island, a nature reserve popular with tourists. Claudia is a physician at the Clínica del Contre, a clinic in Bogotá run by her uncle Camilio Casas.

Even in her early years, Rosario proved to many that she had inherited her parents' intellectual powers. William Rhoads, a retired Agency for International Development employee and neighbor of the Ames family when they lived in Washington, D.C., explains that Rosario was an embodiment of the esteemed intellectual tradition of Colombia. "Perhaps because Colombia had never really gotten filthy rich, the Colombian upper classes who are not all wealthy are still very active in government. So, rather than just sheer wealth as in other Latin American countries, the prestige in Bogotá tended to be more intellectual and Rosario certainly came from that kind of background."[20]

Rosario sees herself as an intellectual. She speaks five languages, reads Shakespeare in English and Baudelaire in French, and can talk with equal fluency in either language. She relishes the cut and thrust of intellectual debate and brings to any discussion the passion of her temperament, which is emotional, selfish, and forceful. Although she would later describe herself as a victim, her early life showed ample evidence that she was a real achiever, perhaps even an overachiever.[21]

The Colombian magazine *Semana* reported that for a "sixties child" Rosario had been surprisingly obedient and "immune to marijuana, the Beatles, and rebellion." Besides being valedictorian of her prestigious high school, she was voted by her classmates as most likely to succeed. According to her 1969 yearbook, her favorite expression was "How aesthetic!"[22] In the early 1970s she worked on her *licenciatura*, finishing it in 1976. Her studies focused on philosophy and literature, which were both taught in the philosophy department at the University of the Andes. Several professors who were her colleagues in the late 1970s have commented that although she likes both literature and philosophy very much, she has a predilection for philosophy.[23]

Before she finished her degree in 1976, Rosario spent a semester at Princeton. Latin American students, unlike European and American students, do not often spend a semester or year abroad; this is in part because of finances. The University of the Andes at one time had had an exchange agreement with the University of Illinois, but it had to let the arrangement lapse because there weren't enough students from Bogotá who could afford to go, year after year. Rosario had this opportunity because her father was given a fellowship to work at his alma mater for two semesters.[24]

Rosario apparently fit in well at Princeton. Her English was quite good, primarily because she had studied at the Colegio Nueva Granada, a bilingual high school, which was also good academically and which was attended by children of English speakers in Bogotá.[25]

On her return to Colombia from Princeton, Rosario began teaching in the department from which she got her degree. In Colombia, professors often will suggest that their better students spend a year or so teaching at a university before doing their Magister, and later their doctorate. And Rosario received this kind of encouragement from the philosophy faculty at the University of the Andes. In her first year of teaching she conducted a half-time course in ancient Greek (philosophy students were required to study Greek and Latin). The next year she taught a course in literary theory.[26] She also taught the role of the city in poetry, and the poets Baudelaire, Eliot, and Lorca.[27] It was during these years that Rosario became acquainted with some of the region's greatest authors and artists, including Nobel laureate Gabriel García Márquez.[28]

Rosario began working on her Magister in 1978 at the National University, the best in Colombia. She pursued her studies there under the direction of Carlos Gutiérrez and did well. She planned to write her thesis on Hegel's aesthetics—it was entitled "Aesthetic Problems in Hegel with Respect to Literature"[29]—but she hadn't yet completed it when she was given the opportunity to go to Mexico.

Greta Wernher, a colleague in the humanities department, described Rosario during that time as "disciplined and responsible."[30] Wernher also has said that Rosario "was a very conservative person. She always followed the instructions of her teachers. As a teacher herself, she was appreciated but not unforgettable, if you know what I mean. She was very formal."[31]

Her adviser Gutiérrez described her as "very intelligent and industrious . . . very hardworking," someone who was "exceptionally good" in seminars, and someone who wrote very good term papers.[32] While she did well in her own studies and in her teaching (her students liked her very much), she didn't get along well with her faculty colleagues at the University of the Andes, criticizing them on both academic and personal levels. She didn't have many close friends. Part of her problem was a simple intellectual arrogance. She was smarter than most people and had no hesitation in reminding them of that fact. She refused to suffer fools and was intolerant of anyone she considered her inferior. She wanted to spend her time taking philosophy or poetry, whereas most of her fellow students wanted to have fun. People do not like being made to feel stupid, and so Rosario found herself alone a great deal of the time.

She did have boyfriends during the 1970s. One was a member (although she wasn't) of the El Noir movement, a left-leaning, sometimes Communist-sympathizing group that was active on Colombian campuses.[33] Professor Piedad Ponnet, a fellow student of Rosario's, recalls two other love affairs; one with a very distinguished and well-known older man who currently teaches literature at the Universidad Pedagógica, and the other with her adviser Carlos Gutiérrez.[34]

Rosario felt that her social background should somehow be providing her with a better life. She was a member of the classic old-guard aristocracy; her family had all the status and connections she could have wanted but none of the money. There is a certain down-at-heels chic in such style, provided the individual has the confidence to carry it off. But for Rosario there was nothing attractive in being poor. She deserved more; she had the brains to have more; her heritage suggested she should have more; so why didn't she? It wasn't exactly that she felt life owed her a living; rather, she was certain that she was deserving of more than life had offered so far.

And these issues became even more pressing when Rosario's father died in 1982. The family quickly discovered that they had no money, and the luxury of being a perpetual student was something that Cecilia could no longer afford. It was Rosario who drew the short straw of heading to Mexico to earn some money while Cecilia worked to continue to send the other children to school. Her move to Mexico occurred as a result of a chance meeting during a family holiday in 1982. The Casas family was vacationing on one of the Islas del Rosario, near Cartagena, where the family had a modest vacation home (their main residence was an apartment in Bogotá). They happened to run into Julio César Turbay Ayala, the president of Colombia, who was a friend of the family and a member of the Liberal Party. When he inquired how the family was doing and asked about Rosario's plans for the future, she replied that she was currently a professor of Greek literature at the University of the Andes and was contemplating going abroad, perhaps to Mexico. Fifteen days after this encounter, President Turbay called and offered her a job at the Mexico City embassy as a cultural attaché. Rosario accepted gladly.[35]

When the Ames case broke, Rosario was portrayed as a diplomat working for the Colombian Foreign Ministry. While this was strictly true, she claims that the reality was really very different.

"I decided to take a break from my studies. First of all I loved Mexico. I have relatives there, two of my aunts, my mother's first cousin. One of my grandmother's brothers was a Colombian diplomat, and he went to Mexico and married a Mexican and never came back to Colombia, so I have two aunts who are Mexican, and lots of cousins, a branch of the family is Mexican. And I'd been to visit them and I really loved the place.

"The president of Colombia was a personal friend of the family and we were so close I asked him, 'Is there any chance that I could get a job in Mexico?' And he said, 'Sure,' and he sent me. I wanted to go to Mexico and he happened to be the president and he happened to send me there. I did not join the foreign service. I was not a diplomat. I knew it was going to be a two- or three-year thing and then I would go back to my studies."[36]

The Colombian Ministry of External Relations—like the foreign affairs ministries of a number of Latin American countries—does not have a well-regulated foreign service, and Rosario's appointment proved useful for all involved. She got a nice job in a nice city in a functional area very compatible with her interests. The ambassador in Mexico City at the time—Ignacio Umana de Brigard—got a top-notch cultural attaché,

one he could rely on, and one who was much better than those who usually fill these positions.[37] Umana, who was also an old family friend, liked
Rosario and found her "extremely diligent, very efficient . . . during her
tenure in the embassy, [she] showed herself to be very intelligent."[38]

The job in Mexico City suited Rosario well. With family already there,
she had an immediate entrée into Mexican society. In addition, she enjoyed the sophistication of the diplomatic circuit. She was very well educated, spoke English fluently, and loved the arts. She met Mark Davison,
an American who was the treasurer of the Diplomatic Association (Am-
cosad). Ostensibly a political counselor at the embassy, he was, in fact,
working undercover for the CIA. She says that he was attracted to her
but that they had nothing more than a friendly relationship. After they
had known each other for a few months, he asked if he could use her
apartment for some meetings, explaining that he was working for intelligence and that he would pay her $200 a month if she agreed to be absent
when he asked.[39]

This extraordinary request is notable on two counts. First, the CIA officer was breaking all the standard opening rules by revealing his cover
and confessing his real job to Rosario. Instead of admitting that he
worked for the CIA, he should either have made up a different story (a
meeting with another woman, a confidential sales conference with a
client) or not used a foreign national's apartment at all.

Second, it is a measure of Rosario's naiveté that she should have
agreed to such an arrangement for such a modest amount of money. Today she seems baffled by her stupidity and wonders with a weary amaze-
ment that she could have been ensnared into something that appeared so
simple but was, in the end, to destroy her life.

"It's the story of my life. I was used by a friend. But look, when I left
Colombia, I was very naive and had led a very sheltered life. I met this
American diplomat who worked in the political section of the embassy,
who was the treasurer of the Diplomatic Association. He asked me out to
lunch, we went to courses together at the Metropolitan Museum and
trips here and trips there and it was fun. The association was a good way
to meet people, and then they had elections shortly after I arrived, and I
ran for secretary and won, and so me and this American were together
on the board.

"Then he asked me if he could use my apartment for meetings. I knew he worked for the Agency but it was out of friendship. If anyone from the CIA had come up to me and said do you want to work for us? No. No way. I'm not interested. What I ended up doing was letting this guy use my apartment for some meetings and I did it out of friendship because I liked him a lot. He would call and I would get out for an hour or two. I don't know who he met or what happened and he paid me $200 a month."[40]

It is almost impossible to believe that anyone—least of all someone as intelligent as Rosario—could be so stupid. But her account is accurate. She rented out her apartment so that the CIA could hold clandestine meetings there, and she immediately entered the CIA database as a source who received money from the Agency. She also became the subject of some interest inside the CIA station in Mexico City. After all, here was this young, vibrant, and attractive woman who had willingly let her apartment become a safe house for covert assignations. The Agency contact had tried to take the relationship further but had failed. Now it was to be Rick's turn.

Rosario's CIA contact introduced the two of them in March 1983, when all three of them took a course at the Museum of Anthropology. To her, he was another American diplomat and she claims that back then she had no idea that he was with the CIA.[41] Again, a more experienced person might have suspected that one CIA officer would introduce her to another, but she insists that she never really questioned Rick about his background. She was content to find yet another older man who could talk on her intellectual level about the subjects that really mattered to her: literature and the arts. There was the added attraction that Ames appeared to have plenty of money and was able to provide her with the kind of lifestyle she believed was her birthright.

Others have a more Machiavellian interpretation of their relationship. Oleg Gordievsky, a former KGB station chief and M16 double agent, recalls that in Mexico, Rosario "moved in circles thoroughly penetrated by Cuban intelligence. . . . It is possible," he continues, "that she was employed to target him, or to persuade him to spy. . . . I should stress," he says, that the idea that Rosario was a latter-day Lady Macbeth is "pure speculation on my part, but it could have happened—the KGB would have taken over from Cuban intelligence when it was apparent how important the case was."[42]

This was a line that was actively followed during the initial post-arrest investigation. A team of counter intelligence officers from the FBI and the CIA interviewed a number of people in the United States, Mexico, and Colombia. They attempted to find a link between Rosario and any other intelligence organization and failed. However unreasonable it might appear at this distance, she was just as naive as she appeared at first glance.

Within a short time of their meeting, Rick and Rosario began a sexual relationship, although sex appears not to have been a particularly important aspect of their love from the outset. Theirs was a mental rather than a physical bonding. However, their romance had an aura of urgency because Rick knew that he would be heading home within six months.

He received a reassignment for that September back to headquarters in Langley. Despite the fact that he had failed at every level of his job in Mexico City and had experienced similar failures in Turkey, it was his record in New York City that counted this time. Ames was rejected by the Latin American Division as deputy chief of station in Bogotá, where his reputation had preceded him.[43] The reassignment back to headquarters was at the behest of another officer, who had worked with Rick in New York; the same officer who had given him such outstanding annual reports.

So the system was able to ignore the failures and focus only on the successes, apparently without any kind of peer review or consideration of the potential consequences. Instead, Ames was promoted to one of the most sensitive positions in the whole CIA, chief of counter intelligence for Soviet operations. He would be responsible for analyzing selected CIA operations involving Soviet assets, reviewing them to ensure they were genuine and that the Agency was not the victim of a Soviet penetration operation. He was the gatekeeper: the man who guarded the Agency's back door to ensure the Soviets had not managed to slip a mole into Langley's heart.

SIX

Sleepwalking to Hell

Three weeks before he returned to the United States, Rick told Rosario that he had been lying to her, that he was not in fact working for the State Department but was a CIA officer working undercover in Mexico. But, he reassured her, he was not into any of the "dirty" stuff but was a simple analyst working for the Intelligence Directorate. This, of course, was just another lie to compound the one on which he had based his relationship with Rosario. It was not the danger that Rosario minded but the fact that he had lied to her about his job and that he worked for the CIA.[1] To Colombians like Rosario, the CIA was almost the personification of evil, the orchestrator of coups, the funder of right-wing dictatorships and fascist guerrilla movements. And now she found herself in love with a man who was working with the very people she had been taught to despise.

"I didn't like it," she recalled. "But by then I guess I was too hopelessly in love, and I decided I could deal with it. But then I never told my family about it, and I should have. If I had told my mother or my family or anybody in Latin America, you know, that the person I had fallen in love with worked for the CIA, I would have been persuaded not to marry him."[2]

This reaction is clear with the benefit of hindsight, but at the time

Rosario must have been more ambivalent. After all, she had willingly taken money from a man she knew to be a CIA officer. Allowing her apartment to be used as a safe house hardly demonstrated the kind of revulsion for the CIA and all its workings she was later to espouse. On the contrary, Rosario was a willing victim who was clearly prepared to compromise her principles for money or, as in this case, love.

In September 1983, the same month he returned to America, Ames formally separated from Nan, who was still living in New York. The couple ratified a "property stipulation" in which Ames agreed to pay her $300 per month for forty-two months, beginning in June 1985 and continuing through November 1989. This placed a new, cumulative debt on Ames of $12,600. Ames also agreed as part of the separation agreement to pay all the outstanding credit-card and other miscellaneous debts, which totaled $33,350.

When he first returned to Washington, Ames stayed with his sister Nancy for a month before finding an apartment in a high-rise at 2300 Pimmit Drive in Falls Church, Virginia. As soon as Rick had found the apartment, Rosario resigned from her job at the Colombian Embassy and headed north to join him. They had already discussed marriage but Rick had not yet secured a divorce from Nan and they both wanted to give the relationship time to settle down before taking the next step. That November, Ames submitted an "outside activity" report to the Office of Security, noting his relationship with Rosario.

The drinking that had become routine in Mexico City followed him to Washington. The incidents in Mexico had been sufficiently serious to provoke a reaction by the CIA station chief, who used back channels to try to get Rick some counseling. He sent a message to the Office of Medical Services at Langley, alerting them that Rick might have a problem. At the same time, the deputy chief of station in Mexico City took him to one side and warned him that this had been done and that he should be prepared for an examination when he returned to Washington.

Once back at Langley, Rick was given one counseling session, but there was no follow-up program of treatment. He was administered blood tests, which proved normal, and he denied to the counselor that he had a drinking problem. The Office of Medical Services was not aware of any incidents of drunken behavior and there was no attempt to contact the Office of Security or the DO prior to the counseling session.[3] The meeting was simply a favor being done for one CIA officer at the request of another. Not surprisingly, given the circumstances, Rick had no difficulty in fooling the counselor and convincing him that all was well.

"There were many much more serious problems of alcohol abuse," Ames said later.[4] His assessment of the Agency culture is right. Regular consumption of alcohol, particularly in the Directorate of Operations, is considered part of the job, not least because the cultivation of sources requires a great deal of social drinking. With such a tolerance of abuse, it is hardly surprising that Ames's performance was considered little different from—and actually much better than—that of many of his colleagues. When the Office of Security conducted a routine background check—such checks are done every five years—on Ames in February 1983, the report said that Ames was a social drinker who was inclined to become a bit enthusiastic when he overindulged in alcohol. In other words, this was merely a case of a social drinker who got a little loud when drunk. There were no attempts to match the reports of long lunches, drunken behavior at embassy functions, or consistently poor performance at work with reports of alcohol abuse.

The return to Washington had meant a promotion and a new title, that of chief, Soviet Operational Review Branch in the Operational Review and Production Group of SE Division. In March 1984, as part of his spycatching duties, Ames was temporarily assigned to a joint FBI–CIA task force that was targeting Soviet Embassy officials in Washington. This was similar to the work he had been doing in New York and identical to Operation Courtship, which had succeeded three years earlier with the recruitment of two KGB officers working for the Soviet Embassy. As part of this assignment, Ames began spending a great deal of time with Soviet Embassy officials based in Washington who had been targeted as possible sources. These contacts were authorized, but as part of the process Ames was supposed to file detailed contact reports, something he had notably failed to do in Turkey, New York, and Mexico.[5]

One potential Soviet recruit assigned to Ames returned to the
U.S.S.R., and so Rick was switched to Sergey Dimitriyevich Chuvakhin,
the embassy's arms control specialist, to see if he could be recruited. But
Ames was already a marked man whose identity was known to the Soviets from his work in New York. The long meetings with Tomas Kolesnichenko, the New York correspondent of *Pravda,* had undoubtedly
been reported to the KGB, and the nature of the Ames discussions would
also have gone into the file. If the roles had been reversed, Ames would
have been marked in the CIA files as a grade 1 prospect, an intelligence
officer who harbored naive views about the unnecessary animosity that
existed between the two superpowers, who was clearly frustrated in his
work and looking for a relationship with someone or something that
would bolster the fantasies he held about himself and his role in the
world. That the KGB, which has a long history of slowly circling a potential recruit over many years, would have ignored such an opportunity
is both unlikely and goes against all the available evidence. So while
Ames was trying to recruit new sources inside the Soviet Embassy, the
KGB was watching him at work and waiting for an opportunity. The se-
ducer was being gently seduced.

Back on home territory and with a boss who seemed to like his work
while he was in New York and was now just as enthusiastic in Washington, Ames appeared to enter a more stable period in his career. His performance appraisals were enthusiastic, even glowing, compared to the
ratings he had received in Mexico. He was judged "above average" and
described as "something of a Soviet scholar . . . [with] considerable experience in working sensitive cases." He was also cited as a good manager.
His supervisor—the same one who had given him the highest possible
ratings in New York—downgraded Ames slightly to a rating performance that indicated he "frequently exceeds the work standards" and his
performance is "excellent." There was no evidence in his file of the
drinking problem that had surfaced in Mexico.[6]

Yet his coworkers from that period recall a different Ames, one who is
difficult to reconcile with the paragon reflected in his annual assessments. "Colleagues still found Ames unsophisticated and lazy, but his
dullness had been replaced by a cavalier attitude and an appetite for
drinking and dancing. Agency hands recall Ames sitting with his feet

propped on his desk, smoking cigarettes and reading old counter intelligence files. He also spent a lot of time chatting in colleagues' offices."[7]

He was again involved in some notable breaches of security. In the summer of 1984 or 1985, after consuming several drinks at a meeting with his Soviet contact, Ames continued to drink at a CIA–FBI softball game until he became seriously inebriated. He had to be driven home that night and "left behind at the field his badge, cryptic notes, a wallet which included alias identification documents, and his jacket." Some recall that senior SE Division managers were either present or later made aware of this incident, but the record does not reflect that any action was taken as a result.[8]

And in the fall of 1984, Ames was sent to New York on a two-week temporary assignment related to the running of a source who was planning to attend a meeting of the UN General Assembly. He decided to take advantage of the Agency's free housing so that he could show Rosario some of the sights. To the surprise of the two others on the mission, Rick took her to the Agency safe house at the San Carlos Hotel, on Fiftieth Street between Second and Third avenues. There, the Agency maintained a number of efficiency apartments for the use of Agency officers passing through New York and for meeting confidential sources.

Such safe houses are understandably kept completely secure, particularly from anyone outside the Agency. If the KGB knew where such a safe house was, they could put the building under surveillance and photograph Agency officers going through the doors and, perhaps, some of their own people on their way to meet with the CIA. To take Rosario there was a clear breach of regulations and immediately compromised the building. Janine Brookner, a fellow officer from the DO, was on the same mission, staying at the same safe house, and she was appalled at such an overt breach of security. She reported Rosario's presence.

"In September 1984, [Brookner] reported [Ames] for violation of Agency policies and procedures including compromising to his foreign girlfriend an Agency safe house, Agency modus operandi, and undercover case officers. The breach, although serious, engendered no investigation or follow up by the Agency. Given the Agency culture, this situation was viewed as a male just doing his thing."[9]

A second CIA officer confronted Ames and reported the matter to senior CIA management in New York. Ames says he complied with a management instruction to move to a hotel room. There is no record that any disciplinary action was taken against Ames in this matter, but both Ames and a headquarters officer recall that when Ames returned to Washington he was told he had exercised bad judgment.[10]

Nonetheless, the incident seems not to have derailed Rick and Rosario's romance and on April 17, 1984, Ames notified the CIA of his intention to marry Rosario. In accordance with CIA policy, this triggered a background investigation of her. On August 27, 1984, Rosario was given a polygraph exam—standard procedure for a foreign national marrying a CIA officer—and she passed without any problem. The Office of Security completed a background investigation of Rosario on November 5, 1984, which included interviews with five of her friends and associates, some of whom commented that "she came from a prominent, wealthy family in Colombia." However, the investigators did not conduct any specific financial checks in Colombia to verify these statements that confused the appearance of wealth with wealth itself. This was an early failure that was to contribute to the disaster that followed.

While the polygraph examination and background investigation did not turn up any derogatory information, the counter intelligence staff of the DO nonetheless recommended that in light of Ames's intent to marry a foreign national, he be transferred from his position as branch chief in the counter intelligence section of the SE Division to a less sensitive position in the Directorate of Operations. This recommendation was accepted by the deputy director for operations (DDO), but no action was taken.[11]

With the pressure of his job and the prospect of his imminent divorce from Nan and marriage to Rosario, Rick was beginning to feel the strain. The divorce settlement, which mirrored the separation agreement, burdened him with a debt of $12,600 over the next four years and committed him to paying off accumulated joint debts of around $33,000. At the time, he earned a salary of around $50,000, so none of these debts was particularly onerous. But since Rosario had come to live with him, his indebtedness had grown through a new car loan, a signature loan, and mounting credit-card payments.

"I felt a great deal of financial pressure, which, in retrospect, I was clearly overreacting to. The previous two years that I had spent in Washington, I had incurred a certain amount of personal debt in terms of buying furniture for an apartment and my divorce settlement had left me with no property essentially. Together with a cash settlement of about $12,000 to buy out my pension over time, I think I may have had about $10,000 or $13,000 in debt. It was not a truly desperate situation but it was one that somehow really placed a great deal of pressure on me. I felt, first of all, that I had let the finances and the household budget slip. We did not live extravagantly by any means. But that through my inability to manage things on my salary, I let things slip. . . . Rosario was living with me at the time . . . I was contemplating the future. I had no house, and we had strong plans to have a family, and so I was thinking in the longer term."[12]

It was these pressures, says Ames, that in April 1985 led him to conceive of "a scam to get money from the KGB." The theory was that he would provide information to the KGB that it would consider revelatory but which was in fact of no value. That way, Ames would get his money but would have given away no secrets.

Ames arranged a meeting with Sergey Dimitriyevich Chuvakhin on April 15, which the Agency and the FBI believed was simply part of a routine series designed to eventually seduce the Russian into working for the CIA. The two were supposed to meet in the bar of the Mayflower Hotel, which lies between the Russian Embassy and the White House. But Chuvakhin was late, and after waiting forty-five minutes, Ames had had several drinks and decided to take matters into his own hands. In what was the first of many extraordinarily foolish breaches of basic security, he simply walked out of the hotel and marched through the gates of the Russian Embassy, where he demanded to see his contact. He handed the Russian an envelope addressed to the ambassador. Inside was a second envelope addressed to the KGB station chief by name. That letter contained two pieces of information and his first demand for money.

The first concerned intelligence the CIA had received six months earlier from a source in the Soviet Union that the KGB was about to send two officers to the West who would appear to be defectors but were in fact double agents. The two had appeared on time and were being run by the CIA, not as doubles but as triples. In his letter, Ames simply told the Russians that the two men were working for the CIA, a fact that was hardly news to the Russians but would appear to confirm Ames's truthfulness.[13]

The second piece of information, which was of much more interest to the KGB, was Ames's real identity. He included his real name, his job description, and a diagram that showed the structure of the SE Division. For the KGB, who had followed Ames's career with interest, this was news indeed. Here was a man whom they had tagged as a potential source who was volunteering high-grade intelligence and who was the most perfectly placed asset they had ever had the opportunity to suborn: chief of the Counter Intelligence Division of the CIA.[14] Finally, Ames demanded a single payment of $50,000 in cash for the information contained in the envelope.[15]

Whether Ames has admitted to all the intelligence that he passed over on this occasion remains one of the outstanding mysteries of the case. There is some evidence to suggest that he actually gave the Soviets other details of Western intelligence sources working in Moscow and in the KGB around the world, but later intensive interrogation and polygraph examinations have failed to clear up this question. What is clear is that the first package of information was enough to convince the Soviets that they had a stunning source who, if handled correctly, might produce even more jewels from the CIA crown.

The Soviets were notoriously stingy with money. Over seventeen years, John Walker, the leader of the Walker spy ring who handed over intelligence to the Soviets worth billions of dollars, was paid just $750,000, and much of that came in small amounts handed over grudgingly. Any approval to pay large sums had to come from Moscow and generally took weeks.[16]

In this case, the Soviets showed no hesitation in meeting Ames's demands. Ames had been targeted nine years earlier, and now was the time to make the first investment in their future. The sum he was asking for, he saw as a single transaction, whereas they saw it simply as a down payment. It is perfectly clear that the Soviet assessment was right: once he had handed over the first—apparently worthless—piece of intelligence, Ames had crossed the line from being Rick Ames, a loyal if drunken CIA officer, to become Rick Ames, traitor.

The Russian Embassy on M Street in downtown Washington, D.C., is located just four blocks from the White House, far away from most of the other embassies, which are located on Massachusetts Avenue. It is a forbidding gray building built in the shape of a U, with the center courtyard facing the street. Its roof bristles with shortwave-radio antennas and the front gates are guarded by security cameras and an intercom entry system. There is a police patrol car permanently parked outside to deal with the protesters who periodically try to daub the iron railings with paint or force their way through the gates. But the visible security is only part of the whole. Inside the embassy, cameras record every move of both diplomats and visitors as they walk down the gray, gloomy corridors. Outside, the FBI keeps a permanent watch on the building from across the street, with cameras photographing every person who goes in and out. Surveillance teams routinely pick up and follow suspected KGB or GRU officers as they go about their intelligence-gathering missions.

From his own briefings at the Agency and from the FBI, Ames knew all about this building and the precautions taken by the Russians as well as the monitoring by the FBI. But he also knew just how inefficient everyone's security really was. The FBI rarely watched its own tapes and the Russians were forced to let down their own guard or nobody—innocent or guilty—would ever get inside the embassy compound. So he knew that when he pushed the buzzer at the right of the embassy's iron gate on the morning of May 15, 1985, he was taking a small risk that would very likely produce a huge reward. After all, Ames had dutifully reported his first trip into the embassy the previous month and no action had been taken.

"There is no way anyone goes into the Russian Embassy," said Ronald T. (Rudy) Guerin, an FBI agent who interviewed Ames after his arrest. "You just don't do that. You get them out. Him [Ames] willing to do that was very strange. Going in a second time was more bizarre."[17] However, Ames's confidence in the incompetence of the system was to prove entirely justified.

He strolled along the short stone path, through the wooden doors, and up to the reception desk, where a plainclothes male receptionist inquired about his business. He asked for Chuvakhin, but instead was escorted to a private room. A man Ames did not recognize entered the room and in fluent English wished him good morning. While the two began an innocuous conversation, the man handed Ames a note. The Russians believed that every move they made inside the embassy was monitored by the Americans. They were sure that directional microphones were aimed at the building, certain that laser microphones were set to pick up conversations by monitoring the vibrations of window glass, and worried that somebody had gotten inside the building and bugged every room.

The note said that the KGB had agreed to pay him $50,000, adding that the embassy wanted to continue using Chuvakhin as a cutout between the KGB and Ames.[18] Two days later, on May 17, Ames met Chuvakhin and received the $50,000 in cash.

Ames had now achieved his goal of earning enough money to pay off all his debts and bank a little for the future. It had been remarkably easy. Becoming a spy was an almost painless experience. There had been no arguments, almost no risk, and the kind of reward he had always believed he was worth but which the Agency had never paid. Looked at in simple terms, this was a straight cash deal carried out by a weak man seeking an easy solution to problems that had grown exaggerated in his own increasingly unstable mind.

But over the next month Ames began to think just how rich he might become and how he could reinforce the relationship that had begun so well. He justified his next huge step along the traitor's road by claiming that he wanted to eliminate any threats to his own position. This is a specious argument, because the sources that the CIA already had in place, including the two inside the Soviet Embassy in Washington, were no threat to Ames. As he well knew, the KGB was rigid about compartmentalization of all sources. Ames's existence would be known only to a handful of KGB officers and he could be certain that the chance of his betrayal leaking to a CIA source and thus back to the Agency was so small as to be irrelevant.

In reality, the Soviets had played Ames perfectly. Without question, they had paid his price, showing him that they understood his real value. They had applied no pressure on him to continue his spying and had not given even the slightest hint that they would blackmail or otherwise force him to commit further acts of betrayal. On the contrary, they were happy to let him hang himself, certain that he would be back for more money and certain, too, that he would need their approval for his selfless acts of bravery that would bring the American and Russian peoples closer together.

They were right. A month after his first visit to the Russian Embassy, Ames made the fateful decision to become a total traitor.

Around six o'clock on the evening of June 12, 1985, Ames was sitting at his desk in the SE Division at Langley. Like all CIA officers of his grade, he had his own modest office in a building that is so anonymous that senior officials insisted on painting the doors in each corridor different colors to improve the morale of those working within. For some minutes he sat surveying the sum of his life as a covert operator: the gray filing cabinet with the security lock, the picture of Rosario on his desk, the pile of paper in his IN tray, the map of the Soviet Union on his wall. It seemed to him then that it didn't appear to amount to very much.

With a dismissive shrug, he finally made the decision he had been edging toward for the past few days. Now, with urgent grasping, sweeping movements, he gathered up the piles of paper that had accumulated on his desk over the past months. With one hand he emptied his OUT tray, with another he lifted a pile of top-secret memos from the floor. Then he swept up all the recent cable traffic that had come in from Moscow Station and all the other outlying parts of the CIA empire that were fighting the Soviet target. One pile after another was shoveled into a plastic shopping bag. By the time he was finished, he had stuffed seven pounds of classified documents into the bag. The haul included information about virtually all the important ongoing cases being handled by the SE Division: information about key sources and methods, the identities of CIA officers working undercover from Langley and abroad, decoded cable traffic, and analyses of different KGB operations. It was a treasure trove.

Ames picked up the shopping bag and closed his briefcase; he walked along the corridor, past the security guard, and through the exit turnstile, and drove back to his apartment. The following day, without any prompting or direction by the KGB or any promise of additional money, he met again with Chuvakhin and handed over the material.

"I'm still puzzled as to what took me to the next steps," Ames reflected later. "The main factor, on balance I think, was a realization after I had received the $50,000, was a sense of the enormity of what I had done. I think I had managed under the stress of money and thinking, conceiving the plan I had carried out in April, I saw it as perhaps a clever . . . not a game, but a very clever plan to do one thing. . . . [I]t came home to me, after the middle of May, the enormity of what I had done. The fear that I had crossed a line which I had not clearly considered before. That I crossed a line I could never step back. And . . . I think in retrospect, it is very difficult for me to reconstruct my thoughts at the time. Before April, I can very well. It was a very rational, clever plan, cut between the middle of May and the middle of June . . . it was as if I were sleepwalking. I can't really reconstruct my thinking. It was as if I were in almost a state of shock. The realization of what I had done. But certainly underlying it was the conviction that there was as much money as I could ever use. If I chose to do that."[19]

"But there was certainly another element, and that was their positive response, which I had fully expected, did make clear to me that there was as much money from the KGB as I could ever ask, or as I could ever conceivably need. That the value of what I had for them was beyond price for them. So, by the middle of June before I was to have lunch with the Soviet embassy cut out or intermediary, I simply in a not very conscious way, I simply delivered my self to them with the information that I had as an act of, some part in desperation, some part in knowing that I would be financially well off, and in a secondary way, also as a measure of protection. While I believed that the KGB would go to very great lengths to compartment and to keep knowledge of me to a very few people in the KGB, other penetrations of the KGB could represent a continuing danger, especially since two of our KGB assets were in the Washington residency. So, there was an element of self-protectiveness to my decision to turn over some of those people. But, on the larger scale, it was an act of, in a sense, a switching of loyalties."[20]

The documents Ames had almost impulsively swept up and turned over to Chuvakhin identified some of the top CIA and FBI agents, including the two working in the Soviet Embassy. The code names of the agents were "GTBlizzard," "GTMotorboat," "GTAccord," "GTMillion," "GTCowl," "GTPrologue," "GTWeigh," "GTFitness," "GTPyrrhic," and

"GTGentile." In addition, he provided the KGB with enough leads to block most of the current CIA operations against the Soviet Union.[21] It was a devastating blow.

CIA officials later described the haul as the "largest amount of sensitive documents and critical information, that we know anywhere, that have ever been passed to the KGB in one particular meeting."

SEVEN

The First Casualty

On May 18, 1985, the day after Ames received his first payment, Oleg Gordievsky, the designated KGB station chief in London, received a telegram from Moscow Center. He was instructed to fly back to Moscow immediately for urgent final consultations before formally assuming his new duties as resident in London. On the surface, there seemed to be nothing particularly unusual about the message: Moscow was always peremptory when it sent a summons; it was always Action This Day or even Yesterday and never Action for Tomorrow. Even so, Gordievsky felt suspicious. For more than nine years, he had been one of MI6's most highly placed agents working deep in the heart of the KGB.[1]

Gordievsky was an unlikely spy for the West. The son of a successful Soviet intelligence officer, he had followed his father into the KGB and seemed destined for a successful and privileged career. The Soviet invasion of Czechoslovakia in 1968 put an end to all that. At the time, Gordievsky was serving as a junior KGB officer in Copenhagen with a brief to recruit sources in NATO. The Soviet invasion caused outrage in the West but also divided the KGB officers into those who opposed the invasion and others who supported it. Gordievsky was in the faction that opposed the attack, and his group bet the invasion's supporters a crate of vintage French champagne that the assault would fail. Gordievsky lost his bet, but the Soviet Union lost the loyalty of one of its most trusted intelligence officers.[2]

Gordievsky knew that Western intelligence routinely monitored all microwave telephone conversations, paying particular attention to any calls going into or out of the Soviet bloc. In the few days immediately after the invasion he made a series of very indiscreet telephone calls to his wife back in Moscow. These were duly picked up by Denmark's intelligence service, which handed their contents over to the British, Denmark's close allies.

To the British, Gordievsky became a marked man, one of those Russians who might, one day, be sufficiently angry to step over the line and begin spying for the West. His career was carefully examined, and it was decided that he had real potential. But it was not until four years later, when he was enjoying an early-morning game of badminton on a Copenhagen court, that an officer from Britain's MI6 approached him. The discussion was brief, but the result was everything the British had hoped. The anger that Gordievsky had felt over the crushing of the Czechs had not cooled with time. He wanted to strike back.

Gordievsky is a quiet, intense man who moves with the short, birdlike movements of the precise thinker. He has wavy, prematurely gray hair and answers questions with the caution and hesitancy of a man who has spent his life in the shadows. But to his SIS handlers, he was a dream, the perfect source. There were none of the unreasonable demands of the neurotic or the unstable. He was always the consummate professional who practiced careful tradecraft and who was entirely motivated by a hatred of the Communist system.

He had a critical role in preventing what might have been a nuclear war between West and East. At the end of November 1981, a circular telegram was sent to all KGB residences in NATO countries as part of a project known as Operation Ryan, which stood for Raketno Yadernoye Napadeniye, or Nuclear Missile Attack. The Politburo had become convinced that, with the arrival of Ronald Reagan in the White House, a surprise nuclear attack on the Soviet Union was likely. They believed the campaign rhetoric used by the Republicans and thought they detected a new fanaticism in America.

Operation Ryan was designed to give the KGB early warning of the preemptive nuclear attack, which, from the outset, was a complete figment of the imaginative paranoia in Moscow. A series of messages over the next three years kept KGB residences around the world apprised of Ryan's progress, with instructions for officers to monitor military traffic, check if the lights were burning late in the White House, and see if the parking lots were unusually full at defense ministries around the world.

The developing crisis became much more serious after the shooting down of Korean airliner KAL 007 on September 1, 1983. While this was a clear error by the Soviet air-defense network, Moscow Center claimed the incident was being used to whip up anti-Soviet hysteria in the West, which in turn would help justify the forthcoming nuclear attack. A further wave of telegrams went out to KGB offices, culminating in one message on November 1983 that reported Western military forces had been placed on a higher state of alert. In fact, NATO was simply in the middle of Exercise Able Archer, an annual command-post exercise that involved no troop movements and no live ammunition. Once the exercise ended, the crisis ratcheted down a notch or two, but still the fifty-strong Operation Ryan team continued to look for early warnings of the impending attack.

Much of this activity was unknown in the West until Gordievsky began passing along the intelligence to his British handlers. He warned that the view from Moscow was so warped that there was a real danger of the Soviets' launching their own nuclear attack to preempt the one they imagined was shortly going to come from America. The problem, Gordievsky explained, was that Moscow believed what it read in the newspapers. If Reagan railed against the Soviets, then he not only believed what he was saying but was prepared to act on it. After all, Moscow Center argued, that is what we would do, and so why shouldn't they act in the same way? The British relayed this intelligence to the White House in the form of a fifty-page paper entitled "Soviet Perceptions of Nuclear Warfare." Unusually, President Reagan read Gordievsky's report from start to finish, with the result that the Republican administration changed its line of propaganda, which gradually reassured the Russians that a preemptive nuclear strike was unlikely.

Gordievsky also had been able to pass over a treasure trove of intelligence, including many of the actual cables transmitted from Moscow

Center, the identity of dozens of moles operating in the West, and the tradecraft used by the KGB around the world. Perhaps as important, he was able to give a vital insight into the thinking of the Kremlin leadership as it took the first tentative steps along the road to political and economic reform. He played a key role in December 1984 when Mikhail Gorbachev, then just a Politburo member but soon destined to become the Soviet leader, visited Britain for talks with Prime Minister Margaret Thatcher. Gordievsky was in the unique position of briefing Gorbachev on what to expect from the British while briefing the British on what Gorbachev had been told to say. At the end of each day, Gordievsky would be debriefed by MI6, which would then pass on his assessment to Thatcher, and the meetings would be adjusted the next day. With such positioning, it was hardly surprising that the visit was considered a great success and that Thatcher thought Gorbachev a man "she could do business with."[3]

Throughout the time he had been spying for the British, Gordievsky's existence had been kept a closely guarded secret among a handful of people within M16. The information he provided, though, had been routinely shared with the Americans, as is customary in such cases. The reports that were sent to Washington were carefully sanitized to disguise the fact they originated with a single person. Despite this, the CIA knew that the British had developed a key source and had been trying to discover just who it was for some years. The reason for the curiosity was in part professional jealousy (just who do they have and how come they have him and we do not?) and in part a wish for reassurance that the person on whom they were pinning so much faith was a genuine source and not part of some complicated game being orchestrated by Moscow Center. MI6 simply refused to answer any of the Agency's questions, but, undaunted, the CIA set up a small team whose task was to try to name MI6's man. One of the members of that team was Rick Ames.

When Gordievsky arrived back in Moscow on May 19, he realized that this was not a routine trip after all. The "urgent" consultations never materialized and despite repeated calls to the office, no one was able to tell him just when he would be needed. He discovered that his apartment had been searched and that he was being followed. It was clear the net was closing, but it was equally clear that the KGB did not yet have the firm evidence it needed to arrest him. Despite the popular fiction, the KGB, particularly when moving against one of its own, was careful to make sure the evidence backed up the allegation.

After a week, he was invited by a colleague to a dinner party at a dacha outside Moscow. The evening was typically Russian with endless courses and huge quantities of vodka being consumed. Soon after the meal began, Gordievsky became convinced that he had been drugged; the joviality ended and questioning began, quickly becoming sharper. Was he an agent for British intelligence? For how long had he been betraying his country?

Gordievsky managed to control his faculties sufficiently to deny everything, and he was taken back to his apartment still a free man. But to add to the pressure, his wife, Leyla, was ordered back from London with their two daughters, Maria and Anna. Gordievsky was informed that he would never be allowed to work abroad again. It was clear that the game was up.

It was only a matter of time before the KGB arrested him and he was charged with espionage. If found guilty, he was certain to be executed. With such a grim future, Oleg began laying his plans for an escape to freedom in the West. His MI6 controllers had always told him that in a crisis they would get him out. It was the kind of reassurance every agent is given by his handlers and only very rarely is it put to the test. On this occasion, Gordievsky managed to contact MI6 through an emergency procedure to tell them he wanted out. The request caused some difficulty in London, where the Secret Intelligence Service was determined to stand by its man. But the SIS also knew that an extraction operation was high risk and might be compromised, with the result that not only would Gordievsky be captured but British intelligence would be exposed as having a hand in what would probably be an illegal operation. That gave the Foreign Office pause and many, including Bryan Cartledge, the British ambassador in Moscow, opposed any action that might upset the delicate relations between Britain and the Soviet Union at this difficult time. The problem was passed around Whitehall until it reached the desk of Prime Minister Thatcher. In typically robust style, she gave her complete support to the SIS. This man has been loyal to us, she declared; the least we can do is show some loyalty in return.[4]

At the beginning of July, Maria and Anna, Oleg's two children, left Moscow for a holiday with relations in the Crimea. Leyla remained in Moscow with Oleg, and he began to lay a series of false trails designed to fool the KGB minders who were watching his every move and listening to every conversation. He had developed the habit of going jogging every day in shorts and a T-shirt, and on Friday, July 19, he left his apartment as usual with a small plastic bag in one hand and set off to jog through the local parks. It was the KGB's habit not to jog after him but to follow by car. They knew his routes well enough, and they were quite confident that he had nowhere to go.

But Oleg diverged from his usual path and made his way to the Leningradsky Vokzal, the station that serves St. Petersburg, northern Russia, Estonia, and Finland. Now dressed in the long trousers he had been carrying in the plastic bag, he bought a ticket on the overnight train to St. Petersburg. By now, he was carrying a set of false papers supplied to him by British intelligence and he was able to pass the security checks that were in place by the time the train arrived at its destination the following morning.

Then Gordievsky boarded a commuter train to Vyborg, which lies eighty miles to the northwest and some thirty miles from the Finnish border. Oleg left the train at a stop before Vyborg; he was met by a car with British diplomatic plates, which contained a secret compartment. Packed inside, he was driven across the Finnish border and met by a delegation from MI6 that included his controller. It was an emotional reunion.

Throughout the trip, Oleg had been shadowed by men and women from MI6 who were determined that he should complete his journey successfully. They were not his traveling companions but observers who were in place in case of crisis. That way, if Oleg was arrested, MI6 might not be directly implicated, but if he simply got into some kind of trouble, then friends would be around to help.

In the post-extraction analysis conducted by MI6, it became clear that someone, somewhere had finally put the pieces together to expose Gordievsky. At first, the SIS was inclined to believe that Gordievsky had simply been exposed by effective counter intelligence work at the KGB. Every agent has a limited life span, however careful the controllers may be to sanitize the intelligence he provides. Gordievsky had delivered a number of Soviet agents to Western intelligence, and the KGB knew perfectly well that there was a leak in Moscow Center. It was conceivable that, in the painstaking way that such molehunts work, they had managed to sift through all the leaks and to gradually narrow the hunt down to Gordievsky as the one name that was common to all the cases. A careful analysis of the traffic from Moscow Center and information from other sources convinced the SIS that Gordievsky's name had come into the frame at some time between April 20 and May 17, 1985.

"Until then the CIA did not know exactly who I was," said Gordievsky. "They knew there was a source, a very good source who was being run by the British. They asked the SIS head of station in Washington to find out from London who the source was and SIS refused."[5]

Oleg's identity may finally have surfaced at the Agency because of a routine report filed to the CIA by the Danish Police Intelligence Service (PET) in 1984 or 1985. Gordievsky arrived in Denmark for the first time in 1966, when he worked as a KGB officer supporting illegal agents (as part of the "N-line" service). This came to the notice of PET because it was the first time any N-line officer had operated permanently in Denmark. PET commenced operations against Gordievsky in the late 1960s together with MI6, but MI6 ended up recruiting him in 1974, on his second tour in Denmark. PET remained closely involved at this stage, because they provided the security for all the covert meetings with Gordievsky, held in a safe house apartment in Skovlunde. Gordievsky supplied PET with invaluable documents detailing Danish agents of Soviet intelligence and other contacts.[6]

When Gordievsky applied for a visa for his formal posting to London in 1984, the fact of his posting was routinely circulated to the CIA, which in turn queried friendly intelligence agencies for any information they might have on the person. It was then that PET inadvertently passed to the CIA information from the Gordievsky file that provided a critical clue to his identity as the British mole in the KGB.

"It was entirely unmalicious," said Gordievsky. "It was one of those stupid mistakes but it was enough to identify me."

The information from PET was the final clue the CIA needed to fill in the blanks about the great British spy, and it was that clue that came across the desk of Rick Ames at the Agency. Although Ames still did not know the precise identity of Gordievsky from the information that came to him, he was able to tell his Soviet contact that (1) there was a high-ranking KGB officer who was a traitor, (2) the traitor had been recruited by the British, (3) he had a background in Denmark, and (4) his CIA code name was "Tickle."

Today, Gordievsky says he is certain that it was Ames who blew his cover, although he concedes that "Ames wouldn't have [my] name at the time. . . . But, Ames would have heard about the kind of information that was coming from me. . . . It would not have been difficult for him to work out that the British had a very important and knowledgeable KGB source with a Scandinavian background working in London. There was only one officer in the London office who fit the bill: me."[7]

After his escape from Moscow, Gordievsky met with Ames many times during debriefing sessions in Washington. The Russian found himself favorably impressed by the CIA officer. "I liked him more than most of the other CIA officers I encountered. His face radiated gentleness and kindness. . . . Ames seemed different. In fact, I was so impressed by him that I thought I had encountered the embodiment of American values: here was the openness, honesty and decency of which I had heard so much. Of course, I didn't know at that point that he had been trying to kill me. When I first appeared at the meeting with him in Washington, I must have seemed like a ghost risen from the dead."[8]

This was an extraordinary confrontation that must be almost unique in the annals of espionage. Here was one of America's great traitors sitting across the desk from the man whom he had betrayed and who had only just escaped with his life. Both were trained observers, skilled in the tradecraft of their business, and yet Gordievsky completely failed to detect any hint of nervousness, any flicker of hesitation in his interrogator. There were no guilty starts, no nervous twitches, just a professional meeting between two professionals. In fact, Ames showed a startling self-confidence at this meeting and at others that were to follow. He was not the weak, vain, and drunken buffoon that he appeared to some of his colleagues. On the contrary, he was a master of his subject and of his emotions, a man so completely in control that he was able to confront Gordievsky and win him over completely.

"That Ames could sit across the table from me, attend meetings with me, and never exhibit a sign of nervousness or betrayal is testament to his mental toughness," said the Russian.[9] Now a rueful Gordievsky realizes just how much Ames was dissembling in those early meetings. He wishes that he had detected the real nature of the man sitting across from him. If he had, many lives might have been saved and much damage avoided. As it is, Gordievsky is simply grateful that he managed to survive.

"He killed over a dozen men," he said. "Of all those he betrayed, I am the only one still alive."[10]

EIGHT

"A Common, Unmarked Grave"

A bookkeeper's son, Dimitri Fedorovich Polyakov was born in 1921 in Ukraine, where he attended military school. He won decorations for bravery when he worked as an artillery officer during World War II, and after the war he studied at the Frunze Academy, the Moscow equivalent of West Point, before signing on as a spy for the Glavnoye Razvedyvatel-noye Upravleniye, or GRU, Russian military intelligence.[1]

In 1956, while he was in his early thirties, Polyakov was given a choice assignment: the Soviet mission to the UN in New York City. There he directed Soviet spies who worked without the benefit of diplomatic cover. It was during a second tour at the UN, from 1959 to 1962, that he made contact with FBI counter intelligence agents in Manhattan. *Pravda* later reported that he first approached the FBI in November 1961 and later met American agents several times at the "Kamerun Hotel," apparently a reference to the old Cameron Hotel on West Eighty-sixth Street. After Polyakov was rotated home for a tour of duty in 1962, the Americans largely lost contact with him, but the post provided him access to GRU penetration of Western intelligence. His next foreign assignment was as military attaché in Burma in 1966, where the CIA took over his handling.[2]

Polyakov turned out to be the ideal recruit. He did not want money for his intelligence but became a spy for ideology, because "it was the right thing to do."[3] In exchange for the secrets he gave, he accepted no more than $3,000 a year, transferred mostly in the form of Black and Decker power tools (he was a carpenter), fishing gear, and shotguns. In addition, he requested lots of trinkets—lighters and pens—that he could give to other GRU officers who did him favors. He considered himself a true Russian patriot who was disillusioned with the Soviet system. Unlike most KGB officers known to the CIA, he drank and smoked little and was faithful to his wife. What mattered to Polyakov were his wife, children, and grandchildren. He wanted his two sons to be well educated and find rewarding professions, which he could guarantee them because of his position in the GRU. The CIA was to aid his career by providing two Americans whom he could show as the fruits of his recruiting. They became double agents for the CIA.

Polyakov's handlers were initially skeptical about his altruism, but eventually understood his perspective. "I think his motivation went back to World War Two," said an unnamed case officer who worked with Polyakov in New Delhi. "He contrasted the horror, the carnage, the things he had fought for, against the duplicity and corruption he saw developing in Moscow." Another CIA officer, who had handled Polyakov's case for fifteen years, said: "He articulated a sense that he had to help us out or the Soviets were going to win the Cold War, and he couldn't stand that. He felt we were very naive and we were going to fail."[4]

Pravda was to give a different, official view of just why Polyakov had decided to become a spy. "What are the sources of his betrayal?" the paper asked. "To explain it all in terms of his not being fully appreciated at his workplace would be naive, although there are such opinions. . . . The situation is not primitive at all. The roots are somewhere very deep. And maybe our 'tree' is such because it is supported by such roots.

"One can track political and ideological change against a background of painful ambition. Somewhere he was misunderstood, and here they are—ambition and love of himself."[5]

Moscow's version of the Polyakov case was published by *Pravda*, which prepared its account with the assistance of the KGB. There are clear discrepancies between the *Pravda* version and that available from Western intelligence sources, with the *Pravda* account continuing to try to maintain the fiction that Top Hat was not a genuine spy for the Americans but a plant by the KGB. According to *Pravda*, the Agency contacted Polyakov in May 1964 by placing a classified ad in *The New York Times* for ten days straight, saying "Moody, Donald F. Please write as you promised. Uncle Charles and Sister Clara are OK."

"This initiative was probably prompted by a CIA hope that Polyakov could tell the agency about Yuri Nosenko." Nosenko had defected to the Americans in January 1964 and was at the center of the dispute between Angleton and other CIA and FBI officers about the existence of a Monster Plot to undermine American intelligence. Some counter intelligence experts say the Soviets soon got wind of the resulting FBI–CIA fight— how remains a troubling question for American counter intelligence experts—and, early in 1965, arranged for "Top Hat," as Polyakov was known, to "give a Soviet spy in England to the CIA as proof he was genuine."[6]

The present came in the form of documents from the Soviet Ministry of Supply that revealed clear knowledge of U.S. missile-guidance technology that had been shared with Britain.[7] The evidence led directly to Frank C. Bossard, forty-nine, a British missile expert employed by the Ministry of Aviation. On his lunch hour, Bossard would pick up a suitcase at the baggage room at Waterloo station which contained his spying equipment and go to a hotel. There he photographed the documents he had removed from the Ministry of Aviation. He received his instructions from Radio Moscow in a code using five pieces of music: "Moscow Nights," "Swan Lake," "Kalinka," "Saber Dance," and the "Song of the Volga Boatmen." The piece of music that was played over the GRU transmitter in Moscow told Bossard which dead-letter box he was to use to dump the secret documents he was copying. It was a clever and almost foolproof arrangement that meant Bossard had met his handlers only once in five years. Without Polyakov, it is highly unlikely he would ever have been detected. Bossard was arrested in March 1965 and later sentenced to twenty years.

Despite this apparent good intelligence, Polyakov fell foul of the paranoia that had already taken hold at the CIA and, to a lesser extent, in British intelligence. Anatoli Golitsin had defected in 1961 with his tales of a massive Soviet plot to destabilize the West. James Angleton had bought all of Golitsin's story and rejected any arguments advanced by Yuri Nosenko that Golitsin was a fraud. Peter Wright, a British MI5 officer, was one of those enticed into the Angleton conspiracy. He was convinced of Golitsin's veracity and just as convinced that Polyakov and another agent in place, "Fedora," were frauds, doubles planted by the KGB and GRU to try to undermine Golitsin, the greatest defector of all time. Both Top Hat and Fedora claimed that the Soviet ICBM program was encountering numerous difficulties and that the United States was far ahead. This assessment of Soviet capabilities was important to the debate about whether the Soviets had sufficient hard-target kill capability to base their military doctrine on preemptive defense.

These allegations, too, were used by Angleton and Wright to play into their grand conspiracy. As they saw it, with Bossard sacrificed to establish Top Hat's veracity, he had moved on to his bigger agenda, which was to discredit Golitsin by establishing that Nosenko was legitimate. Top Hat was also attempting to give the West a completely false sense of security by claiming that the Russians were less advanced in their nuclear and space program than they really were.[8]

It was all nonsense, of course, a despairing cry into the wilderness of mirrors that Wright and Angleton perceived as their real world. Fortunately, there were enough serious intelligence officers in both the CIA and the FBI to fight off the undermining of the man who was to turn out to be one of the most successful American sources of all time.

Through his high-level access, Polyakov was able to tip off the West to several moles: Army sergeant Jack E. Dunlap, who gave National Security Agency secrets to Moscow officials and committed suicide in 1963; Army lieutenant colonel William H. Whalen, a GRU spy on the joint chiefs' staff from 1959 to 1961; Air Force sergeant Herbert W. Boeckenhaupt, who transmitted cryptographic and code information to the GRU; Navy yeoman Nelson C. Drummand, who passed Navy secrets to the GRU; and Bossard.

When Polyakov was posted to Burma, the CIA again used the columns of The New York Times to keep in touch: "Moody—Donald F. I was pleased to learn how lucky you are. See you soon. Everything is fine. John F."

Any suspicions that he may have been a Soviet plant were allayed by the quality of the information he provided. In the late 1960s, while running the GRU's key listening post in Rangoon, Polyakov gave the CIA everything the Soviets collected from there on the Vietnamese and Chinese armed forces. Rotated back to Moscow as head of the GRU's China section, he photographed crucial documents tracking that country's bitter split with Moscow. A CIA specialist on Sino-Soviet relations drew on rich detail from a Soviet source—who he later learned was Polyakov—enabling him to conclude confidently that the Sino-Soviet split would persist. Of course this was used by Angleton as another convincing piece of intelligence that showed what a fraud Top Hat was. It was the idea that the Sino-Soviet split was a myth that drove Angleton and was at the heart of Golitsin's claims. However, Polyakov's paper was used by Henry Kissinger, helping him and Nixon forge their 1972 opening of China.

Polyakov's promotion to general in 1974 gave him access to intelligence that crossed almost every branch of Soviet intelligence. He handed to the Americans the Soviet "wish list" of foreign military technology that the GRU were tasked with stealing or buying in the West. The CoCom list, as it was called, not only told the Americans what the Soviets wanted but illustrated clearly exactly where the gaps were in the Soviet armed forces and their military-industrial base.

"It was breathtaking," recalls Richard Perle, an assistant secretary of defense in the Reagan administration. "We found there were 5,000 separate Soviet programs that were utilizing Western technology to build up their military capabilities."[9]

It was Polyakov's list that encouraged President Reagan to push hard for Western restrictions on the export of technology to Communist countries. The restrictions on exports turned into one of the contributory reasons for the eventual bankrupting of the Soviet economy as it failed to match the West in the arms race.

Polyakov often copied documents with film that could be developed only with a special chemical known to him and his handlers. If the film was processed normally, it would come out blank. He met his U.S. contacts in a variety of places. In Rangoon, he saw them in back alleys. While he was in Moscow, CIA technicians built Polyakov a device into which information could be typed, then encrypted, and transmitted in a

2.6-second burst into a receiver in the U.S. Embassy in Moscow (this transmitter was given to him by CIA agent Paul L. Dillon in India). At other times, Polyakov would speak into a hidden tape recorder on the banks of the Yamuna River in New Delhi, India, while his CIA contact pretended to fish. He would also photograph documents with self-destructing film and then hide the film in hollow, fake stones, dropping them in meadows for pickup by CIA operatives.

With such tradecraft, Polyakov copied more than a hundred issues of the journal *Voyennaya Mysl'* (Military Thought), the classified strategy journal of the Soviet general staff. The insights and frank assessments provided by this important journal enabled analysts to understand how military and political leaders thought about the use of force and their beliefs about their potential for victory in a nuclear war. A close reading of the journal showed the American analysts that far from being "crazy warmongers," as they were often portrayed in American propaganda, the Soviet military were little different from their counterparts in the West.

By the late 1970s, Polyakov had achieved almost legendary status within the Agency. His access was so good and his commitment so high that there was no longer any serious attempt to ask him to provide particular types of intelligence. He knew what the Americans wanted, and they knew that he would do his best to provide it. His abilities were so legendary that on days when his batch of intelligence documents arrived, one CIA officer said, "it was like Christmas."[10]

After Polyakov was unexpectedly ordered back to Moscow in June 1980, an emergency meeting with his CIA handlers was organized. The Agency was worried that perhaps Polyakov had been betrayed and that he was heading home for interrogation and execution. The CIA officer tried to reassure his source.

" 'You know, if anything happens, you are always welcome in our country,' the American began to babble, like a nervous lover. 'I hope the day will come when I can sit down openly with you and have drinks and dinner in the country.' The Russian fixed him with steel-blue eyes and replied quietly and evenly. 'Don't wait for me. I am never going to the United States. I am and I will die a Russian.' 'But what will be your fate,' asked the American, 'if your spying is discovered?' The reply came in Russian: *'Bratskaya mogila'*—a common, unmarked grave."[11]

It was a false alarm that time, and it appeared that once again Top Hat was going to continue with his careful life as a top CIA spy. He continued to deliver the goods until July 1985, a month after Rick Ames had swept his desk of all the classified material at hand and turned over his shopping bag to the Russians. Whereas Oleg Gordievsky was given sufficient time to organize his escape, no such luxury was allowed Polyakov, then head of the KGB's China station. He was arrested in July and after years of brutal interrogation was executed on March 15, 1988.

No one knows where Polyakov is buried or how he died. When Russians are sentenced to *vyshaya mera*—the highest measure (of punishment)—the condemned is taken to a room and made to kneel, then is shot in the back of the head, a tradition begun by Joseph Stalin and continued today.

The arrest and death of Polyakov was a massive loss for American intelligence. For years he had been providing top-grade intelligence to the CIA, and over those years, his various handlers had learned to admire the courage of this extraordinary man as well as to respect the ideals that motivated him. He was judged to be the most careful of agents and his disappearance was a mystery to the counter espionage experts at Langley.

"He was a big catch, and went on for a very long time," says James Nolan, formerly the FBI's top Soviet counter intelligence specialist. "There aren't many who start out as medium-grade officers and rise to the rank of general."[12]

The general was a master of discretion and had successfully avoided arousing suspicion among his GRU comrades for more than two decades. Polyakov's disappearance was picked up within two weeks by the Agency when he failed to make a routine drop in Moscow. The British had already passed on the fact that they had had to pull out Gordievsky, and the level of that loss was only just beginning to be understood. And now there was Polyakov, the best the CIA had.

Whereas Gordievsky was seen as a strictly British problem, the fact that Polyakov had been burned was something for the Agency to sort out. His handlers refused to believe that he could have made a mistake. He had been living too long in the half world of the spy to be caught out in some elementary trap set by the counter espionage experts in the KGB. Everything pointed to a betrayal from within the Agency.

Everything pointed to the fact that Edward Lee Howard had passed on the intelligence that Polyakov existed. The CIA had hired Edward Lee Howard in 1981, and as part of his training for an initial assignment in Moscow, Howard had been given access to the details of certain CIA operations in the Soviet Union, including identifying information on several CIA sources. In 1983, after Howard admitted during a polygraph examination that he had used cocaine while on the CIA staff and had stolen money from a woman's purse, he was fired. Over the next year, he had grown increasingly embittered against the Agency and decided to get his revenge by telling what he knew to the Soviets.

But further investigation revealed that there were two problems with this analysis. First, Howard had not been specifically briefed about Polyakov, and so he did not have the intelligence to pass on. Second, the Agency heard from other sources that Howard had given some bare information to the Russians about the existence of a well-placed CIA mole inside the KGB—not the GRU, which is where Polyakov worked.

Based on that scant information, the CIA knew that the KGB would not have been able to act as fast as it had done. The KGB must have had other intelligence, but exactly where it had come from was unclear. Some within the Agency, particularly Gus Hathaway, who was then head of counter intelligence at the CIA, became convinced that while it might be convenient to lay the blame for Polyakov's loss on Howard, they should actually be looking for another mole buried deep within the Agency.

To his handlers in the Agency, Polyakov was known by different code names—Top Hat to the FBI, "Bourbon" to the CIA, and, on occasion, "Donald" and "Roam." In the Ames court documents, he was GTMillion and GTAccord. Polyakov, hailed as one of the great "Three P's," along with Oleg Penkovsky and Peter Popov, was regarded by American officials as one of their most important foreign assets.[13] His fate was concealed by Moscow until January 1990.[14] Years later it was Jim Woolsey, the director of central intelligence, who provided a fitting epitaph for the man who had managed to fill twenty-five drawers at Langley with top-secret intelligence. Polyakov was the "jewel in the crown" of the Agency. His work "didn't just help us win the Cold War, it kept the Cold War from becoming hot."[15]

Meanwhile, both the British and the Americans had lost their two best sources inside the Soviet Union to Ames's treachery. Here were two men, Polyakov and Gordievsky, who were spies because of what they believed. They were betrayed by a man who believed in nothing except the financial rewards of his work.

NINE

The Year of the Spy

For a brief, terrifying moment as Rick Ames read through the cable from the CIA station in Rome, he felt his heart beat wildly as his blood pressure soared. Struggling to focus on the paper, he sensed disaster, his career as a Russian spy exposed only a month after he had handed over his treasure trove of material to his new masters. An image of his immediate future flashed before him: the arrest, the ignominious exit through the corridors of Langley with colleagues and friends seeing the handcuffs and understanding the perfidy.

The top-secret message that arrived from Rome on August 1, 1985, gave the first details about the defection of Vitaly Yurchenko, a man who could have all the details about Ames's treachery. Yurchenko was the deputy chief of the KGB's First Department of the First Chief Directorate and responsible for all operations in North America and Canada. He would thus be in a position to name all the sources controlled by the KGB in the area and brief the CIA on the methods and tasks of the KGB officers working in America. Potentially, this was a stunning coup, and Ames had been chosen to get Yurchenko safely back to America and organize a team to handle his debriefing. Aside from Ames, there were three key players involved in the debriefing of Yurchenko and the analysis of the information he provided. Clair George was deputy director of operations, head of the CIA's clandestine service, a post he had been appointed to by DCI Bill Casey and which he had held for a year. George, a thin, spare man, was a veteran of CIA operations in the Far East and the Middle East. He had been station chief in Beirut and Athens and, more recently, had masterminded Casey's efforts to overthrow the government of Nicaragua. He would later be badly tarnished by the Iran-Contra affair and forced to resign from the Agency. But for now, he was the most important power—aside from Casey himself—at the Agency.

Gus Hathaway was head of counter intelligence at the CIA and Ames's direct boss. Hathaway had a justified reputation for being taciturn and for the kind of subdued formality that was more common among a previous generation of covert operators. Hathaway had run sources in Eastern Europe and had earned a reputation as a tough, very aggressive officer who was respected by colleagues and his counterparts in foreign intelligence services. Hathaway had recently returned from a tour as station chief in Moscow and so had a very clear idea about both CIA sources in the Soviet Union and the capabilities of the KGB. His job was to uncover any penetration of the CIA, or indeed of American intelligence, by the KGB. If he had a target, it was Ames, the very man whom he had personally briefed to handle Yurchenko.

The third man was Burton Lee Gerber, the head of the SE Division and a former Moscow station chief like Hathaway. At fifty-two, Gerber was eight years younger than Hathaway but he appeared just as conservative, with that innate caution that seems to be a hallmark of so many senior CIA officers. For Gerber, the defection of Yurchenko represented a considerable coup. If handled right, his debriefing would offer prizes enough for everyone.

It was with mixed feelings that Ames received this news. Clearly, the fact that he was being trusted with such a responsible job was a measure of the confidence the Agency retained in him. But it was possible that Yurchenko might have sufficient information to identify Ames, the new source of which the KGB was undoubtedly very proud. As he flicked through the first cables from Rome, he searched anxiously for any information that might suggest Yurchenko knew of his existence. It would be the first thing Rome Station would have asked about, the question on everyone's mind: Was there an enemy within? The answer appeared to be that there might be a couple of embarrassing sources working for the KGB but neither of them sounded like Ames.

"It was apparent to me when I read the cables that Yurchenko didn't know anything about me so that put my mind at ease," Ames recalled. "And so, I spent the next twenty-four hours or so organizing, you know, the safe house, the reception at Andrews, and reading his file and preparing the initial debriefing. I went out to Andrews and met him and we took him to the safe house and I played the key role in the first day and a half, two days, of debriefing.

"From the psychological point of view, there was never a time that I can recall where I sat in a meeting, organizing a reception for Yurchenko or something else like that and sort of said in the back of my mind 'If they only knew.' I kept these things very apart in my mind. I really did."[1]

Just how relaxed Ames really was at the prospect of meeting Yurchenko is unclear. Certainly he was sufficiently nervous the night before the Russian's arrival at Andrews to get so drunk that he almost overslept.[2]

When Yurchenko arrived at Andrews Air Force Base on board an American Air Force executive jet, he was immediately taken to a CIA safe house in northern Virginia and the debriefing began. To the eager CIA team, Yurchenko appeared something of a typical Russian. He was a big bear of a man with a gravelly voice and droopy black mustache, the kind that was fashionable in America in the 1960s. He spoke English fluently but with a heavy Russian accent and was missing the tips of two fingers of his right hand, which had been caught in a winch when he worked as a repairman on Soviet submarines while doing a stint in the Navy.[3]

Ames's relaxed approach to the meeting was almost shattered at that first meeting. In answer to that all-important question about the mole, Yurchenko explained that "something" had happened at the Washington station, something so important that the KGB station chief had actually flown home for consultations. Ames knew that that "something" had been his own recruitment. The fact that Yurchenko brought up the information helped convince Ames that his defection was genuine. Of course, he could do nothing to prevent that information from getting out, because every question and every answer of the interrogation were faithfully recorded. But he need not have worried. The Agency failed to follow up the Yurchenko tip, apparently believing that the defector was reading too much into a routine consultation between the station chief and headquarters.[4]

In the first twenty-four hours of his debriefing, Yurchenko, who knew exactly what kind of intelligence his handlers wanted, was able to finger two important sources inside American intelligence, but the identity of both was vague. The first was a man he knew only as Mr. Long, who had first walked into the Soviet Embassy in Washington in January 1980 offering to sell American secrets. He had offered details on a secret National Security Agency project known as Ivy Bells, which involved tapping into undersea telecommunications cables that the Soviets thought were secure. It had been one of the NSA's most successful secret projects and had yielded volumes of intelligence about the codes and plans of the Russian military command. The man would later be revealed as Ronald W. Pelton, who worked at the National Security Agency and had passed to the Soviets many of America's most sensitive communications secrets, including codes.

Yurchenko also revealed that a second source, code-named "Robert," worked for the CIA. He knew nothing else about the man apart from the fact that he had traveled to Vienna to meet with the KGB in 1984 and that he had been assigned to Moscow by the CIA, and so knew the names of many CIA sources in the Soviet Union and the methods used to contact them. Yurchenko added that, for reasons he did not know, Robert had never actually taken up his Moscow post.

To both Gerber and Hathaway, the identity of Robert was immediately clear. The fears they had had all along about Edward Lee Howard were simply being confirmed. And yet the situation they found themselves in could have been avoided. The moment Howard had been dismissed, the FBI should have been alerted that a potential security risk was out on the street. In fact, the Agency did everything possible to cover up the details of Howard's hiring and firing, evidently too embarrassed to admit the mistake. Even after the Agency heard that Howard had been considering selling secrets to the Soviets, they simply took him to see the CIA's chief psychiatrist, who counseled him and sent him on his way. Again, although there was now clear evidence of an intention to betray his country, the FBI was not informed.

Now that Yurchenko had come up with his damaging leads, there was no longer any question of covering the case up. Still, it was a full five days before the FBI was told of Howard's existence, and even then the Bureau was given only a partial account of who he was and who his friends were. This was to so hamper the FBI's investigation that it would be unable to gather the evidence it needed to arrest him.

And so on September 21, some six weeks after Yurchenko had identified him, Howard and his wife, Mary, left their home in Santa Fe, New Mexico, for a meal at a nearby restaurant. After the meal they headed home, with the FBI tail car in tow. Then, using a technique he had learned at the CIA's own training school at Camp Peary, Mary slowed the car down, Howard flicked open the side door and rolled out into some bushes by the side of the road. Immediately a dummy, complete with wig and clothes, popped up into the passenger seat, reassuring the tail car that Howard remained inside.

Howard turned up in Moscow a few weeks later and from there was able to continue his betrayal of many of the American sources inside the Soviet Union. It was a defection that could easily have been avoided, had the CIA dealt with the situation openly and had the DO not been so concerned about its own image within the Agency and outside.

For Yurchenko, there was little satisfaction in the Americans' exposure of the traitors toward whom he had pointed them. Many defectors go through a period of depression after leaving their home country, and Yurchenko was no exception. Although he had been promised a cash payment of $1 million and a generous salary for life, he missed his own country and particularly missed a woman who was attached to the Soviet Embassy in Canada who had once been his mistress. The CIA arranged for him to travel north to see the woman, but the meeting was not a success, because Yurchenko's offer to her of setting up a new life in exile was spurned.

In Yurchenko's case, the CIA appears to have gone out of its way to alienate him. The Agency had promised to keep his identity secret, but leaked his defection to the papers. It promised not to reveal the intelligence he had handed over, but then circulated videos of his debriefing and told the press just how he had fingered both Howard and Pelton. Yurchenko felt lonely and betrayed. On the night of Saturday, November 2, he went out to Au Pied du Cochon, a French bistro in George-town, accompanied by one of his CIA minders. He left the table to get some fresh air, hailed a taxi, and took it to the Soviet Embassy com-pound on Wisconsin Avenue. He was immediately let in and became not just the highest-ranking KGB official to defect to the United States but the most senior official ever to redefect to the Soviet Union.

Some intelligence officials believe that Vitaly Yurchenko was sent to protect or monitor Ames's espionage activities. "I can envision a sce-nario where Yurchenko was sent to see if Ames was for real and test the quality of his reporting," says Harry (Skip) Brandon III, who retired in January 1994 as deputy chief of counter intelligence for the FBI.[5] After Yurchenko returned to Moscow, the Soviets could compare what he un-covered with what Ames had given them. Yet, although Ames was re-sponsible for debriefing Yurchenko they were never alone, because Yurchenko was under a twenty-four-hour CIA security watch. Brandon also attempts to explain the possibility that Yurchenko was sent to pro-tect Ames. Those subscribing to this theory believe that Yurchenko gave up Edward Lee Howard and Ronald Pelton specifically to deter a full-blown CIA investigation for a penetrated agent. Angelo Codevilla, a Senate Intelligence Committee staffer at the time of the Yurchenko de-fection, described the CIA as "relieved" when Yurchenko failed to un-cover other active moles.[6] That may be so, but there is really no evidence that Yurchenko was a plant of some kind.

Bob Gates has a simpler explanation: "I think there were two things that were catastrophic from our standpoint. One was when we let him go to Canada to try to reignite an old relationship and the woman rejected him. Then we thought he needed a break and took him to Las Vegas and suddenly not only was he not a clandestine operative but nobody gave a shit that he was a colonel in the KGB. And he couldn't write a check and he had a hard time ordering breakfast. It was the little stuff. Each day it was hard for him and he didn't get any deference like he had in the So-viet Union and all of a sudden it was very boring.

"It was a classic case where a spur-of-the-moment defection so frequently goes sour. The guys who have done best are those who worked in place for a long period of time and then come over with some preparation."[7]

After Ames was exposed, the whole Yurchenko file was reviewed in the light of the wealth of information that had now surfaced, and the CIA reinvestigation of the case concluded that Yurchenko was a genuine defector. It also concluded that the content of the twenty or so meetings that Ames had with him was relayed in its entirety to Ames's Soviet controllers in their Washington embassy. Ames was debriefing Yurchenko, typing up his notes of the meeting, and making a copy for his controller. This substantially devalued much of the intelligence that Yurchenko was handing over but was insufficient to save either Howard or Pelton from discovery.

But if Yurchenko had not been sent as a blind to cover up the Ames betrayal, it is clear that after his return to the Moscow fold he was given clear instructions by his KGB handlers to protect the man whom he had known as "Phil" during his interrogation. At a press conference after his redefection, Yurchenko named two of the three CIA handlers but omitted all mention of Ames. This was later the subject of a running joke in the Agency—that Yurchenko had omitted to mention Ames on the instructions of the KGB. It was a joke based entirely on the truth.[8]

The Yurchenko defection was not allowed to interfere with Rick's personal arrangements. Two days after Rick escorted Yurchenko to his safe house in Virginia and finished the first debriefing, Rick and Rosario were married at a Unitarian church in Arlington, twelve days after his divorce from his first wife, Nancy Jane Segebarth, was finalized. Although the full details of the divorce are unclear—the judge sealed the papers for a hundred years—Rick's McLean High School classmate Michael Horwatt, who handled the divorce, said it was "uncontested and uneventful."[9]

Rick and Rosario's wedding ceremony was short, and few attended. Rick apologized to his guests at the reception for serving only wine, commenting that his recent divorce had financially devastated him, leaving him "poor."[10]

During their courtship, it had seemed to Rosario that Rick always had plenty of money. In Mexico he was living the life of a CIA officer abroad, which meant that he was banking his salary and benefiting from a very generous expense allowance. As Rosario was on the CIA books as a person receiving money from the Agency, Rick was able to charge legitimate expenses while entertaining her. When they returned to America and to Washington, there was a brief change in the lifestyle that Rick handled by going deeper into debt, which partly accounted for his later decision to spy for the Soviets.

But once the money started flowing in from his new paymasters, Rick was forced to devise a cover story that he hoped would account for what he expected would be a significant change in their fortunes. He explained to Rosario that he had made a number of private investments while he was a student in Chicago. These had been done with a fellow student known only as Robert, and they had proved so smart that they continued to produce large amounts of income. Until just before their arrest, Rosario believed that the hundreds of thousands of dollars of income were generated entirely by these investments. This sophisticated, well-educated, and intelligent woman chose to accept this story and made no effort to find out just who "Robert" was or to ask Rick just why in all their years of marriage she had never been introduced to the man who had turned out to be such an important benefactor to herself and her family. She also chose never to question Rick as to just why all the money from his investments was never declared to the Internal Revenue Service on the family tax returns.

Today, when questioned about such basic flaws in her claims to be an innocent victim, she angrily maintains that she simply believed what she was told. "He liked to live well but not extravagantly," she said. "When I got married to Rick, when he had already started what he was doing, I married a man with investments. He said he had extra income other than just his salary that came from investments he made when he was at the University of Chicago. I'm not a person who's ever been interested in finances. He is not a lower-class person, and the class of people I belong to, it's just a normal type of life for me. There was nothing, no sudden change. People think that all of a sudden in the middle of our marriage, you know, all of a sudden money started coming in. No, when I married Rick, he had already started doing what he was doing and that's why it's all so unforgivable because when he married me, he had already made all the choices."[11]

The second lie Rick had to create was at the Agency itself. He was surrounded by mid-level bureaucrats in an organization that does not pay particularly well. His colleagues all suffered from the usual middle-class problems of high taxes, low income, and big mortgages, subjects each and every one of them would discuss with the others from time to time. Rick was clearly the exception, and was to become even more of an exception as time passed. Marriage to Rosario was to provide the perfect cover for him. He simply let it be known that he had married money, that Rosario's family were well off and that they provided additional financial support for his family. It was simple enough to arouse some envy but no suspicion. However, as Rick himself acknowledges, this was a high-risk strategy that could have been exposed at any time.

"I told Rosario that while I wasn't doing anything illegal, it was not entirely proper that I do this and that I was cutting a corner here (with my investments). So she understood that. What did concern me, however, was the extent, was the possibility that someone might say to her, my your family is very well off. And she would say what are you talking about? My family, her family was well known for never having money. . . . If you asked anybody in the family, they would say they don't have any money. Her mother and father were . . . well known for not being wealthy."[12]

But during all the time Ames was spying, it is amazing but true that in an organization filled with people trained to observe and to question, nobody saw the obvious extravagance and thought on a single occasion to ask either Rick or Rosario about the source of their wealth. This cadre of trained professionals chose to ignore the first thing counter espionage experts are told to look for when hunting a spy—unexplained wealth—and instead took at face value the gossip that had been carefully planted by Ames.

Even before the Yurchenko drama had begun to unfold, American intelligence had been rocked by a series of spy scandals that were merely crowned by the Pelton and Howard affairs. In total, there were eleven spies arrested in America in 1985, among them John Walker, who headed the Walker spy ring and handed over communications codes that caused billions of dollars of damage to the American armed forces;

Jonathan J. Pollard, the Israeli spy; and Lawrence Wu-tai Chin, a spy for the Chinese. So many agents were uncovered in 1985 that the Reagan administration nicknamed it the Year of the Spy.

But if it was a good year for the counter intelligence people, it was also an exceptionally bad year for those running sources inside the Soviet Union. Adolf Tolkachev was a military researcher in Russia who passed the CIA the Soviets' most precious secrets on their "stealth" radar research throughout the 1970s as well as other valuable Soviet defense secrets, including research in aircraft technology and electronic guidance systems and countermeasures. On June 13, 1985, Tolkachev was arrested while meeting his controller, Skip Stombaugh, an Agency officer working as a second secretary at the embassy in Moscow. He was executed in November 1986.[13]

Other Soviet contacts began vanishing about the same time. In a perfect piece of duplicity, the KGB ordered Valeriy Martynov, one of the two officials in the Soviet Embassy in Washington who had been recruited as part of Operation Courtship, to escort Yurchenko back to Moscow, where he was arrested.[14] Nine days later, Martynov's wife, Natalya, received a message, ostensibly from her husband, asking her and the children to join him in Moscow. The letter claimed he was stuck in Russia after an old knee injury had flared up, and he was likely to be there for some time. As soon as she arrived in Moscow, Natalya was taken in for questioning and learned for the first time that her husband was a spy for the Americans. Over the next two years, she visited him four times in jail and on each occasion he showed obvious signs of a brutal interrogation. Finally, he was shot by firing squad on May 28, 1987. It took nine days for the official notification of his death to reach Natalya, because the message had been sent to the wrong address.

Natalya has never met Ames and had not heard of him until his arrest and long after her husband had been killed.

"He betrayed my husband, and my husband was executed simply because of Ames," she said. "Of course he knew what would be the end result and if he says now that he did not know, he lies."[15]

Sergey Motorin, the other Operation Courtship recruit, was caught the day after meeting with his U.S. handlers, just after Martynov had been summoned back to Moscow. Like his colleague from the KGB,

Motorin suffered months of brutal interrogation before being shot. Others began disappearing, too: a double agent posted in Nigeria and one posted in Southeast Asia.

In October 1985, the CIA learned that a second intelligence asset in a European country, who traveled to Moscow in August on home leave, had never returned to his post. In December of that year, the CIA discovered that this asset had also been arrested. In January 1986, the CIA ascertained that a third source posted in a European country had been taken into custody by Soviet authorities in November and returned to Moscow.

These agents were the best that the CIA had managed to recruit within the Soviet Union. Almost at a stroke, Rick Ames had managed to unravel years of work by both the CIA and the FBI, destroying the networks that had been so carefully established. There had never been such a casualty list in the history of American intelligence. And the losses were only just beginning.

According to the CIA analysis, Edward Lee Howard had known none of these agents. Thus, while Howard's treachery had initially clouded the picture, it was clear to the SE Division of the Directorate of Operations by the end of 1985 that the defection of Howard alone could not explain the disastrous events that were unfolding.

Indeed, throughout 1986, the CIA continued to learn of Agency operations that had been compromised to the Soviets. As one CIA officer put it, "they were wrapping up our cases with reckless abandon." This was, by all accounts, highly unusual behavior for the KGB. If the KGB had recruited an agent within the CIA, the last thing it would likely do— according to the prevailing wisdom among the Agency's professional spycatchers—would be to draw attention to the agent by suddenly rolling up all the cases he knew about. But the shock of the intelligence that Ames had provided had been felt all the way up to the Politburo. There was consternation at the level of CIA penetration of the Soviet security structure, and the political leadership had taken precisely the action that defied all conventional intelligence wisdom. In fact, the KGB officers had argued against that action: if they began to arrest the sources who had been betrayed by Ames, that would provoke a massive manhunt by the American counter intelligence units that would be bound to expose their source. This would be crazy, particularly as Ames had only just surfaced and they had yet to begin to tap his real potential. But the conventional argument was lost on the political leadership and the arrests began, to the astonishment of Ames himself. He had a complete understanding of how the intelligence world worked, and so when he handed over his gold mine, he was certain that nothing would happen for several months and that the arrests, if they ever happened, would take place over several years.

"I had a very valid and legitimate presumption that when I provided all that information to the KGB that they wouldn't do any such thing as what they did. I presumed that as they had done in many other cases, as any intelligence service would do, or counter intelligence service, they would have been extremely concerned over the need to protect not only my identity, the fact that I was a source, but that they had such a source."[16]

By the time the first arrests began to surface within the intelligence community and the leaks started to appear in the press, Ames had left his job to begin language training prior to a new assignment in Rome. Of course, he had heard about the arrests and the disappearances on the gossip network and had made the connection between his betrayal and the disaster that was unfolding for the Agency. It was then that he began to understand the potential consequences of what he had done, and he became frightened that he was about to be arrested. Later the KGB would apologize to him for its actions.

The curious part of this episode is that in the first moments of his betrayal, Ames appears to have thought little or nothing about the consequences of what he was doing. Then, seduced by the money, he committed to betray again, handing over the documents and information that led to the deaths of so many trusted CIA sources. He was then confronted by the real fear of imminent discovery, the apparent certainty of arrest and imprisonment, with all that would mean: the loss of wife and family, the disgust of his colleagues, the loss of all his friends. And yet, in all the attempts he has made to justify what he did, in all the hours that have been spent interviewing him, there appears to have been not a single moment when he hesitated. There was not a second when he paused and thought about the road he had taken, debated with himself whether he should abandon his new friends in the Soviet Embassy. He showed no remorse for the men he had killed, the people who had trusted their lives to the CIA and whom Ames had executed as casually and certainly as a murderer sweeping a crowded shopping mall with a machine gun. Far from demonstrating any regret, he remained completely determined to continue with his life as a traitor. At last, he had found a role in his life that he felt was worthwhile.

TEN

Defending the Faith

Apparently oblivious to the turmoil going on around him, Ames continued his meetings with Chuvakhin, his Soviet cutout. Permission had been given for these meetings by Lee Gerber, his boss in the SE Division, and had also been authorized by the Courtship team. To prepare the ground for these meetings, Ames had told the Operation Courtship team that the Russian was a likely potential recruit whom he was courting. After each lunch, he would file a report on the meeting, describing what the Russian had said and how he was playing hard to get. Yet there seems to have been little attempt by either party to check on what was happening.

"Rick was trying to play a funny game, you know, because in one sense he was—he wanted to make it look good enough so that everybody would want to continue the operation, but on the other hand not make it look so good that people would start to focus on it. And not to make it look so good that when Rick decided to withdraw from it, that someone else would want to take over the case."[1]

At first, these meetings were taken quite seriously by his superiors, but as 1984 moved into 1985 and five meetings turned into ten and ten moved toward twenty, there was a growing disbelief that the Russian would ever come over. But there was a clear sense that this was Rick's case, that he should be allowed to develop it if he wanted. Rick played into this casual attitude and then exploited a clear disconnect between the Courtship team and Langley. At first he filed his contact reports to the field office and copied them to Langley. By July 1985, Ames occasionally reported meetings to the CIA, which passed some details on to the FBI. Then he simply stopped filing reports and each side was under the impression that the other was getting the paperwork. The FBI was aware that the meetings continued and requested that the CIA follow up to ensure that Ames submitted formal reports of the meetings, as required by both organizations. "There were two or three times that our people either went over there and finally actually sent a communication over asking CIA why aren't we receiving any of the reports of these meetings. But the reports were never forthcoming and neither CIA nor FBI followed up. Also, the reports that were made were not shown to his current bosses in SE."[2] The FBI presumed that the CIA knew of the meetings and that Ames was simply slow in getting the paperwork done.

Even now, this apparent inability of the CIA to persuade one of its own men to comply with elementary procedure still rankles at the FBI. The Bureau's records clearly show that the Agency was asked many times about the obvious difference between its own surveillance records of Chuvakhin and the number of times Ames actually reported meetings. This was the most elementary flag that should have drawn an immediate response from the CIA. Almost the only way the Russians run an agent is through dead drops and regular face-to-face meetings. The fact that Ames was having the latter might have suggested he was also servicing the former.

"There was some pressure by us with the CIA for them to obtain the reporting from them on those contacts," said John Lewis, deputy assistant director at the FBI, who later helped in the hunt for the mole. "And I have to say that was never adequately addressed at that time. Once he transferred to Rome, we have records where we asked the CIA to please go to Rome and ask him about these contacts. Unfortunately for everyone, that was not done."[3]

In fact, Ames was meeting with Chuvakhin at least once a month and handing over a cornucopia of material. During this period, he established a pattern that he was to continue throughout his career as a spy.

He would go to work at Langley and either print out from the database or copy documents that flowed across his desk that he thought might be of interest. This included information about sources, double agents, tradecraft, communications codes, and the identity of CIA officers working in Langley and in the field. It was a vast dump of material that is literally without precedent in the annals of espionage. There was no attempt to filter, to select the few choice gems that really sparkled. Instead, he would fill his briefcase or plastic shopping bags, take them home, and then hand them over to his contact.

Usually handlers will try to direct a source to critical pieces of information that are of high value. This helps establish a master-servant relationship that makes the source feel needed. In this case, the Russians made no such attempt to control Ames, recognizing, perhaps, that when he was left alone, he produced more and better intelligence than they could ever demand and would ever normally expect an agent to deliver.

Realizing his value, the Soviets ensured that Ames received regular payments, which ranged in size from $20,000 to $50,000, all in cash. The Russians clearly understood that whatever other, complex motives he might have, Ames responded well to large sums of money.

Ames maintained several local bank accounts in his name, as well as in his new wife's name, where he would regularly deposit the cash he received from the Soviets. When Ames received a payment from the KGB, he generally broke it down into smaller cash deposits—in increments under $10,000—in order to avoid bank-reporting requirements that might have led to inquiries by banking regulators.

In Moscow, the First Chief Directorate of the KGB established a small unit that was dedicated entirely to handling the Ames product. It was to be the most productive of any section of the KGB and, in fact, would become completely overwhelmed by the volume of material that Ames was to deliver. After its initial unprofessionalism in arresting so many sources, the KGB became totally obsessed with protecting its prize. The Ames unit was kept small to prevent the risk of leaks, but this stopped it from processing all the material he produced. Instead, unit members had to make rapid priority decisions to act on some intelligence while stockpiling other pieces for later examination. Eventually the backlog was to become almost unmanageable. It is a measure of the depth of Ames's betrayal that now, more than a year after his arrest, this unit is still working full-time processing that backlog of intelligence.

What Ames was doing was not simply naming names. He did plenty of that, but he also did much more by betraying the methods by which the CIA recruits sources and then runs them. So, he was betraying not just the substance of today but the style of tomorrow. Armed with the initial bursts of information, the KGB was able not just to stop CIA penetration of the Soviet target; by developing a deep understanding of the inner workings of the Agency the KGB was also able to run a series of successful operations against the Agency. It knew to a fine degree just what deceptions might work and why. By the end, it knew, too, the identity of just about every single covert operator in the SE Division and many of the men and women working elsewhere in the Agency. It was as if the KGB had been invited to Langley to look over the personnel files, the training files, and the intelligence provided by every major source operating in and around the Soviet Union. Even now, after all this time and the exhaustive debriefing of Ames, the CIA still does not fully understand the extent of Ames's betrayal.

As case after case collapsed, the SE Division at the CIA was in turmoil. Gus Hathaway, whose responsibility it was, began the search for clues as to who or what might have caused the losses. In such cases, the analysis of what has gone wrong in an operation tends to be lengthy and complex. In some rare instances the source of the betrayal is clear—Kim Philby turns up at a press conference in Moscow, for example. More usually, there is no simple answer and the investigation begins with an underlying assumption that every source has a limited life span. Whatever the precautions, there is an expectation that a source will eventually be compromised. After all, the other side is working hard to plug any leaks it knows may be in its own ranks or simply to discover leaks that it suspects may be there. A source may just be unlucky or an officer running the source may be compromised or the tradecraft may become obsolete.

These are all routine solutions to the complex problems of counter espionage, and they are the solutions that the investigators naturally look for. In this instance, there were twenty or so major cases that had been compromised by Ames in a few short months. About half of the cases could be directly attributed to Howard, whereas the others remained open. The CIA knew as a matter of historic fact that if the Soviets had developed a source within the Agency that they were still running, they would not have done anything so stupid as to arrest in such a short period the people he had betrayed. That would compromise the source and provoke an instant investigation. That went against all standard intelligence practice, both in the Agency and in the KGB.

In this case, it proved impossible for the counter intelligence (CI) team to project their investigation beyond the confines of what had always happened in the past, to reach into the Kremlin and try to measure the impact of all these agents being named at once by a single source. It was simply inconceivable. It was therefore also inconceivable that the Soviets should have been so horrified at the extent of the penetration of the Soviet political, military, and industrial structure that they felt they had to defy convention and take immediate action.

So the investigators looked elsewhere. The first and most obvious answer was that the Soviets had somehow managed to penetrate the communications between Langley and its field officers. A series of dummy messages was sent over a three-month period at the end of 1985 to try to flush out a Soviet response. There was no reaction of any kind, and the Agency concluded that the penetration problem lay elsewhere.

As the investigation moved into 1986, there was no sign of any real progress. No human source had been identified, and there were no clues suggesting that there might actually be one. The communications lead had been tested and found secure. There was no indication that the Soviets had managed some massive coup that at a stroke had given them access to all the most secret files. There was simply no answer to the question of why there had been so many key sources blown in such a short time. Reluctantly, Hathaway and his team concluded that without further evidence there was essentially no answer, that each of the compromises could be explained by individual failures by the source, by the handlers, by the tradecraft, or by the successes of the KGB. As a result, the investigation ground to a halt.

Despite his signing off on the initial investigation, Hathaway himself retained some doubts about whether they had been looking in the right place. He had a nagging suspicion that it was a mole and not simply a series of coincidental mistakes that had brought down so many sources. But without evidence, there was nothing he could do. However, when Oleg Gordievsky came to Washington in February 1986 as part of his general debriefing, Hathaway arranged for a private interview with him. The two men talked for over an hour, and while Hathaway never specifically asked Gordievsky if he thought there was a mole in the CIA, the questions went around and around the same subject. Had Oleg any idea how he might have been betrayed? Who knew what he was doing? Just how effective were the CI people in the KGB? Gordievsky, who had no real idea of the extent of the damage done to the CIA's efforts inside the Soviet Union, was an experienced enough intelligence officer to understand the tenor of Hathaway's questions.

"He suspected, no he knew that there was a mole and he wanted me to help find him," said Gordievsky. "He was very worried."[4]

By the fall Lee Gerber, chief of the SE Division, and Hathaway were to become so obsessed by the thought of a killer working among them that they barely noticed the early unraveling of Irangate.[5]

Just in case the investigation was wrong and the rot ran deeper than anyone really believed, the SE Division was restructured at the beginning of 1986 to refine compartmentalization. Cases were handled by fewer people, new coding systems were introduced to sanitize files, and access to those files was further restricted so that no single person or group of people had any clear idea of just how many sources were being handled within the SE Division at any one time and who those sources were.

The investigation by Hathaway and Gerber had been conducted under the watchful eye of Bill Casey, who had been appointed director of central intelligence by President Ronald Reagan on January 28, 1981. Casey was an old covert warrior from the days of the Office of Strategic Services. He had served with the OSS in London during World War II, sending clandestine teams into mainland Europe to harass the Germans and gather valuable intelligence. He brought with him to Langley his memories of those halcyon days when wartime allowed anything to happen provided it was a good idea that produced results. But, contrary to the popular myth, Casey was not just a wild man ready to do anything to achieve the results he wanted. He was a savvy political operator who understood that Reagan wanted to achieve some significant successes against the Soviet target and Communism. But he also appreciated that this was not the OSS but a mature intelligence organization with a rule book that needed to be followed.

However, Casey came to the Agency ready to do battle with the sharp swords at his disposal and instead found a number of very blunt instruments that were of little use. Instead of a lean fighting machine staffed by young men and women filled with initiative and enthusiasm, he found a largely moribund bureaucracy. He found the people suspicious of him as an outsider and resentful of any instructions or ideas that were generated from outside.

"The DO had become like the military," said Bob Gates, who in January 1982 was appointed deputy director of intelligence, or DDI, by Casey. "Each officer had to check off certain boxes in order to advance. For a DO officer, going outside that organization for an assignment elsewhere in the Agency, with rare exceptions, did not help one's career and often harmed it. More and more the recruitment process had led to new officers looking very much like the people who recruited them: white, mostly Anglo-Saxon, middle to upper class, liberal arts graduates, mostly entering in their mid- to late twenties, engaging hail fellows well met. Few non-Caucasians, few women, few ethnics even of recent European background. In other words, not as much diversity as there was among those who helped create CIA and the clandestine service in the late 1940s.

"No one who failed to fit the [DO] mold could get in. Few could get out to broaden their experience either within CIA or elsewhere in Washington. And with too few exceptions, they resented and dismissed anyone from outside their ranks who had the temerity to offer insights or advice on how to do their job better. Outside critics? What could someone who had never recruited an agent or made a dead drop or lived in some godforsaken hellhole in the Third World know about operations? New kinds of information and new ways to get it? If information isn't stolen, it isn't worth having. Counter intelligence? Can't beat the polygraph, and besides, Angleton went too far and paralyzed operations."[6]

But Casey was determined to take on the DO and turn it into the cutting edge of the CIA. From the moment he arrived at Langley, he tried to force change on the DO, encouraging it to be less timid and more imaginative, and to deliver the kind of intelligence that would be of real value to the DI and thus to the president. At every step he was to be frustrated by the entrenched interests of the DO, who successfully managed to fend off any significant changes. This was to have two important consequences. Casey was forced to short-circuit the DO to accomplish his mission, and so he sought out those, both inside the CIA and outside, who were prepared to take the risks to do the job. This led to some serious mistakes such as Iran-Contra.

Second, the failure of Casey to persuade the DO to make changes served to reinforce its own perception of itself as an organization that was self-sustaining. It really didn't matter what outsiders thought or what the politicians wanted. The DO would sail smoothly through the ups and downs of different administrations, making judgments about what was or was not important from its own perspective. It became a cardinal belief among DO career officers that they were the elite. They simply knew better than anybody else what was right or wrong and they would never go outside to the amateurs for help or advice. It was this attitude that was to be the cause of so much unnecessary loss of life and destruction during Ames's years of betrayal.

By the fall of 1981, after only ten months as DCI and well before Ames began his career as a Russian spy, Casey had clearly lost faith in his ability to change the DO's ways. On October 15, he wrote to John Stein, the DDO: "Despite months of discussion of areas of rebuilding, neither the DCI nor the DDCI know what is being done." He demanded a report on the closer integration and expansion of the effort to obtain information from the business community under the DO, the rebuilding of covert action and paramilitary capabilities, the expansion and improvement of nonofficial cover, and the strengthening of counter intelligence. Nothing of significance was done.[7]

It was against this background that the Howard and compromised cases landed on Casey's desk in 1985. He saw them as another illustration of the sloppiness of the DO, and he decided to try to use them to force through some of the changes he had been demanding for so long, with so little success. He ordered his own review of the compromised cases to try to understand just why there had been so many failures in such a short time. His investigation ended by supporting the SE Division's own conclusions: that there was no single explanation for the sources' all being compromised at the same time. In April 1986, Casey called a meeting of senior staff from the DO to discuss the different reviews, and he was told simply that the investigation was ongoing. He was also told that the SE Division had managed to recruit a number of other sources, who remained in place and had not been blown. This tended to support the view that each of the compromised cases had its own explanation. The whole series of disasters was just a ghastly coincidence. That trained professionals in the intelligence business should have allowed themselves to accept such a feeble explanation is little short of bizarre. After all, in the course of one year, the CIA had lost all its important sources inside the Soviet Union, a blow to its effectiveness that nobody in the Agency had ever experienced before. It is clear that there was a determination to search everywhere—anywhere—for an explanation of the losses that did not involve looking inward to try to find a source within Langley. The memories of the ghastly destruction wreaked by Jim Angleton's paranoia were all too fresh in the minds of many senior CIA officers. Nobody wanted to repeat any aspect of that period, particularly without the kind of hard evidence that was always lacking in Angleton's investigations. There were genuine fears that morale in the SE Division, which had only just begun to recover, would plummet once again and that the personnel who had been carefully built up over the previous ten years would start moving away. So the choice was simple enough: go with the evidence, do nothing, and the SE Division remains intact and continues to function; or dig deeper and risk another long period of agony that risks destroying everything rebuilt since Angleton was fired in 1974.

But the Howard case had provoked other reactions, and both John Stein, the CIA inspector general, and the President's Foreign Intelligence Advisory Board (PFIAB), which acts as an independent advisory body to the president, began their own investigations. Casey was furious when he read the IG's first draft, and he wrote on November 11 that it "was not tough enough" and "needed to pinpoint failures and to make specific recommendations." The second draft did not make him any happier, and he wrote to the IG on November 26: "I am troubled by the failure to discuss any specific responsibility for the appalling confusion and inattention to detail in the DO's handling of this case."[8]

The Stein report did more damage than that set out by Casey. The IG had suggested that his investigation produced some evidence that some of those who had been compromised had made their own mistakes.

"There was evidence in subsequent years that some of the people who were shot did things that were self-destructive, like volunteering for other intelligence services, and this lent weight to the notion that those operations had collapsed largely of their own accord," said Milton Bearden, a member of the SE Division at the time, and its future chief.

"The Stein report said that each operation had the seeds of its own destruction. That report caused some difficulty in SE, and while it is true the operations can carry the seeds of their own destruction, the impact of this report helped take some of the momentum away from the notion that these eight or ten sources had been compromised by a mole."[9]

Despite the Stein report and the lack of any other corroborating evidence, some involved in the investigation maintained that the source of all the problems was a still-hidden mole. Among those believers were Hathaway and Paul Redmond, deputy director of the SE Division.

In April, six months later, the PFIAB issued its own report, which specifically identified serious institutional and attitudinal problems in the CIA's handling of counter intelligence cases. The PFIAB report noted in particular that "senior CIA officers continued to misread or ignore signs that Howard was a major CIA problem. This myopia was partially ascribed to a fundamental inability of anyone in the SE Division to think the unthinkable—that a DO employee could engage in espionage." The report went on to recommend that CIA component heads report counter intelligence information to the Office of Security, and that the Office of Security serve as focal point for informing the FBI of such matters.

On June 4, 1986, Casey sent a memorandum to DDO Clair George: "I am appalled at the handling of the Howard case as described in the recent PFIAB report." He went over the warnings ignored, the delays in bringing the case to the attention of the FBI, the lack of leadership to give the case focus, the reluctance to recognize a major counter intelligence problem until too late, and "above all an astonishing complacency and seeming unwillingness to accept, even as a possibility, a DO officer committing espionage for the Soviet Union." He stated that the DDO and the SE Division deserved censure and that "efficiencies and process, organization and attitude that contributed to this catastrophe must be corrected and I hold you personally responsible to do so."[10]

He added that the DO division and staff chiefs were to be instructed that "the DO must be more alert to possible CI cases in the ranks." In the future, any suggestion of such a development was to be shared with the director of the Office of Security, and the chief of the Counter Intelligence Staff. Also, the DCI charged the chief of the SE Division to take personal responsibility in the future for the selection of division officers for particularly sensitive posts.[11]

The letter from Casey became something of a legend within the Agency for both its toughness and its tone. "I worked closely with Casey for five and a half years," said Gates. "He never wrote a letter that strong to any other CIA officer."[12]

Despite the firmest of instructions from the DCI, every aspect of his letter was ignored by Clair George and the DO. Not a single individual of importance was censured for his part in the Howard case; punishment was restricted to low-level employees. There was no real change in the DO's way of doing business, and all the problems that had been identified by both the IG and the PFIAB reports remained in place. If action had been taken after the Howard debacle, then Ames would likely have been caught much earlier. As it was, Ames prospered because the CIA in general and the DO in particular learned no lessons from the Howard affair and blithely went on to repeat precisely the same mistakes.

While the CIA was wading through its massive losses, Rick suffered a loss of his own. Rachel Ames, his mother, died in her sleep of a heart attack on May 18, 1986, at Rick's home, after attending the graduation at the Naval Academy of her grandson Stephen Carleton.[13] The funeral service was in Falls Church's First Presbyterian Church, even though she had been active in the Unitarian Church. Her three children, rather than a minister, performed the eulogy. They read poetry and other inspirational texts. Rick's sister Alison was ill with cancer and walked with a cane at the service.[14]

Rick attended the funeral with Rosario, and according to Rachel's friend Myra Myers, appeared very sad. Rachel's will, which had been drafted in 1971, had left all her possessions to Carleton, but he had, of course, died before her. So Nancy became the executor of Rachel's estate, which was divided equally among the three children.[15] Although Rick had moved to Rome by the time the estate was finally settled, he signed a letter on September 29, 1986, disclaiming his portion of the estate. Charles Dixon, Rachel's lawyer, explained that such a disclaimer is sometimes signed so that a person can avoid paying inheritance tax. At the time, Dixon thought this was a generous gesture by Rick, because Alison needed what little money there was in the estate to pay for her cancer treatment. Of course, Rick had no need of the money himself, given his other sources of income.[16]

After the first flurry of betrayals, Rick's behavior settled down to a more consistent series of leaks and compromises. Having fingered the most important people, he now began to work his way fairly steadily through the CIA's list of secondary sources. First on the list was Vladimir Potashov, a military expert at the prestigious Institute for the Study of the USA and Canada (IUSAC). Potashov had moved to Moscow in 1966 as a seventeen-year-old student and graduated as a mathematician from the Moscow Physics-Technical Institute. He eventually earned a doctoral degree in history. As a senior military analyst at IUSAC, he had a nice apartment and a car. Fluent in English, he was allowed to travel abroad and by the mid-1980s had published two books and about a hundred articles on disarmament and had earned an international reputation in the field.[17]

While on a business trip to Washington in 1981, he had been approached by a CIA officer who asked him if he would supply regular reports on Soviet acceptance of President Reagan's zero-option nuclear proposal, under which the United States would cancel its planned deployment of mid-range missiles if the Soviets agreed to eliminate all their SS-4, SS-5, and SS-20 missiles. Potashov said he agreed, knowing that it was "deathly dangerous," because he wanted to support disarmament. His decision to spy for the Americans was based on what he described as ideological reasons, and he received no money. His was intelligence that gave some insight into just where the Soviets were moving on disarmament issues at a critical time for NATO and America. And he was able to point the Americans in the direction of Mikhail Gorbachev as the Soviet leader most receptive to disarmament initiatives.

As Potashov left work for home on July 1, 1986, about 6:30 p.m., he noticed a green van parked near his car. "As I pass, three men grab my back and then two come in front. They lifted me into van and then opened my mouth and put stick across it. Stick was eaten by hundreds of dogs maybe, it was such a smell." He was taken to Lefortovo, where he was brought before three KGB officials who accused him of treason. "I thought I'd be shot," he said. "I never knew any story of people arrested by KGB who ever get out again. I never knew anyone who go into Lefortovo and get out."

Potashov has a vivid memory of the gun the KGB interrogator always showed him during their sessions, even when Potashov's defense lawyer was there. Potashov recalls that as a cruel joke his interrogator once asked if Potashov wanted his forehead marked with an anticorrosion liquid. When Potashov asked why, the interrogator said, "We'll mark you with a star on your forehead." Potashov responded, "So that your soldiers won't miss?" The interrogator said, "No, so the bullet won't rust going through."[18]

His interrogators knew of his reports, even of letters to which they could not have had access in the U.S.S.R. Two things probably saved his life. First, he never told the interrogators facts they could not have known already. And second, Soviet policy had moved to support the "zero option" by the time of his trial.[19]

He was not allowed to hire his own defense attorney, but had to take one assigned him by the military court. After a year's interrogation, he had a six-day trial and was found guilty. Potashov was charged with "betrayal of the motherland." He asserts, to the contrary, that he and other prisoners at Perm-35, a labor camp, "didn't betray our motherland. We tried to change it so that things would progress to the way things are now."[20]

He was sentenced to serve thirteen years in Perm-35, located eighty miles outside Perm, which is among the most notorious of the forced-labor camps. With its guard dogs, watchtowers, and cement walls, the camp was known for its harsh treatment of political and religious dissidents.[21] Normally, political prisoners are segregated from ordinary criminals, but Potashov "was deliberately put in a railroad car with 15 men who had been convicted of murder and were being shipped for treatment of tuberculosis for the seven-day trip [*sic*]. 'Those seven days I remember as days of hell,' he said."[22]

At the time, Perm-35 had only thirty-eight prisoners. Another inmate, Boris Yuzhin, was also an Ames victim; he was a former Tass correspondent who had been recruited by the FBI while he was stationed in San Francisco in 1972. He continued this relationship on a second stint in California from 1978 to 1982, though he said he was never approached by the CIA in Moscow. He was arrested in 1986 in Moscow and was sentenced to fifteen years for high treason. For five years he was kept in complete isolation from the outside world, not even knowing where he was being held. He was later to be released at the same time as Potashov.[23]

The camp had ten rows of barbed wire and guard towers with machine guns. "Inmates were frequently punished by being placed in a *shizo,* or solitary-confinement cell. 'It contains a wooden plank fastened to the wall on which to sleep, with no bedding or blankets and a cement stump on which to sit,' noted Representatives Frank Wolf and Chris Smith in a 1989 report based on their visit to the camp. 'The cell, and the punishment, is designed to make the natural cold of a Soviet labor camp that much more severe—that is, the unbearable cold temperature is used as torture.' "[24]

When he was arrested, Potashov had been married for three years. His young wife, Veronica, never wrote or spoke to him again, because she was afraid of the authorities, he said. They were divorced while he was in the gulag. " 'The KGB confiscate my apartment, my car, all my possessions—and they confiscate my wife too.' Potashov's father, who had been director of the biggest diesel engine–manufacturing plant in the Soviet Union, was dismissed from his job after Potashov's jailing and placed on a miserly pension."[25] Potashov says he appealed to the courts in 1989 to retain the fees for his book, *War or Peace,* or donate them to a good cause. The court agreed in 1989 to donate the fees to "peace-making."[26]

He was finally released in February 1992. Eventually he managed to escape to Poland and then obtained political asylum in America. He now lives in North Carolina, and works as a technical writer for a consulting firm.

Sergey Fedorenko, who had been run by Ames during his assignment to the UN, had dropped from sight since his return to Moscow in 1977. Restrictions had been placed on his travel and he knew that, for the time being, his academic career had stalled. What he did not know was that toward the end of 1986, Ames had fingered his old friend as a CIA source.

At the time, Fedorenko did not know that he had been betrayed. All he knew was that he had been taken in for questioning by the KGB and that he was under continuous surveillance. It appears that the KGB decided not to arrest Fedorenko for a number of reasons. Ironically, Sergey Fedorenko survived because he was a known enemy of Potashov, whom he considered an orthodox Communist and a second-rate academic. He believed that Potashov had plagiarized the Richard Smoke and Alexander George classic *Deterrence in Foreign Policy* and attempted to publish a book very much like it as his own. When Potashov was arrested, Fedorenko and others named on a KGB blacklist were taken in for questioning by the KGB, which was eager to discover just why he was so disliked. There was also the fact that Rick was unable to provide documentary evidence that would stand up in court and that the academic had a number of well-placed friends in senior government positions. There must also have been the calculation that only a handful of CIA officers knew about Fedorenko's work for the CIA, and his arrest might just have proved the final nail in Ames's coffin.

After twelve years in isolation, Fedorenko was once again allowed to travel. He was invited to take part in an academic conference on arms control at the Center for Foreign Policy Development at Brown University, where he cochaired a panel with Lynn Davis (now undersecretary of state for international security affairs), and at which Joe Nye and Strobe Talbott participated. While at the conference, Fedorenko met Rick and an FBI agent for dinner at the Madison Hotel. The men talked for four hours that night.[27]

After that conference, Fedorenko came to the United States about five times, as well as to Vancouver, Canada, in the summer of 1990, when he was part of a high-level delegation led by the chief of the Ministry of Foreign Affairs legal department.[28] He had some computer diskettes that contained draft papers on military restructuring under way in the Soviet Union, and he wanted to deliver them to Ames.[29] He tried to schedule a trip to visit him in Washington, D.C., but was unable to make it because he had no visa and was short of cash. As a result, Ames arranged for the visa and established an account for him in northern Virginia, using his own address on the account. Fedorenko later made the trip but the information he had was of little interest to the Agency.

Later that year, Fedorenko decided to bring his wife to the United States, and he moved to northern Virginia, where he lived for over a year before asking for political asylum.[30] At the time, he continued to provide the CIA with information and analysis of Soviet policy. And soon after he moved, Fedorenko reestablished regular contact with Rick. The two would spend long evenings talking about the state of the world, often in the comfort of Rick and Rosario's home. Once again, the two men found they shared a great deal, with their cynical view of the political world in which they both lived and worked. But after a while in Washington, Fedorenko had a few disagreements with his handlers in the CIA, and he moved to Cambridge, Massachusetts, in the spring of 1991. He then taught at Tufts University and served as a visiting professor at the Naval War College in Newport, Rhode Island. He currently teaches international relations at Salve Regina University in Newport.[31]

It was not until Rick's arrest in February 1994 that Fedorenko discovered the true nature of his "friend." Today, Fedorenko is the only known American source in the Soviet Union to have escaped either death or prison as a result of Rick's betrayal. That alone is a mark of distinction. But what also sets Fedorenko apart from the rest is his intimate relationship with Ames. Rick was clearly able to betray a man—and in Fedorenko's case, a close friend—without any hesitation and then sit down with him over a few beers and discuss the state of the world as if nothing could ever come between them.

Rick was scheduled to leave for his Rome assignment in July 1986 and completed his language training at the end of April. On May 2, he was ordered to take a routine polygraph test, his first since 1976. Ames would subsequently state that he might not have made the decision to commit espionage in April 1985 if he had known that he was going to be polygraphed the next year. Ames recalls being "very anxious and tremendously worried" when he was informed that he was scheduled for a polygraph exam in May 1986.[32]

In part, Rick's fear was illustrative of one of the real values of the polygraph: few understood its capabilities, and therefore it was assumed the machine could see deep into people's minds to prize out even the most hidden secret. This was far from the truth, and if he had known the reality, Ames could have afforded to be much more relaxed. A special report prepared by James K. Murphy, special agent of the Laboratory Division of the FBI, states that the polygraph is a reliable, albeit imperfect, piece of investigative technology when used properly.[33] Murphy cites several problems with gauging the precise reliability of the polygraph. First, it is difficult to simulate psychophysiological reactions of a criminal suspect in a laboratory study—it is difficult to imitate emotions such as fear and guilt when no crime or deceptive act has been committed. Additionally, it is not possible to fully determine the accuracy of the polygraph by studying results in actual cases, because the complete truth regarding the crime and its circumstances remains unavailable.

There have been a number of formal studies focusing on the validity of the polygraph. One published in 1978, which measured the results of polygraph exams under laboratory conditions, concluded that they have an accuracy rate of more than 90 percent when properly conducted. Psychology and neuroscience professor William Iacono of the University of Minnesota has written that statistics provided to Congress by the Department of Defense on its use of counter intelligence polygraphs revealed that of 12,306 tests only 23 were failed, and 8 of these 23 received their security clearance anyway. If the polygraph were even 90 percent accurate, one would have expected about 1,000 people to fail, just by chance. The Defense Department has suggested that sometimes examiners, believing the rate of spying to be low, try hard to pass people on their polygraphs. Unknown to polygraph examiners in this study, nearly half of the 207 research subjects had engaged in simulated acts of espionage prior to taking the test. Of these, 66 percent were passed by polygraphers from four different intelligence agencies, including the CIA.[34]

Iacono indicates that there are two basic types of polygraph tests: "control question" or "specific incident" tests, and national security tests.

The former type typically is used in criminal investigations to question subjects about a particular problem or event. The subject is first asked a control question, which investigators assume will elicit a predictable response in the subject. The polygraph measures this response in terms of the subject's breathing, heart rate, and galvanic skin response. The subject is then asked a question relevant to the specific incident or event, and again the polygraph records the subject's response. Investigators compare the responses to the two questions, and any discrepancies may indicate that the subject is lying. O. J. Simpson, for example, might be asked the control question "Have you ever considered hurting someone to get revenge?" and then be asked a relevant question such as "Did you stab Nicole Simpson?" in order to compare his respective responses.

"If the responses to the relevant question (assuming the subject answered 'no') are much larger than the responses to the control question, then one assumes the subject was lying. If the responses to the relevant question are more or less similar to those on the control subject, then one assumes the subject is telling the truth," said Iacono.[35]

The national security test differs from the control question test "in that it concerns not specific behavior, but general misbehavior." Because the subject is not asked a particular control question, investigators have developed other methods of assessing discrepancies in the subject's responses. One such method is called a "card test," in which investigators ask a subject to pick one card from a pack of twenty to twenty-five held by the polygraph examiner. The examiner then goes through the pack and asks the subject if each card was the one he had picked. The subject is instructed to answer "no" to every question, even when the examiner asks about the card he had indeed chosen. Because the machine is rigged to record which card the subject did pick, his response when he answers "no" to the card he had chosen is evaluated.

Another method for establishing a " 'control set' of responses" in a national security test is to "let the questions serve as controls for one another." Investigators typically ask a subject questions in groups of ten and covering a variety of topics, such as "Have you ever had a homosexual encounter?" or "Do you take illegal drugs?" or perhaps "Have you ever intentionally divulged any classified information?" The investigators measure the responses to these questions, and if one response seems more intense, or more vivid, than any of the others in the group, the investigator presses the subject to discuss that particular question in more detail. This heightened response is significant because "given a variety of threatening stimuli, a person will give greater psychological attention to that area which he perceives to hold the greatest threat to his well-being at that time."[36] Iacono explains that this method is effective because investigators pose the questions "without telling the subject which of the questions the examiner believes is associated with an untruthful response, so the subject starts talking about anything they think might have cause the alleged problem."

Because the national security test lacks a control question/relevant question scenario, it is not specifically designed to be a lie-detector test. Instead, it is useful for obtaining admissions, as investigators evaluate subjects based on their ability to explain themselves. Iacono believes that the national security test is a particularly effective investigative tool, because "it is intimidating enough, and people take it seriously enough because the stakes are high—a job on the line, etc.—that they start divulging things about their personal or professional lives that no one had known."[37]

During his polygraph, Ames was tested on a series of issues having to do with unauthorized contacts with a foreign intelligence service, unauthorized disclosure of classified information, and financial irresponsibility. He gave consistently deceptive responses to issues related to whether he had been "pitched" (i.e., solicited for work) by a foreign intelligence service. The CIA examiner noted Ames's reaction to the pitch issue—but apparently detected no reaction to the other counter intelligence issues covered by the test. When Ames was asked about his reaction during the session, he explained that he was indeed sensitive to the pitch issue because, he stated, "we know that the Soviets are out there somewhere, and we are worried about that."

Next the CIA examiner asked a series of follow-up questions relating to the pitch issue, in order to ascertain why Ames had appeared to give a deceptive response. Ames responded that since he had worked in CIA's SE Division, he had been involved in pitches to potential assets. Also, he hypothesized that he might be known to the Soviets because of a recent defector. He further stated that he thought he might be reacting because he was preparing to go to Rome in July 1986, and had some concerns that he might be pitched there. From this, the polygrapher surmised that Ames had gotten his concerns off his chest, and there was nothing more to tell. Once again, the polygrapher went through the CI questions on the polygraph machine, focusing on the pitch issue. This time, the CIA examiner deemed Ames truthful and concluded the examination, characterizing Ames as "bright [and] direct." The examiner's supervisors concurred with the assessment that Ames was nondeceptive.

Even though the CIA examiner passed Ames on this exam, the deception indicated in Ames's response to the pitch issue in 1986 was never resolved, according to the FBI, which examined Ames's polygraph charts in June 1993. Also, in the opinion of the FBI, significant deceptive responses by Ames were detectable to questions dealing with unauthorized disclosure of classified material. No additional testing or explanations for these deceptive responses, however, were noted in Ames's polygraph file.

For many years, the CIA, along with many other American government departments, has placed a heavy reliance on the polygraph as the machine that can detect the liar. This dependence on technology rather than human instinct or knowledge is peculiarly American (British intelligence rejected the use of the polygraph in the late 1980s because of its unreliability). However, the CIA should have known to look beyond the results of the polygraph test, since even Bill Casey admitted to acquaintances that "with some Valium and a sphincter muscle trick he learned in the OSS he could flatten the spikes before they occurred on any [lie-detector] machine."[38]

Others are just as skeptical. "Polygraphs can be somewhat effective against Americans, who usually feel guilty when they sin, lie, or have too much fun. They break into a sweat and breathe erratically. But against foreigners, Cubans for example, the machine is absurd. The fact that the institution even talks about the polygraph after all its failures just shows how conservative, arrogant, and lame the place has become."[39]

Iacono suggests that Muslims, or perhaps other Middle Eastern peoples who may believe that it is a duty to lie about certain issues to a non-believer, could elude such a test. "If I were in charge of a foreign intelligence service," he says, "I would certainly spend a few thousand dollars for a polygraph machine, hook my agents up to it, and explain what sorts of questions the Americans would ask, as well as what the countermeasures are. I could train anybody to defeat the exam."

Although there are studies that "have concluded the polygraph to be 99 percent accurate, with an almost matching reliability rate," Iacono warns that the test is by no means immune from deceit.[40] He contends that an "easy way" to distort the polygraph results is to "exaggerate the responses to inconsequential questions." Subjects who tried to subtract small increments from a large number without making any mistakes as soon as an examiner began asking them an inconsequential question were found to be able to generate enough stress to match their response to a relevant question. On an even more basic level, subjects simply began pushing their toes onto the floor when a control question was asked, which, Iacono reports, "also leads to a larger response to the control question than one would ordinarily find."[41]

In fact, a relative dearth of studies about the polygraph and its use in subject testing has hampered the debate about its effectiveness or validity. Most people involved in the administering of such tests are bound to secrecy about their work, making definitive results difficult to obtain. Iacono does cite one prominent study from the Department of Defense Polygraph Institute in Alabama, in which about two hundred subjects were told to breach security and release information from a top-secret file. When they were later polygraphed, two thirds of the supposed offenders were not even detected by polygraphers from a host of intelligence agencies and groups. There were, however, several confessions about unrelated, previously occurring security breaches by the participants in the study. As Iacono explains it, the validity of the test lay in the fact that "people were intimidated enough by the poly that they volunteered damaging information even though they were aware doing so could hurt them." Clearly the test does wield some legitimate power. But because of the criticism these results received in the press, the DOD has since deemed all further studies from this institute as classified.

━━

Ironically, at the very time Rick was taking and passing the polygraph, Congress was launching the first of what would turn out to be a large number of investigations into the failures of American intelligence. This study, carried out by the House Select Committee on Intelligence, was specifically designed to look into the failings of the Howard case. In the light of what was to follow, it is worth examining in some detail just what the committee found and the recommendations it made on February 4, 1987.

Over the past several years, a dangerous upward trend in successful espionage operations against the United States has occurred. Present and former U.S. Government employees with access to sensitive classified information have played the key roles in each operation. Damage to U.S. national security has been significant and is still being estimated.

Overall, the Committee perceives a serious management failure in the U.S. intelligence community. Major flaws exist in implementing existing security procedures, including the granting of too many security clearances, improper document handling, violations of the need-to-know principle, poor supervision of personnel with access to classified information and a lack of coordination between agencies on security matters, to name but a few shortcomings. Underlying all of these problems has been a lack of either urgency or top priority at departmental and lower levels with respect to needed security changes, despite the high priority given to counter intelligence issues over recent years by the White House and by the Congressional intelligence committees. Once the glare of public scrutiny leaves the problems of espionage and security, the Committee is concerned that the political will to advance security programs and maintain high levels of attention and necessary funding for their implementation will not be sustained. The very size of the U.S. national security community, its complexity and lack of unitary management and the historically lower priority assigned to security concerns have produced cynicism and failure to change in the past and could once again.

The Committee went on to identify a series of security failures that could have been a blueprint for the problems that would later emerge with the investigation into Ames: the intelligence community relied too much on polygraphs; security checks were lax and background checks generally failed to reveal problems with drugs, alcohol, and sex; most American spies had money problems, and that was their prime motive for spying; the "need-to-know" principle was constantly compromised, so that too many people had access to too much classified intelligence; and there was a systemic weakness in security and counter intelligence in the intelligence community.

In its report, the committee made the following key recommendations:

1. U.S. intelligence agencies should undertake a coordinated review of their hiring practices.

2. The President should authorize an independent group of experts outside the intelligence community to examine thoroughly the damage to U.S. intelligence capabilities resulting from recent espionage cases and to urge needed adjustment of U.S. intelligence collection techniques.

3. All U.S. intelligence agencies should be required to report as appropriate to the Director of the Federal Bureau of Investigation or the Director of Central Intelligence information they possess which raises a suspicion of possible espionage.

4. U.S. intelligence agencies should institute a rigorous need-to-know policy to govern access to classified information and back that policy by disciplinary action against employees who breach that policy.

5. The Director of Central Intelligence should consider establishing a system for dissemination of intelligence with minimal source identification, restricting full knowledge of sources only to those who absolutely need to know.

6. The executive branch and the Congress should work to standardize, expedite, and adequately fund the security clearance

process. The Secretary of Defense, in consultation with the Director of Central Intelligence, should examine whether the Defense Investigative Service (DIS) can serve adequately the personnel security background investigation needs of the military departments and defense agencies and should consider whether such departments and agencies should undertake their own background investigations and whether they should contract with private firms for such investigations. The Congress should carefully examine the budget request for DIA within the FY 1988 Defense budget review process.

7. Background investigations should focus more on the financial status of the subjects of the investigation.

8. Periodic reinvestigation of personnel with access to sensitive compartmented information, i.e. the nation's most sensitive intelligence secrets, should be given priority equal to that of initial investigations.

9. Legal and administrative mechanisms should be established to ensure that agencies which possess information of security relevance on an employee or applicant for employment of another agency share that information with that agency.

10. The National Security Council, the Attorney General, the Secretary of Defense, and the Director of Central Intelligence should review jointly executive branch policy with respect to former government personnel and personnel of government contractors who have access to sensitive compartmented information and consider changes, such as requiring exit interviews and a separation non-disclosure agreement, to deter post-employment unauthorized disclosures of classified information.

11. The leadership of the House of Representatives should examine the feasibility of establishing uniform security procedures for House committees, offices and organizations which meet or exceed executive branch standards.

12. The Federal Bureau of Investigation should establish a program of rewards for information leading to the arrest of individuals for espionage.

13. Strict, rigidly applied communications and computer security practices should be established within the U.S. Government.

14. The Attorney General, the Director of the Federal Bureau of Investigation and the Director of Central Intelligence should consider realigning some FBI surveillance resources to high priority intelligence targets. The Congress should carefully weigh the amount of resources requested for this purpose in the FY 1988 budget review process.

As Casey had already discovered, attempting to change the way the Agency does business is a tough, if not impossible, task. If it so wished, Congress could have legislated many of these changes and forced the Agency to act. But, as usual, any attempt from outside was fiercely resisted by those inside. A fierce lobbying campaign began to undermine the committee's findings and to argue that any further oversight of the intelligence community would actually contribute to a reduction in both the quality and the quantity of intelligence disseminated to the policymakers in Washington. This is always an easy case for the Agency bureaucrats to make. Touch us, the argument goes, and the whole house of cards might come tumbling down. It takes a tough and aggressive congressman backed by the full weight of the president to go up against the full might of the intelligence community. For now, it was easier to mouth the words and do nothing to implement the recommendations.

ELEVEN

La Dolce Vita

Ames arrived in Rome in July 1986, and it proved to be a perfect spot from everyone's perspective. It gave Rick ample opportunity to continue his activities and to do the maximum damage, far away from any suspicious prying eyes in Langley. Rosario loved the life of a well-placed diplomat's wife: the parties, the social scene, and, above all, the opportunity to explore one of the most civilized cities in Europe. At last she felt she was enjoying the kind of life for which she had been bred and educated.

The American Embassy is located on the Via Veneto, the street made famous by Fellini in *La Dolce Vita*. The three-story rose-pink building was built in 1885 as the residence of Italy's Queen Margherita and has been home to the embassy since just after World War II. During the 1950s and 1960s, when the Via Veneto was the center of Roman society, and the paparazzi pursued famous movie stars, intellectuals, and filmmakers in the street's many cafés, embassy staff frequented the same spots. In fact, the left-hand side of the street was known as the Italian Bank (like the Left Bank of Paris) and the right-hand side, on which Doney's, the historic café, stands, was regarded as the American hangout.

If the Via Veneto was once the haunt of film stars like Sophia Loren, by the time Rick and Rosario arrived, such sights were largely part of its famous past. By the mid-1980s the area was beginning to take on the scruffy look that is the hallmark of large areas of Rome. But still, for a diplomat and his wife with plenty of money and time on their hands, it was an attractive base from which to explore the architectural and artistic glories of one of the great European cities.

His colleagues back at Langley seemed happy that Rick had left. He had been recommended for his new job by his supervisor in the SE Division, and the assignment had been approved by the European Division chief, the same man who, when stationed in Ankara in 1972 as Ames's supervisor, recommended that he would be better suited to work at headquarters because of his poor performance in Turkey. A message from CIA headquarters to Rome, advising of Ames's forthcoming assignment there, described him as "highly regarded by SE Division management," but in fact his transfer overseas was seen as a good way to move a weak performer out of headquarters.[1]

As a branch chief of the Soviet and counter intelligence programs, Ames had had access to the true identities of CIA agents, the details of planned agent meetings, and copies of the intelligence reports produced by these agents. He participated in weekly staff meetings where intelligence assets and potential asset recruitments were discussed. He coordinated double-agent operations of the U.S. military services and received sensitive intelligence reports about worldwide events. The post had provided Rick with a measure of responsibility that he wanted, and easy access to the kind of material he knew that the Soviets would need if he was to continue to satisfy them and thereby keep the cash flowing.

His move to Rome would change not only his job within the Agency, but also his relationship to the Russians. For Christmas 1985, Rick had used some of his Soviet earnings to take Rosario back home to Bogotá to visit her family. And Bogotá provided a location in which Rick could work out how he would maintain contact with the Soviets, who were eager to establish some kind of relationship with a new handler. They felt that moving his cutout from Washington to Rome at the same time that Rick moved there would be an obvious signal that even the CI people at the Agency would not miss. They had instructed Rick to get away from Rosario's family for a few hours and make his way to the Russian

Embassy in Bogotá. There he was introduced to "Vlad," an officer from the KGB's counter intelligence directorate, who became his controller for the next few years. Vlad told him that when he arrived in Rome, he would meet Aleksey Khrenkov, code-named "Sam II," who was a serving diplomat at the Soviet Embassy in Rome. Ames would meet with him regularly, and on occasion Vlad would come to Rome for longer conversations and to renew what he explained would be a long and mutually prosperous relationship.

For the first couple of months, Rick's handlers in Rome left him alone to find his feet and work his way around the CIA station. Then Vlad and Rick scheduled a meeting in October on a busy street; this appointment was supposed to cement a new stage in their relationship. In fact, as often happened, Rick needed to have a drink or two or three in advance of this rendezvous to steel his nerves. He arrived at the meeting place drunk and an hour early. Sitting on a nearby bench to wait for Vlad, he realized he needed to urinate. He found a convenient lavatory and while urinating noticed that he was passing blood. What turned out to be a prostate infection placed Rick in a drunken panic and he turned up for his appointment with Vlad in a very confused state. For the Russian, encountering a drunken, panicked source, the occasion can hardly have been reassuring. But, like the effective controller he was, he assured Rick that all was well and confirmed the arrangement with Sam II, the cutout at the Rome Embassy. Vlad suggested a second meeting the following night, when he would have some cash for Rick. However, Rick was so drunk that he completely forgot about the arrangements for the following night and failed to turn up.

"When I saw him later, six months, nine months later, I apologized for that. And I had earlier told him in a letter about the infection and everything, which had all cleared up. But when I told him about it, it was very interesting. I said, you know, I am sorry about missing that meeting and all the problems associated with that and I said, you know, I had, I simply had had too much to drink, both before the meeting and then during the meeting, because we sat at a café and I continued to drink. And he dismissed it. Just like an Agency manager."[2]

However, before the two men parted, Vlad said something that managed not just to penetrate the drunken haze but to register. Vlad warned

Ames that the CIA believed it had been penetrated, that there was a mole deep inside the organization. "He said, we're trying to find effective ways of diverting attention, and one of the ways is to create the impression that there's a commo problem"—that is, to invent a communications breach in an attempt to shield Ames.[3]

Several weeks later, the U.S. Embassy in Moscow had what appeared to be a huge security breakdown. The embassy, the CIA station inside it, and a new embassy still under construction were discovered to be filled with covert listening devices. Who was to blame for the breaches of security? The victim chosen for sacrifice was Sergeant Clayton Lonetree, a young Marine guard at the embassy. Lonetree had been the subject of a long-term KGB operation since his arrival in Moscow in 1984. He had been targeted not least because he came from a background remarkably similar to Rick Ames's, a background that had produced weaknesses that it was only too easy for the Soviets to exploit.[4] Clayton's parents, both Native Americans, met at an Indian center in Chicago in 1961, when his father, Spencer, was nineteen and his mother, Sally Tsosie, only sixteen. Two months later Sally was pregnant with Clayton. Though they never married, Sally and Spencer struggled through a troubled relationship for two years, producing another son, Craig, shortly before breaking up. A short time later, Sally found herself pregnant again and drove her children to an Indian mission in New Mexico, where she worked as a cook. Four months after her daughter, Valerie, was born, Sally abandoned her children and returned to the Navajo reservation in Arizona where she'd grown up. Clayton was five years old and never got over the sting of her rejection.

After the boys had lived at the mission for five years, Spencer invited them for a Christmas visit to his home in St. Paul, Minnesota. When they arrived he sued Sally for custody. Spencer's family was a distinguished one. His father had been chief of the Winnebago Indians of Wisconsin. His uncle Mitchell Red Cloud, a descendant of Chief Sitting Bull, won the Congressional Medal of Honor during the Korean War, and Spencer himself was an active and respected participant in Indian affairs. Spencer had also been a championship long-distance runner in his youth, and believed that second place was for losers—a philosophy he expounded relentlessly to Clayton. Though Spencer was known as a drunk, he insisted on running each morning before dawn, waking his sons to join him by banging on their bedroom door and shouting, "C'mon, girls!"

In high school Clayton struggled to meet his father's high standards, but could never raise himself up out of second place. During this time he developed a strange fixation upon Adolf Hitler and the Third Reich, once handing a teacher a notebook with slogans such as "The Holocaust is a lie" and "Hitler lives" written all over it. In 1980, while still in high school, Clayton signed up with the Marines, partly to escape his over-bearing father and partly because he believed military service would look good on his record should he decide to run for public office.

Considering the well-documented tactics of the KGB, the last candidate for posting in Moscow should have been a single, immature man. And yet that is precisely the type of soldier the State Department and Marine Corps had been sending since 1934. So it was not at all unusual that Clayton Lonetree, a young man of low intelligence but with grandiose expectations of himself and a consuming need to be loved, was posted to Moscow in 1984. From the beginning of his posting Lonetree, then twenty-two, established himself as a mediocre Marine, repeatedly drunk and showing up late for guard duty.

"He was a loner, not very articulate, borderline in the mental category," said Master Gunnery Sergeant Joey Wingate. When the Marine Corps decided to promote Lonetree to sergeant a few months after his arrival, Wingate objected but was overruled. Even after Lonetree was found asleep on guard duty in the summer of 1985, and Wingate recommended that he be demoted and sent back to Quantico, Lonetree continued to guard the CIA station in Moscow.

Though it was strictly against regulations for the Marines to fraternize with foreign nationals from many countries, including the U.S.S.R., it was widely known that a number of the men were carrying on affairs with Soviet women. In the beginning Lonetree was wary of Soviet employees, but in time he began to look at fraternization as no big deal. Then, the year after he arrived in Moscow, Lonetree spotted a woman crossing the compound whom he would describe to a friend as the most beautiful woman he had ever seen. When he stopped her, demanding to see her identification card, he was surprised to find she was Russian.

In September 1985, while riding the Moscow subway, Lonetree had what he thought was another chance encounter with the woman, but it was more likely a KGB setup. Violetta Sanni was a twenty-five-year-old Ukrainian Jew who worked initially as the ambassador's receptionist and later as an interpreter. She dressed stylishly and spoke almost perfect English. With her large gray eyes, fair skin, and attractive figure, Violetta was irresistible, and Lonetree quickly became infatuated with her. Using Violetta as the honey, the Soviets began to spin a trap around Clayton, who, having recently been disciplined, was ready to walk right into it.

When Lonetree took Violetta to the Marine Corps Ball in November, an act in direct violation of the rule against fraternization, no one appears to have been shocked or indeed to have said anything at all. The two became lovers in January 1986, though apparently titillating sex was less of an attraction for Clayton than the love and affection Violetta showered on him. Actually the two managed to be alone together only four times. Soon, Violetta introduced Lonetree to her "Uncle Sasha," a man she described as a lawyer interested in American culture. Sasha was, in fact, a high-ranking Communist Party member and KGB agent named Aleksey G. Yefimov.

Following standard KGB procedure, "Sasha" forged a relationship with Lonetree, asking him questions about life in the United States and talking about subjects such as World War II and Hitler and Marx and Stalin. In time, however, Sasha's innocent questions gave way to more probing inquiries about embassy life. Sasha wanted to know whether Lonetree had ever been in the ambassador's office and what the security arrangements were generally. The questions were always asked in a casual manner and setting, such as during a walk with Violetta. One day Sasha produced a list of questions that had been compiled by a friend who was a KGB general. "I knew after this meeting that Sasha worked for the KGB," said Lonetree during his confession.

Lonetree exposed the names of CIA employees such as Michael Sellars (who was expelled for spying) and Murat Natirboff, who was widely known to be the CIA station chief. Sasha repeatedly asked Lonetree to plant bugs in embassy offices, and repeatedly Lonetree refused. But when Sasha requested plans for the seventh floor (known to house the CIA), Lonetree said he would try to get them. Lonetree stole the plans three weeks later and handed them over to Sasha. Then Sasha laid out more than three hundred photographs of embassy personnel and asked Lonetree to arrange the photos showing who was married to whom, and Lonetree complied. Sasha then had Lonetree flip through an embassy phone book and describe the functions of each person. Lonetree also went over the embassy's floor plans with Sasha, marking sensitive spaces, secret doors, and security devices on the seventh floor. Under Sasha's probing, Lonetree gave a detailed description of Ambassador Arthur A. Hartman's desk, presumably so the KGB could design a listening device for it.

Though by this time Lonetree was clearly being handled by the KGB as a spy, he continued to believe that the encounters with Violetta and Sasha were strictly social. He simply could not bring himself to face the fact that his lover was a KGB plant and that her affection for him a sham.

In March 1986, Lonetree was transferred to the Vienna Embassy, where he received letters from Violetta proclaiming her love. He continued to meet with Sasha and provided information about the Vienna Embassy personnel and floor plans. Lonetree was paid $3,600 for the material, $1,000 of which he spent on a handmade Viennese gown for Violetta. When Sasha offered to smuggle Lonetree back to Moscow for a visit with Violetta, in exchange for photographs of U.S. employees believed to be CIA agents, Lonetree jumped at the chance. But as he, Sasha, and his new handler, Yuriy V. Lyson, began making plans for the rendezvous, the stress became too much for Lonetree. He began drinking even more heavily than before, and on December 14, 1986, strode up to the Vienna CIA station chief at a Christmas party and confessed. He told the man, "I'm in something over my head. I need to talk to you about it."

Thinking he could save his neck and get the girl, too, Lonetree concocted a preposterous plan whereby he would return to Moscow as a double agent and flush out Edward Lee Howard. He even imagined himself swooping down, rescuing Violetta from Moscow, and returning to the United States a hero. Eventually the CIA decided that the plan was too risky and instead turned Lonetree over to the Naval Investigative Service to face criminal charges for espionage.

After a sensational trial, Clayton Lonetree was sentenced to thirty years' imprisonment at Fort Leavenworth, Kansas. The sentence was later reduced to twenty-five years, in exchange for Lonetree's full cooperation in providing details of his recruitment by the KGB.[5] Lonetree's attorneys now allege that he was persuaded to confess in order to divert attention away from Ames, and they are heading back to court to try to have him exonerated.[6] The prosecutor also believes that the case should be reopened in light of the Ames case.[7]

For at least two years after the Lonetree case surfaced, the Agency and other parts of American intelligence were engaged in a huge damage-limitation exercise in an attempt to understand the extent of the KGB's penetration of the embassy's security. There was a widespread assumption at the time that Lonetree had managed to pass over to the Soviets many of the communications codes used by the embassy and that he had allowed the KGB to understand where bugs should be planted for maximum effect and in some cases actually helped them to plant the listening devices. While there was fury that Lonetree should have betrayed his country, there was a measure of relief in the Agency that there was at least an explanation for many of the losses that had been incurred. Of course, it was only much later, when the whole episode was placed in its proper context, that Lonetree was relegated from the role of master spy to the part of bit player in the whole drama.

Lonetree achieved exactly the diversion that the KGB had wanted. Their initial assessment of the Agency's response to Ames's betrayals had been dead right. The CIA was indeed taking another look at the series of compromised sources in 1985–86 and searching for answers to some of the unresolved questions. Even before the Lonetree debacle, in October 1986 the CIA management took its first significant step to resolve the compromises. The chief of the counter intelligence staff named a four-person analytical group, known as the Special Task Force (STF). Agency officials now knew that as many as thirty CIA and FBI Soviet operations had been compromised or had developed problems between 1985 and 1986.[8] (Each case represented an individual who was providing useful information, but who may or may not have been a fully recruited individual.)

Two of the team members were experienced Soviet-operations officers who also had significant counter intelligence experience. The other two were retired operations and counter intelligence specialists. The senior CIA managers who ordered the creation of the Special Task Force did not require that the team include individuals trained in investigative techniques or financial reviews. Rather, they were looking for seasoned officers who had operational or counter intelligence experience, and who understood the Directorate of Operations. There was a commonly held belief, apparently shared by successive deputy directors for operations, that a small team was preferable because it reduced the chance that a potential mole would be alerted to the investigation.[9] While this was a reasonable point of view, the level of the disaster caused by Ames's betrayal should have led to a departure from tradition. After all, someone or something had effectively destroyed the SE Division's operational capability. Dealing with that problem required more than a business-as-usual approach.

The STF was tasked to look at all the cases known to have been compromised and to identify any common features among them. Some of the questions the task force considered were:

1. What CIA offices were involved in the compromised cases, or had known about them?

2. Within these offices, which CIA employees had access to the information?

3. How many of the compromises could be accounted for by the Edward Lee Howard betrayal, and of those remaining, how many could be explained by other factors, such as poor operational procedures by CIA officers?

The STF analyzed all of the compromised cases, searching for patterns or other indicators that could shed light on the catastrophe. The task force did not create a formal list of suspects who had access to the compromised information and did not initiate investigations of specific individuals who were considered likely suspects. Nor did the team conduct a comprehensive analysis of cases that had *not* been compromised, which might have shed light on the similarities among those cases that had been compromised.[10] CIA management was supportive of the STF review, but did not apply pressure on them or attach great urgency to the investigation:

"People ask me whether [my supervisors] bugged me about [the investigation]. I said, no, they didn't bug me about it because they don't call up their doctor every five minutes and say, do I have cancer. I mean, they did not put a lot of pressure on us, but they encouraged us. . . . The problem was that we didn't make progress in it and we didn't get any answers."[11]

In October 1986, the same month the CIA established the Special Task Force, the CIA and FBI learned that two Soviet sources who had worked closely with the FBI had been arrested and were about to be executed. The FBI responded by creating its own six-person analytical team, known as the "ANLACE Task Force," which worked full-time to analyze the compromise of its two sources. An anlace is a short dagger—which the team hoped they would plunge deep into the heart of the mole. On the team were Tim Caruso, now assistant special agent in charge of Russian intelligence in New York, and James Holt, a counter intelligence specialist. They worked in a dark, windowless room known as "the Vault."[12]

The CIA and FBI task forces shared some information informally, and in December 1986 held the first of eight "off-site" conferences to discuss the compromised intelligence sources. The CIA briefed the FBI regarding the compromises it was aware of, and the FBI in turn provided briefings on a series of investigative leads it had received in the mid-1970s, but could not resolve, which related to possible penetrations of the CIA. The FBI believed these old leads might hold the key to the 1985–86 compromises. The December 1986 off-site meeting with the FBI prompted at least one CIA participant to raise concerns to the chief of the CIA's SE Division about the FBI's inquisitiveness regarding CIA's organization and activities. Pointing out that the FBI had disclosed its own "dirty linen" at this meeting, the CIA participant wrote that "a conscious decision has been made here concerning the degree to which we are going to cooperate with, and open ourselves up to, the FBI."[13]

In general, the FBI gave the CIA information pertinent to its cases and provided detailed summaries of its own compromises as it learned of them, whereas the CIA jealously guarded its own operational files. After the Howard case, the Bureau and the Agency had signed a memorandum of understanding that was supposed to codify just how much information should be shared and when. The concept was a brave attempt to break through the years of distrust, but it failed dismally. At every single review conference, which took place every two years, the Agency generally declared itself happy with the way things were going, whereas the Bureau appeared with a long list of complaints spelling out just how uncooperative the CIA was continuing to be.[14]

At the second joint meeting between the CIA and the FBI, in March 1987, the head of the CIA's counter intelligence staff praised the cooperation between FBI and CIA officials and noted that "the concept of SE Division, Office of Security, CI Staff, and the FBI working together is something previously unheard of."[15] From the CIA's perspective, although the CIA and the FBI had experienced problems in working together in the past, the Ames case was later seen as an exception: "All in all, coordination between CIA and the Bureau on the Ames case was exemplary."[16]

The Lonetree case caused particular concern to the task force. The idea that the KGB had managed to physically penetrate the American Embassy in Moscow was horrifying, because it suggested that the KGB might have been walking the halls planting bugs at will. It might even have been able to gain access to CIA files and make copies.

For almost a year, this was to be a major focus of the investigation, but by the end of August 1987, most of the STF was persuaded that the Lonetree case was a "dry hole" in terms of explaining the 1985–86 Soviet compromises. While the STF was able to rule out Lonetree as the cause of the compromises, the possibility of a human penetration remained, nevertheless.[17]

Before and after the Lonetree incident, the KGB undertook a concerted effort to draw the CIA's and FBI's attention away from any possibility of finding Ames. The KGB tried to spread the word that it was, in fact, Edward Lee Howard who was responsible for any compromises. And in a worldwide campaign of disinformation the KGB suggested through a series of careful leaks that some of the sources thought to have been compromised were actually alive and well and that others might have been lost for reasons unrelated to any kind of mole within the CIA. KGB officials passed along information that suggested some of the losses

(ABOVE LEFT) Aldrich "Rick" Ames, from his 1959 McLean High School yearbook. *(courtesy of McLean High School)*

(ABOVE RIGHT) Rachel Ames, Rick's mother, who taught at McLean. *(courtesy of McLean High School)*

Rick in happier times—wittiest in his class. *(courtesy of McLean High School)*

Rick, backstage at the
University Theater,
University of Chicago.
*(courtesy of the Department
of Special Collections,
University of Chicago
Library)*

CIA headquarters at
Langley, where Rick filled
shopping bags with top-
secret documents.
*(UPI/Bettmann
Newsphotos)*

William Webster, the DCI who for more than a year was not told about the worst security leak in the CIA's history. *(Associated Press)*

Bob Gates, the DCI who first heard about Ames from the newspapers. *(Associated Press)*

William Casey, the DCI who fought for reforms at the CIA and failed. *(Associated Press)*

James Woolsey, the DCI who became yet another of Ames's victims. *(Associated Press)*

Vitaly Yurchenko, who defected and then returned to the U.S.S.R. after being interrogated by Ames. *(Associated Press)*

Oleg Gordievsky, the MI6 source in the KGB who is the only high-level spy to have survived Ames's betrayal. *(courtesy of Oleg Gordievsky)*

Dimitri Fedorovich Polyakov, code-named "Top Hat," who was betrayed by Ames and shot. *(Associated Press)*

Edward Lee Howard, the CIA officer who defected to Moscow just before Ames began his deadly work. *(Associated Press)*

James Jesus Angleton, whose paranoia about a CIA traitor almost destroyed operations against the U.S.S.R. *(Associated Press)*

Clayton Lonetree, the Marine guard at the U.S. Embassy in Moscow who at first was blamed for Ames's spying. *(Associated Press)*

Ames walked into the gates of the Russian Embassy under the noses of the FBI.
(Jaimie Seaton)

2512 North Randolph Street, the $540,000 house Ames bought for cash. *(courtesy of James Adams)*

Having walked into a trap set by FBI agents, Ames, leaning on his Jaguar, is frisked before being handcuffed and charged with espionage. *(FBI Photo/John Hallisey)*

The Post-It note recovered from Ames's trash, which was the first confirmation that he was an active spy. *(FBI Photo)*

I AM READY TO MEET
AT B ON 1 OCT.
    I CANNOT READ
NORTH 13-19 SEPT.
    IF YOU WILL
MEET AT B ON 1 OCT
PLS SIGNAL NORTH U
OF 20 SEPT TO CONFI.
NO MESSAGE AT PIPE.
    IF YOU CANNOT MEE.
1 OCT, SIGNAL NORTH AFTER
27 SEPT WITH MESSAGE AT
    PIPE.

The traitor unmasked and in chains. Ames after receiving a life sentence for spying. *(Associated Press)*

Rosario Ames on her way to jail after admitting her role as a spy. *(Associated Press)*

might have been due to poor tradecraft or effective counter intelligence work (a perspective that was reflected in the Stein report). One source who had been arrested by the KGB was allowed to contact an official in America to give the impression that he was still operational, and the KGB continued to service the dead-letter drops of others. To help add an air of authority to these careful leaks, the KGB used previously reliable CIA sources who had been identified by Ames but whom the KGB allowed to keep running for precisely this kind of campaign. Once these sources had outlived their usefulness, they, too, were arrested.

This barrage of information, some of it conflicting and none of it supporting the theory of a mole inside the CIA, had to be evaluated on its own merits. Each lead had to be checked—often in very difficult circumstances—and each question resolved. For the CIA and FBI investigators, this was an almost impossible task. Some of the information, such as the false intelligence, could be checked, and many of the sources could be verified through personal contact or other emergency procedures. But this all took weeks and months to resolve, and none of it appeared in the end to mean very much. It was standard operating practice for the KGB—as it was for the CIA—to sow disinformation in the enemy ranks whenever and wherever possible. So while the Agency recognized there was some kind of worldwide campaign under way, it was not until much later, when the Ames case was reviewed with the knowledge that there had indeed been a mole, that the disinformation effort's true significance was understood. Until then, it was a huge and very successfully managed distraction that kept the investigators well away from what should have been their central concern.

In September 1987, at about the time the CIA Special Task Force had begun to conclude that the Howard case could not explain the earlier compromises, the FBI ANLACE Task Force concluded that it could go no further with its own analysis. While it believed that Edward Lee Howard could have been the source for one of its two blown operations, it found no explanation for the compromise of the other source.

Nonetheless, a few months earlier, in May 1987, a joint meeting had been held to discuss progress on solving the mystery of the compromises. In an effort to develop new leads, CIA and FBI officers agreed to launch a new initiative to recruit Soviet intelligence officers who could shed some light on the problem, despite the fact that such information might well come at a high price. The two agencies would attempt to identify Soviet intelligence officers worldwide who might currently be, or might formerly have been, in positions giving them access to information regarding the 1985–86 compromises. This recruitment initiative continued until the time of Ames's arrest in 1994. Despite repeated efforts to develop sources, the program succeeded in producing only relatively marginal results over the period of its existence. Meanwhile, the news on the 1985–86 compromises worsened when, toward the end of 1987, the CIA learned that three additional Soviet sources, all recruited before 1985, had been arrested, and that one had been executed.

In that same May of 1987, William Webster was appointed director of central intelligence. With his experience as director of the FBI, he should have been a powerful force for driving cooperation between the Agency and the Bureau. Indeed, during his time as DCI, he did take a number of positive steps to improve cooperation, even to institutionalize it, through the establishment of a number of different bodies. But, whatever his instincts, he was to be left unaware of the existence of the investigation and even of the suspicion that a high-level mole might have penetrated to the heart of the organization he was heading. This omission is almost unbelievable given the nature of the damage that Ames had wreaked and the fact that the most important division of the CIA under Webster's control had virtually ground to a halt. At the very least, he might have expected to be fully briefed on the investigation within a week or two of arriving at Langley. In fact, it was to be a year and a half before he was even informed that an investigation was under way, let alone told the dimensions of the damage that had been done to the most secret operations of the Agency he was running.[18]

It is difficult to overstate the dimensions of this extraordinary lapse. Webster was the man charged with fighting for and defending the CIA against its many critics. Yet the culture within the DO was such that there was nobody prepared to let this outsider in on the SE Division's shabby little secret: that it had virtually stopped functioning and was producing little intelligence of any serious value. Instead, all those involved chose either to ignore the chain of command or simply to close ranks and hope that they would be able to solve the problem themselves.

It appears to have been a simple coincidence that gave Webster any knowledge of the investigation at all. Dick Stolz had been appointed DDO, and he simply ran through with the DCI some of the matters that he felt were high on his agenda. Among them was the investigation into the penetration. According to Webster, at that time there was not "a judgment there had been a human penetration."[19]

Webster believes that there were several reasons why the CIA endeavors against Ames didn't proceed as fast as they could have. First, "historically, almost every awareness or identification of moles has come from information supplied by our own recruited agents inside the hostile intelligence service, but no leads were forthcoming on the loss of the Soviet assets in the first several years. There was no specific reason to attribute the loss of the assets to a leak from CIA; there might have been a communications penetration; perhaps the KGB was simply doing good security work. There could have been separate reasons that the assets were lost."[20]

In any case, says Webster, the issue of how the sources were neutralized "remained basically an analytical task from 1985 until the early '90s without specific leads following the principal losses in 1985–86. As a matter of fact, in the late 1980s, the analytical inquiry faltered from lack of new investigative leads or new methodology."[21]

In February 1988, yet another joint conference was held between the FBI and the CIA task forces. While the task forces had concluded that in all likelihood Lonetree had not allowed the Soviets to enter the U.S. Embassy in Moscow, the conferees remained focused on the possibility that a technical penetration of the embassy could explain the majority of the earlier compromises. The joint meetings of the CIA and FBI task forces now covered a wide range of counter intelligence topics, not all of which related to the 1985–86 compromises. A representative of the CIA Special Task Force did note a continuing effort to analyze Soviet operations by computer to determine the reason for the 1985–86 compromises, but little tangible progress was cited.[22]

In the spring of 1988, the CIA opened an investigation of an SE Division employee (not Ames) who had access to some, though not all, of the compromised cases. The employee had made numerous damaging admissions during the course of previous polygraph examinations (none relating to security issues per se), and had difficulty getting through routine polygraph examinations over the course of his CIA employment. Relying upon a 1988 tip from a CIA employee that this officer was spending large amounts of money at a level not explained by his salary, the CIA Office of Security opened a financial investigation of the individual. While the investigator determined that the employee had indeed spent far in excess of his salary, the employee was able to demonstrate that the money had come from his spouse's inheritance. The CIA decided to remove this individual from access to sensitive operations. This yearlong investigation, which proved to be unrelated to the 1985–86 compromises, significantly diverted the sole investigator assigned to the compromised cases.

The staff of the Special Task Force was also distracted during this period by the effort required to create a new coordinating office for counter intelligence. On April 1, 1988, Webster established the DCI's Counter Intelligence Center (CIC), which included the participation of people from the Defense Intelligence Agency, National Security Agency, State Department, FBI, and various military branches. He also established the Intelligence Group for Counter Intelligence under the leadership of the director of the FBI. Later he was to establish a Security Evaluation Office to help the State Department set up and evaluate standards for counter intelligence at U.S. embassies. That same year, he signed a memorandum of understanding with the FBI affirming that the CIA would share information with the FBI if the Agency noticed any problems that fell under the jurisdiction of the FBI. In theory this should have been a milestone toward improving relations between the two organizations, but it was to be another three years before the directors of the Bureau and the Agency really started working together. With that example from the top, it is hardly surprising that all the different bureaucratic shuffles did little to change the reality of the difficult relationships on the ground.

As part of the reorganization of counter intelligence into the CIC, the CIA Special Task Force looking into the 1985–86 compromises, which had been a part of the counter intelligence staff of the Directorate of Operations, was subsumed within a new Investigations Branch of the Security Group within the Counter Intelligence Center. This branch had responsibility for all cases involving possible human penetrations of the CIA. The deputy chief of the Security Group and, concurrently, the head of the new Investigations Branch, was the same CIA officer who had previously been in charge of the Special Task Force.

In June 1988—three years after Ames's most damaging disclosures to the KGB—the KGB instituted the most elaborate of its ploys to direct attention away from Ames. The KGB had one of its officers pass information to the CIA concerning five of the cases Ames had compromised. The information suggested that each of the cases had been compromised due to poor tradecraft on the part of either the source itself or the CIA officers involved. While the opinion of CIA officers varied as to whether the new information was genuine, it clearly created a stir and required time-consuming analysis over the next two years.

When the CIA–FBI task forces met again on July 20, 1988, they had little to report, because most of their energies had been diverted trying to set up the new Counter Intelligence Center. But the teams agreed that sixteen significant Soviet sources had been compromised in the 1985–86 period and that Edward Lee Howard had certain knowledge of only three of the cases, and potentially might have known details about seven others. That left six cases that he could not have known anything about.

On October 13, 1988, the CIA and FBI task forces met yet again. The officials discussed the progress of the related counter intelligence investigation, which was attempting to find out whether the KGB had been able to penetrate a particular office of the CIA. The investigator assigned to the case reported that he had thus far reviewed the access of ninety employees assigned to the office in question. While reporting the investigation had produced ten suspects, including Ames, the investigator noted, "there are so many problem personalities . . . that no one stands out." However, none of the ten seemed likely to be responsible for the 1985–86 compromises. Essentially, the inquiry had run out of places to go. With no overt compromises on the scale of the first batch, it seemed as if the mole—if there ever had been one—had gone to ground. With no new leads and no new ideas, the investigation was simply marking time.

What is striking about this period is that the counter intelligence effort received such a low priority. The setting up of the two task forces and the cooperation between them were clearly the start of what should have been a productive relationship. The teams swiftly learned that Edward Lee Howard was not the source of all the betrayals. But, because it appeared that the 1985–86 disasters were merely an unfortunate "spike" in the otherwise smooth intelligence graph, the impetus appeared to go out of the investigation. It is true that Ames had done the most damage in the first few months of his spying, while he was still in the SE Division and had had access to the 301 files, the documents that actually identified key agents in place in the Soviet Union. Both the Agency and the FBI talked frankly about the devastation that had been caused by those betrayals and the fact that the Agency was effectively left without any operating sources inside the Soviet Union. At this stage, there seems to have been no real attempt to match the people who had access to the 301 files with the timing of the betrayals. Nobody asked the critical questions: Who knew? and Why did the betrayals stop? The answers to those two questions would have produced a very short list of names, among them that of Rick Ames.

The stream of disinformation that emanated from Moscow was seen in Washington as simply a series of leads that needed to be examined. The idea that the KGB, which everyone in the intelligence business respected as a clever adversary, might have been waging a concerted campaign of disinformation did not occur to anyone. Instead, each lead was followed and then discarded as an isolated event. As the compromising of sources appeared to stop, so the high priority initially given the investigation was replaced with a feeling that the series of events in 1985–86 might simply remain an unexplained mystery. By the end of the 1980s, so much energy had been expended on the investigation that there was none left to pursue the real leads to the real villain.

For both the KGB and Rick Ames, this was good news indeed. The fact that the KGB had managed to successfully distract the Agency and the FBI was exactly the reassurance Rick wanted. He knew that the people he was really working for not only valued him enough to pay him properly but were clearly smart enough to fool the idiots back home. He was ready to get down to some serious work.

TWELVE

Frustrating Marriages

Immediately after Lonetree was convicted, Rick wrote his handlers a letter that was later described as "a renewal of marriage vows." "My commitment remains in force. . . . You can trust completely that I am at your service. This is a commitment that has grown on me and has gotten to the point that I can see your commitment deserves the same from me."

The Soviets mounted another diversion at this time. In 1986, when Ames told his handlers in Rome that he feared he would be considered a suspect, the KGB instructed one of their case officers in East Berlin to tell a CIA contact that he knew Moscow had learned of the penetrations through a leak in the CIA worldwide secret communications facility at Warrenton, Virginia. For almost a year, the CIA investigated its own personnel at Warrenton, and Ames again went unnoticed.[1]

With his back now effectively covered by the carefully orchestrated diversions, Ames felt free to begin his lengthy relationship with Sam II, whom he was to meet at least twelve times over the next three years. In addition, there were to be three further meetings with Vlad. Using exactly the same tactic he had devised for his meetings in Washington, Ames told the CIA station chief, Alan Wolfe, that Khrenkov (Sam II) was a potential recruit and received official authorization to hold meetings with him. As before, Ames appeared initially enthusiastic about the evolving relationship but then began to downplay it in case it should begin to receive too much attention inside the office. In fact, oversight of the meetings appears to have been so lax that he need hardly have bothered. Ames failed to submit reports documenting many of these meetings, but this was almost routine for Ames by now and nobody appears to have questioned this clear breach of regulations or to have followed up on the contact meetings to see just how the alleged seduction of Sam II was progressing.

Some of Ames's colleagues in Rome suspected that he was not reporting all of his meetings with the Russians. Ames's supervisor was aware that he was in contact with a Soviet Embassy officer, but apparently did not query him about the relationship or ensure that he was documenting all of his contacts.[2] One of Ames's subordinates in Rome suspected he was not fully documenting the relationship between himself and the Soviet official. She had searched the office database to see whether Ames was reporting all of his contacts and discovered that he had not. Even so, she did not turn him in.[3]

Sam II would meet Ames for lunch, dinner, or a drink, and there would be an exchange of information for money, which was often hidden inside a box of cigars. Typically these payments ranged from $20,000 to $50,000 per meeting. For the more important appointments with Vlad, Ames would be picked up by Sam II in his car and then taken to the Soviet Embassy. Ames would pull a hat down over his eyes and crouch down low in the seat just in case the car was photographed going through the embassy gates. He would spend the next three or four hours with Vlad drinking vodka and discussing the information that he had passed to him and what the Russians would like to see in the future.

The volume of material crossing Ames's desk was huge, and most of it arrived as a matter of routine. He was the end of the paper chain, and much of the material was supposed to be shredded in his office. Frequently, such was the volume of paper that there were two copies of key material, and so he was able to shred one and keep the other. On other occasions, he simply failed to shred the material. It all proved remarkably easy.

"I wouldn't characterize Rome Station as being a center of a lot of sensitive operational activity. But the nature, the nature of the DO and the paper flow and the accelerating bureaucracy meant that there was a tremendous amount of material about Directorate of Operations policies and plans and resources that would get sent to all stations," said Ames.

"I was [supposed] to destroy the paper. And it wound up with me. Typically, I would meet with my cutout in the early evening. And I would simply stay in my office until 6:00 or so, gather up, quickly gather up, review and gather up information that I thought would be of value. Put it in envelopes in a shopping bag and leave the embassy."[4]

While he certainly had stunning access, his position in Rome was very different from the role he had in Washington. Back at Langley, Ames was privy to the top-secret 301 files. In Rome, there was no need to know that specific information. Instead, Ames knew a great deal about day-to-day CIA operations and also learned more about CIA operations in Eastern Europe (aside from the U.S.S.R.) than he had in Washington. Thus, he was able to compromise a number of networks operating in Communist countries. He revealed the identity of a Hungarian official, code-named GTMotorboat, who was voluntarily giving Ames classified documents dealing with Eastern European security matters. GTMotorboat subsequently disappeared, and the CIA made many attempts to contact him, but without success.[5] GTMotorboat was later executed, and a number of other Hungarians working for the Americans were arrested and jailed.[6] Ames also compromised a CIA network in Czechoslovakia and damaged CIA operations across the whole of Eastern Europe.

By gossiping with colleagues and trying to bridge the need-to-know walls that existed between different officers in the station, Ames tried to supplement the wealth of material at his disposal. One officer told FBI investigators that Ames was always asking a lot of questions, saying he was keeping abreast of intelligence information.[7] Other former colleagues in Rome reported that near the end of Ames's tour, he often asked questions about cases that had no relation to his past or current post, but none of the people in the station saw anything particularly unusual in this kind of questioning, and nobody thought to report Ames to the Office of Security.[8]

It has been alleged that, while in Rome, Ames let the Russians plant secret recording devices in his apartment that allowed them to monitor conversations with his guests.[9] This is specifically denied by the CIA, which carried out a detailed search of Ames's apartment after he was uncovered and also questioned him at length about the allegation.[10]

In anticipation of large cash installments from his Soviet friends, Ames traveled to Switzerland in early December 1986 to open account number 0835-206582-62 in his own name at the local branch of Crédit Suisse with a cash deposit of $40,000. He also opened a second account, number 260880-32, known as the Crédit Suisse B account, in the name of his mother-in-law, Cecilia, and specified himself as the sole trustee. Many of his cash deposits in these accounts were in large amounts—one deposit, for example, was for more than $300,000. The CIA investigation later determined that Ames deposited a total of at least $950,000 into the Swiss bank accounts while he served in Rome. Between January 1987 and August 1991, more than thirty-one cash and wire transfers were made from his own account, known as the Crédit Suisse A account, to his and Rosario's account with the Dominion Bank of Virginia. These transfers totaled $718,900. There were also eighteen wire withdrawals from Cecilia's account over the same period totaling $1.091 million, with $240,000 going to the Ameses' bank accounts in Virginia and $165,000 going to other investment accounts in America.[11]

In August 1987, he filed a false income-tax return, from Rome, for the 1986 tax year, reporting his total income as $64,973, nearly $20,000 less than his most recent Soviet cash installment.

In order to discourage undue scrutiny of his finances by banking officials, Ames avoided frequent or high-dollar electronic bank transfers from Rome into his Swiss bank accounts, instead traveling to Switzerland on several occasions with large amounts of cash, which he deposited directly into his accounts. Some of these trips were made without the knowledge of his supervisors, in violation of regulations requiring that all overseas personal or business travel by CIA employees be approved by CIA officials.

Rick and Rosario began to enjoy the fruits of his betrayal while in Italy. Debriefings of officers who served with him indicate there was a general awareness among his coworkers that Ames was affluent. One officer has described Ames's spending as "blatantly excessive," and stated that everyone knew and talked about it. Many of his colleagues knew that Ames and his wife took numerous personal trips throughout Europe—to Switzerland, Britain, and Germany. One colleague knew that the Ameses had telephone bills totaling $5,000 monthly.[12] In fact, the Rome security officer brought Ames's spending and drinking habits to the attention of the senior CIA officer in Rome, but the perception that Ames had created—that Rosario came from a wealthy family—seemed to defuse any security concern over the Ameses' extravagant spending habits. No mention of these issues was included in Ames's personnel or security file.[13]

Those who knew him in Rome admit that he also began to openly flaunt his newly acquired fortune. Vincent Cannistraro, a former CIA officer, recalls that Ames "had a number of items that would have caused anyone observing him to say that he had a lot of money." Cannistraro, who has traveled and lived abroad frequently during his tenure with the CIA, and is quite familiar with the crowded Italian streets, most frequently traversed by tiny old Fiats and motor scooters, describes Ames's Jaguar as "ostentatious in the local context." Ames showed off other expensive items, including a Duraflex camera, a second car, and expensive suits. Cannistraro recalls that Ames's material possessions were much more memorable than his personality or appearance. "He was nondescript—unremarkable."[14] Milan's daily *Corriere della Sera*, on the other hand, reported that Ames was a high-society figure, a "fixture" in Rome's trendiest nightspots.[15]

In early 1989, Ames continued to make cash deposits in his Crédit Suisse accounts—and continued turning over valuable information to the Soviets.[16] On March 6, he deposited $150,000 in cash in his Crédit Suisse B account.[17] The following week, he typed another message on his computer to his Soviet friends, which disclosed classified information relating to national security and defense and the identities of more double agents.[18] Apparently, the contents of the memo to the Soviets were valuable. About a month later, on April 24, 1989, Ames made two cash deposits, totaling $140,000, in the Crédit Suisse A account.[19]

Ames's job performance in Rome was mediocre to poor. Of the four job-performance evaluations he received during his Rome tour, the first two commented positively on his personnel-management skills, but noted he needed to do more work in developing new leads. In his second evaluation, Ames's supervisor wrote, "He handles ongoing cases; his efforts to initiate new developmental activity of any consequence have been desultory." This was an extremely critical evaluation of an operations officer. The last performance appraisal in Rome, written by a different supervisor, noted Ames's performance was inconsistent and that "his full potential has not been realized here in Rome." One of Ames's senior managers commented that he felt Ames had been a "terminal GS-14" and a lackluster, "middleweight" case officer.[20]

As in previous tours, Ames was persistently late in filing financial accounting of his official expenditures. Ames blames this on sheer procrastination on his part.[21] In fact, his supervisor in Rome confronted him with this problem, leading Ames to close out his operational account and use his personal funds to pay for job-related expenditures. He submitted his expenses for reimbursement, but one of his supervisors made him reopen his operational account.[22]

Ames's job performance was further marred by his alcohol dependency, which resurfaced in Rome and was well known within the office. Once again, however, there was no official record made of his drinking problems. In post-arrest debriefings, former colleagues stated that Ames would go out for long lunches and return to the office too drunk to work. One of his Rome supervisors recalled that Ames was drunk about three times a week between 1986 and 1988. Another colleague commented that in 1987 Ames was very upset when he failed to get promoted, and he began to drink even more heavily. Yet another supervisor reportedly once described Ames to a colleague as "one of the worst drunks in the outfit."[23]

On at least two occasions, Ames's alcohol problem came directly to the attention of his supervisors. In the first instance, he returned from a meeting with Sam II and was unable to write a message for transmission to Washington, as directed by his supervisors. On the second occasion, he became drunk at the ambassador's July 4 celebration in the gardens of the embassy.[24]

"Rosario was visiting Bogotá at the time and so I started drinking, and my own pattern of sort of semi-binge drinking is that while I might drink too much, or more than I should, I could often stop and not get totally drunk and incapable. But on a very few occasions, the inhibition would stop and I would just keep drinking. And that is what happened at that reception. And I have no recollection of the latter half of the reception, and I walked home and passed out on the street beside my apartment building. And I woke up in hospital.

"This didn't give rise to my counseling. . . . My Chief of Station, when he saw me in the hall the following Monday, he looked at me, there was never any discussion of what had happened. He looked at me and he said, 'you should be more careful.' . . . And I gave him kind of a, probably a kind of a hangdog and apologetic look and said I know I have . . . that was really a . . . I must . . . that was really something, to that effect. And that was that."[25]

The issue of his drinking was not always handled so indirectly. At one point, when a superior criticized Ames's failure as a recruiter and his continuous drinking, Ames is said to have responded sarcastically, "I should listen to him? *He* has a drinking problem."[26]

Despite the huge cash benefits and the lavish lifestyle, the personal relationship between Rick and Rosario virtually collapsed during this period. She found that the sweet, kind intellectual she thought she had married was in fact a drunken monster. During the first year of the assignment, Rosario became pregnant and then had a miscarriage. At the same time, their sex life became increasingly difficult.

"Our marriage was deteriorating rapidly. . . . Rick started becoming indifferent, showing less and less interest in, let's say, the sexual part of our relationship, which was very hurtful to me," she said.

"He was very good at manipulating and using because without really saying much he had me totally convinced that it had to be my fault. I was either too skinny or too hysterical or too something."[27]

Despite these problems, Rosario managed to become pregnant in 1988 and she gave birth to Paul the following year, an event she described as "a miracle really because we were not having a normal sex life."[28]

Even the pregnancy and later birth were seen by colleagues as a contributing factor to Rick's poor performance. Rick was often called out of meetings by his wife when she wanted to discuss something about the baby. "[This] is something that isn't usually done during important intelligence operations."[29] After the birth of Paul, sex was a low priority for

Rosario, and Rick had no interest. But when she wanted to reestablish a sexual relationship, she discovered that Rick was impotent, a condition that was to continue until his arrest.[30] This condition, combined with his drinking, was a visible sign of the toll that was being taken on Ames by his spying.

"There are two kinds of 'erectile dysfunction,' " explained Dr. Ronald Moglia, a professor and director of the graduate program in human sexuality at New York University. "We don't use the word 'impotent.' The word has a strong psychological effect, meaning 'useless.' There are two kinds: primary and secondary. Primary means a man never had an erection. Secondary—probably the case with Ames—means at some point in his life a man is unable to have them. Almost all men have some kind of erectile dysfunction at some time in life."[31]

Fifteen years ago, the assumption was that most cases of impotence were caused by psychological problems. Now the thinking is reversed. In practice, however, the distinction between the two is blurred, because physical problems make people feel anxious and stressed-out. And then if someone then becomes impotent on top of that, his emotions are going to go into a tailspin.

The physical factors known to cause impotence include high blood pressure, diabetes, smoking, alcoholism, aging (to some extent), heart disease, some two hundred or more prescription medications, and even extensive bicycle pedaling—basically anything that impairs blood flow or circulation to the penis. Unless a person has a condition such as diabetes that absolutely leads to impotence (or alcoholism, which often does), it's difficult to say exactly what the precise medical cause is. That's because there's no medical way to test the cause of poor circulation to the penis or microscopic damage to the veins.

From a medical perspective, Ames was a prime case for impotence as a heavy smoker and an alcoholic, but he was also deeply psychologically disturbed. Ames had chosen to follow in his father's footsteps by working as a CIA officer, and then to compete and beat his father he became not just a spy but a double agent. According to Dr. Bonnie Anthony, a Maryland psychoanalyst who specializes in impotence, Ames was caught in a vicious circle. "It's tremendously stressful, psychologically speaking, to best one's parents. You drink more to alleviate the stress. You try to drink it away. You anesthetize yourself. One place you also anesthetize is in the penis. More stress and anxiety follow. That anxiety alone can be enough to stop an erection.

"In other words, you can't screw two people at once. So if screwing Dad is the unconscious focus of Ames's activities, then he has no time to focus on his wife."[32]

Rosario kept secret her deteriorating relationship with Rick, and he had no friends in whom he could confide the information. Instead, the two were seen by other officers in the station as a problem couple who were going through a rough time, including a series of noisy public fights. But such marital problems were not that unusual at the Agency, and while there was counseling available, there was no official mechanism to force Rick and Rosario to get help. Instead, they were simply left to get along with their personal business.

Although Ames's performance had been mediocre at best and his alcohol abuse was well known, his superiors extended his two-year assignment in Rome for another year. CIA headquarters approved the extension to July 1989.

Near the end of his Rome assignment, between May and July 1989, the KGB provided Ames with three documents that were later retrieved during the FBI investigation into Ames's activities. The first was a financial accounting of what the KGB had provided Ames by that time. The letter read (including grammatical and typographical errors):

Dear Friend,
    This is Your balance sheet as on the May 1, 1989.
*All in All you have been appropriated . . . 2,705,000$
*From the Times of opening of Your account in our Bank (December 26, 1986) Your profit is . . . $385,077$ 28¢ (including 14,468$ 94¢ as profit on bonds, which we bought for You on the sum of 250,000$)
$ Since December 1986 Your salary is . . . 300,000$
*All in all we have delivered to You . . . 1,881811$ 51¢
On the above date You have on Your account (including 250,000$ in bonds) . . . 1,535,077$ 28¢

P.S. We believe that these pictures would give You some ideas about the beautiful piece of land on the river bank, which from now belongs to You forever. We decided not to take pictures of housing in this area with the understanding that You have much better idea of how Your country house (dacha) should look like.

Good luck.

Just why the Russians believed that Ames would want to defect and live in the Soviet Union is not clear. Certainly in the extensive debriefings that took place after his arrest, there was never any suggestion that his life's ambition was to retire to a dacha near Moscow. On the contrary, there is ample evidence that he intended to continue spying for as long as possible, retire from the CIA, collect his pension, and then go and live on his farm near Bogotá, with occasional forays to the shopping malls of London and Paris to keep Rosario happy. A miserable life in Moscow does not exactly square with that ideal, but his Moscow handlers clearly believed that he needed the continued reassurance that not only were they paying him well but that they were thinking about his long-term future.

In June, the KGB contacted Ames again in Rome, forwarding to him a copy of communications plans to be used when he returned to CIA headquarters in Virginia. The letter provided future payment arrangements and described the type of information that they were interested in receiving from Ames. The Soviets reassured Ames, in this letter, emphasizing that his security was their "main priority." In addition, they reminded him to avoid CIA "mole traps."[33] It proposed dates in the coming year for Ames to pass documents and receive money through clandestine communication sites, also known as "dead drops." The new communications plan also called for Ames to meet with his senior KGB officer at least once yearly outside the United States. Meetings were planned for Bogotá, Colombia, on the first Tuesday of every December, with additional meeting sites, such as Vienna, Austria, listed as alternative sites as needed.

But the reassurance that the KGB gave Ames at the end of June was that which he understood all too well. He received another installment from the KGB and he made three more cash deposits in the Crédit Suisse B account, totaling more than a half a million dollars.[34]

The third document the FBI later recovered was a nine-page letter which showed that Ames would be given another $300,000 in two meetings prior to his departure from Rome. This letter was unusually long. Most communications from his handlers were never more than a page and a half, written in medium-sized block letters in pencil or pen. This letter again spelled out Ames's Soviet handlers' priorities, which included "penetrations of military organizations, political organizations and other organs of the Soviet state. It also asked for information on potential recruits for the Soviets at the CIA and information on U.S. military plans for Eastern Europe and the U.S.S.R."[35]

The letter also specified the iron meeting site that was to be Ames's fallback if he should be compromised. In KGB jargon, an "iron meeting site" is the location where a meeting will take place regardless of what happens to an operation—compared with a drop, which has to be clean before a meeting can occur. If Ames should be compromised, the Soviets guaranteed, someone would appear at the iron meeting site—in this case, the Unicentro Mall in Bogotá.

With arrangements in place to continue his spying, Rick was now set to return to Washington. Professionally, Rome had been a wonderful experience. He had developed his relationship with his Russian controllers, the men who really understood his true value. They had paid or promised nearly $2 million and he knew that if he continued to deliver—and who was to stop him?—then the money would continue to roll in. He had developed a lifestyle that was the envy of his colleagues.

His personal life had not fared so well; there were problems with Rosario, and he was not so deluded as to fail to see that he was slowly being crushed beneath the weight of the stress of his double life. But on the plus side of the ledger was the arrival of little Paul, a son he genuinely adored and who would remain the focus of what little affection he had left to give after the lie he was living had squeezed most of the emotion from him. With the arrogance that increasingly came to dominate his thinking, Rick regarded his CIA colleagues as a bunch of amateurs. He had left enough clues that even a bumbling Inspector Clouseau could have picked them up, and yet nobody suspected a thing. The more he spent, the less he worked, and the more obvious his meetings with the Russians became, so apparently the less attention did anyone pay. He would tell himself repeatedly in those weeks before his return to

Washington that he had been right to betray the Agency: it deserved no less; it was simply a bunch of useless individuals with no role and no future. It was the Russians who were going places, who understood him and his world. They deserved him.

Washington and all it presented beckoned. He looked forward to the transition with eager anticipation. He had more money in the bank—or rather his Swiss bank accounts—than he could possibly spend. But he was going to give it his best shot. If the Russians deserved him, then he also was entitled to spend some of the fruits of his hard work.

THIRTEEN

Return to Base

On July 20, 1989, Rick and Rosario flew back to Washington, D.C. The return to Washington meant opportunities both at home and at work. Rick was appointed chief of the Western European Branch, External Operations Group, a post he assumed in September. It involved overseeing case officers working with sources in Western Europe. These cases largely involved information collected in Europe from the diplomatic corps in various Western European capitals about other countries around the world. He was chosen for this position by his former boss in New York, who thought that Ames had done a good job at the Agency.[1]

This time, the appointment did not come without some opposition from within the Agency. The man who led the charge against Rick was Milton Bearden. He had first met Rick in 1985 when he had returned from Khartoum to become deputy chief of the SE Division. He was there during the first molehunt in the immediate aftermath of the catastrophic losses in the Soviet Union, and some within the Agency blame him in part for not taking stronger action at the time. But Bearden had been reassigned to Khartoum at the same time that Rick went to Rome. Now they both found themselves back in Langley, with Bearden promoted to be chief of the SE Division. Bearden did not want Ames back in his shop, and when the CIA placement board met in the summer of 1989 to discuss a number of future appointments, including Ames's request to return to the SE Division, Bearden launched a fierce attack against Ames. He claimed that Rick was a second-rate operator who had no role in the SE Division and that he should be consigned to some other area in the CIA where he could essentially mark time until he either left or was retired. Despite this less than ringing endorsement, Personnel overruled the objections and Ames was appointed.

"I had to take Rick," said Bearden. "They said, 'Well, here he is, and he's got a clean poly.' "[2]

Clearly, the Agency wasn't yet onto Rick. As he later remarked, this position would have been one of the last places for him to be assigned if the CIA had had suspicions about him.[3]

In early September, Ames completed the transition from Rome to the Virginia suburbs, with the purchase of a rambling, spacious, blue-gray home on North Randolph Street in Arlington. The five-bedroom, professionally landscaped house was located in a quietly wealthy neighborhood, among equally majestic homes owned by former government officials and Washington lawyers. What was unusual about the purchase was not its price, but that Ames paid for the $540,000 home in cash. He paid in full at the time of purchase, informing the title-insurance agent that the money came from an "inheritance" from his wife's family.[4]

Although this suspicious purchase went unnoticed by the CIA, neighbors began to inquire about the financial status of the Ames family. According to neighbors, it was "common knowledge" that Ames paid cash for the house, because he purchased it through a real estate broker named James Ross Ward, a retired Navy captain, who, with his family, also lived on North Randolph Street.[5]

"[That it was] an all-cash sale, raised a lot of eyebrows," says Arlington neighbor William Rhoads. Five months after the Ameses moved in across the street, two FBI agents called at the Rhoads house during the day to ask questions about the new neighbors. As a former government employee himself, Rhoads was familiar with the security-clearance procedure and tried to be as cooperative as possible with the agents. Although he knew that Ames had paid cash for the house, he did not want to say anything that might deny Rick his clearance. Instead, he suggested to the FBI that it might be worth their while talking to Ward to get the full circumstances surrounding the purchase. Apparently this suggestion was not enough to spark a thorough inquiry of Ames's financial status.[6]

The cash payment for the home was not the only purchase that raised eyebrows. "It was obvious they had quite a lot of money, because in addition to purchasing the house for cash, they spent a lot of money fixing it up and a brand-new Jaguar and Honda Accord showed up in their driveway at the time they moved in," says Rhoads.[7] There were less obvious signs of wealth as well; Mrs. Tommye Morton, who lived across the street from the Ameses and occasionally sipped cocktails and shared Camel cigarettes with the spies, said that "although this is a nice neighborhood and most of us have cleaning ladies once a week, they had full-time, round-the-clock help." Rick and Rosario had a Philippine couple who lived with them when they first moved into the neighborhood. And Rosario always dressed nicely and had "good-quality clothes."[8]

Neighbors are full of anecdotes about just how normal and nice a couple the Ameses were. They aided one neighbor who was in a car accident nearby and needed help to get back home. They were founding members of the neighborhood association and regularly attended meetings. They doted on their son, Paul, and gossiped with neighbors about the difficulty of getting him into a good school—"Getting Paul into preschool is as tough as getting into Harvard," Rick told one friend.[9] Even with the benefit of hindsight, there is nobody who knew the Ameses who noticed anything different about them. They simply seemed a normal, loving, and unobtrusive family.[10]

However, a different portrait emerges from the various nannies that Rick and Rosario hired to look after Paul. María Trinidad Chirino, who worked for the couple for eleven months and was paid $275 a week to do so, says that she was ordered to keep Paul out of the home for most of the day and was not supposed to be alone in the house. Chirino told FBI investigators that she would take Paul to parks, and to neighborhood swimming pools, and to visit with nannies who worked in neighbors' homes. In the winter, she recalled, she took Paul to the Ballston Common shopping center before the stores opened, just to keep the child warm.[11] Chirino, whose eleven-month relationship with the Ameses ended bitterly, says she was forbidden to enter certain rooms in the

Ameses' home.[12] "I wondered why she didn't want me in the house," Chirino recalls. "It just wasn't right."[13]

In a news conference following the Ameses' arrest, Chirino criticized Rosario, calling her obsessively secretive. She also questioned Rosario's penchant for spending money: "I could not understand. There was too much luxury if she was going to school all day. . . . I always thought he spent more than what he makes." Chirino claims she was fired when she attempted to prevent Rosario from hitting Paul. She also asserted that Rick Ames tried to push her.[14] It has been impossible to find any corroboration for these allegations, which directly contradict the impression of friends and colleagues that Rick and Rosario were loving parents.

One of Chirino's daughters, Ivania Bedoya, accused Rick Ames of physically threatening her when she tried to collect two weeks' pay after the Ameses fired her mother in October 1990. Chirino took the couple to court in an attempt to recover the wages, but lost.[15] Jacqueline Clark, the founder of A Choice Nanny franchise, Chirino's employer, says that although her company's files on the Ameses include poor-communication complaints from both Rosario and Chirino, there was never any record of physical abuse and no indication that the nanny was forced to stay outside the house for long periods with the child.[16] There is no corroborating evidence from doctors, neighbors, or coworkers that either Rick or Rosario was ever physically abusive toward their son. On the contrary, within the constraints of Rick's work at the Agency and his spying, and Rosario's studies, they do seem to have been devoted parents.

Once back from Rome and settled into his new home, Rick carried his masterful charade to new heights. After years of regularly passing classified information via face-to-face meetings with his Soviet intermediaries, he now began relying on the dead drops that the KGB had written him about that summer. For much of this century, the Russians have used exactly the same methods of communicating with their sources. One side places a chalk mark at a designated site and the other side sees it and knows that a package needs to be collected or dropped off. Once the dead drop has been serviced, the chalk mark is erased so that the signaler knows the message has got through. It is a simple but remarkably effective method of communicating that has served the KGB very well. They used exactly the same system for keeping in touch with the Walker spy ring and, despite the enormous publicity surrounding that case, decided to stick with tried-and-true methods for communicating with Ames.

They provided him with four different sets of signals and dead drops. NORTH, a telephone pole on the corner of Military Road and Thirty-sixth Street in Arlington, was for the Russians to tell Ames that he should pick up a message at PIPE, a drainage pipe in Wheaton Regional Park. The other sets were for Ames to tell the Russians he had left a message for them. A chalk mark on the side of SMILE, a mailbox at the junction of Thirty-seventh and R Streets in Northwest Washington, connected to BRIDGE, a pedestrian footbridge spanning Little Falls Parkway where it runs under Massachusetts Avenue. ROSE, at the junction of Garfield Road and Garfield Terrace, near the foreign embassies that line Massachusetts Avenue, was linked to GROUND, a site under a bridge at the intersection of Pinehurst Parkway and Beech Drive. And BITE, a mailbox at Twenty-eighth and Dumbarton in Washington, connected with CREEK, a pedestrian footbridge in the Langley-Hampshire neighborhood park off New Hampshire Avenue in Prince Georges County.

SMILE, ROSE, and BITE were all sites that the Russians could see while driving on their normal routes to work, and so Ames would place his chalk mark before 8:00 a.m. so that his handlers could note it as they commuted to the embassy downtown. NORTH was on Ames's way to work, and so he would pick their signal up as he drove from Arlington to Langley.

From 1990 until 1993, face-to-face meetings with his handlers took place only outside the United States. Ames met Vlad in Vienna in June 1990, but missed an October 1990 meeting because he mistakenly went to Zurich rather than Vienna. In December 1990, Ames made his next contact in Bogotá, where he was introduced to his second KGB case officer, "Andre." Ames did see Andre in Bogotá in December 1991 and in Caracas in October 1992, and had his last operational meeting with the Russian in Bogotá in November 1993.

However effective the operational side of his life may have been, his blatant personal lifestyle was finally beginning to attract the attention of colleagues. Everyone had noticed the Jaguar, the expensive Gucci watch he had picked up in Rome, the smart shirts and suits, and his apparently limitless appetite for all the fine food and wine that Washington had to offer. For most of his colleagues in the SE Division, he was simply a lucky guy, someone who had been fortunate enough to marry money. But in November 1989, a woman who worked in covert operations and who knew Rosario's family wrote a letter to her supervisors pointing out that Rick's lifestyle was completely incompatible with the salary he was earning from the Agency.[17]

She said that she had known him long enough to contrast his behavior before he went to Rome, when he seemed as poor as everyone else, with his lifestyle since he had returned. She knew he had paid cash for his home, bought two new cars, and seemed to be living well beyond his means. The explanation that he could afford the extravagance because of Rosario's family's wealth was not true. She knew Rosario and her family and said that while they might know the right people in Colombia, they had no money to go with their social pretensions. She was convinced that an investigation was needed. In fact, so convinced was she that Ames was earning money in addition to his Agency salary that she continued to bombard the Office of Security with details of the extensive landscaping work being done in Rick's backyard, the $50,000 kitchen remodeling, and the foreign travel.[18]

Finally, the act of this one woman, who broke the division's vow of silence, was enough to prod the slumbering beast into action. An investigator from the Office of Security assigned to CIC, who usually handled investigations of CIA employees in connection with suspected penetrations, opened a routine financial inquiry on Ames. He queried the U.S. Customs Service for any information on currency transactions involving Ames. The investigator also examined public records and discovered that Ames had purchased his Arlington home for $540,000 and there was no record of a mortgage.[19]

The inquiries that were made about Ames within the division were cursory and never went beyond the most superficial questioning of colleagues. This was hardly surprising, because anyone from the Office of Security was considered a pariah by any other Agency employee, especially somebody from the Directorate of Operations.

"You have to understand that everybody in CIA hates the Office of Security and that Security is the enemy rather than the friend," said Bob Gates, the former DCI. "The DO people regard the Office of Security

people as just a bunch of dumb gumshoes with no operational sophistication or anything else and that's why they're not going to tell the Office
of Security."[20]

It was hardly surprising, then, that the investigator's inquiries were focused not inside the Agency, where he might get the fastest answers, but
on neutral outside agencies that would not give him a lot of grief just for
asking questions. In January 1990, the Treasury Department responded
to the currency-transaction request and identified three "hits" involving Ames: a $13,000 cash deposit into a local bank account in 1985; a
$15,000 cash deposit into the account in 1986; and, upon his return from
Rome, a conversion of Italian lire into $22,107.[21]

Even when the Agency was armed with this new information, there
was no added urgency to what was still a routine inquiry. No link was
made between the allegations of one woman that raised questions about
Ames's spending habits and the security leaks of four years earlier. The
financial investigation was simply boring routine that would probably
lead nowhere, and the security probe had virtually stopped for lack of
new evidence. Part of the reason was that those at the top had lost interest in the subject, and most in the Agency at any level did not believe in
the existence of a mole. Since there were no major compromises from
1986 to 1989, there was really no further evidence to help ascertain
where the problem was, or indeed whether there was still a problem.

"When I returned in 1989, I thought at the time that it was impossible
that there was a mole, and the proof to me that there wasn't a mole
was that the dog didn't bark," said Milton Bearden. "By this I mean that
we were running a lot of operations that were yielding very good information, and if there had been a mole, those operations would have been
compromised, and that wasn't happening. These people were surviving
and it was inconceivable to me that we could have continued these sorts
of operations if there really had been a mole."[22]

By now, the single holdout who believed in the existence of a mole was
Paul Redmond, who remained a lone voice in the SE Division calling for
a more vigorous investigation. It was not until the beginning of 1990,
when he was transferred to be deputy chief of the CIC, that he gained
sufficient authority to order more resources to the inquiry.

The CIA now had two vital pieces of evidence in the mosaic that would eventually come together to finger Ames: the letter from the woman that had exploded the myth about Rosario's being the source of the wealth that Rick so flagrantly displayed, and the evidence of a number of unexplained cash deposits into his local bank that were in excess of what he could have saved as a CIA employee. The connection could hardly have been clearer, and yet nothing was done.

The single investigator assigned to look into Ames's cash resources was sent on a two-month training course in January 1990, and nobody was assigned to take up the case while he was away. He was able to read the significance of that as well as any other competent bureaucrat: the higher-ups had no interest in Ames, and he therefore saw no reason why he should give the case priority either. As the only investigator working in counter intelligence, he had plenty of other, more pressing cases, and so he switched his attention to those. Not surprisingly, it would be over a year before there was any formal request for action.[23]

Oblivious of the net beginning to close slowly around him, in mid-December 1989, Ames typed another letter to his KGB contacts, transmitting national defense secrets, including the cryptonym of a Russian intelligence officer in the KGB who was secretly cooperating with the CIA, whose identity Ames had given them previously. Because the SE Division was reorganizing, Ames served only a short time as the Western European Branch chief. After only three short months, he was made chief of the Czechoslovakia Operations Branch, a post he assumed in December 1989.[24]

In preparation for his new job, he signed a Sensitive Compartmented Information Nondisclosure Agreement with the CIA on December 7, 1989, in which he stated that he would never divulge information that could "irreparably injure the United States, or be used to the advantage of a foreign nation, without prior written authorization." Signing such an agreement is standard practice for a CIA officer moving from one department to another, where he will gain access to new files.

Rick's new position may seem like a demotion, since he had earlier served as chief of operations for Western Europe, but in fact the Directorate of Operations moves people around as necessary, more often than the Directorate of Intelligence. People are moved to positions because of last-minute changes in personnel needs as people travel or as particular accounts "heat up." In the fall of 1989, Eastern Europe was experiencing a revolution, and the DO was short-staffed, given how fast important news was breaking overseas and how vital it was to know about these events. Since people keep their grade level at the Agency basically regardless of where they serve, Ames's move to chief of a country branch from a continental branch was basically a lateral move.[25]

Nonetheless, the move did marginalize Ames's access to the kind of information the KGB was interested in. It was unwelcome news to his Russian controllers, and they pushed him to get a transfer to some assignment where he would have greater access. Just as the Agency was struggling to cope with the collapse of Communism, so the KGB was desperate to retain its special entrée into the darkest secrets of the CIA as a way of keeping ahead of the game and retaining political stature at home. As a result, Ames approached his supervisors in January 1990, saying he wanted to return to a position where he could handle sensitive Soviet cases again. His supervisor subsequently stated that he thought Ames's approach was "brazen," and he advised Ames he would get back to him. The supervisor never did.[26]

Milt Bearden had by now seen through Rick and decided that he was deadwood in the division. "Rick was a slug," said Bearden. "I mean, a good part of the situation at SE was like four generations of sleeping with your sister. As Communism was falling apart and the Warsaw Pact was slipping under the waves, getting good intelligence from those places had gone beyond doing dead drops in Prague or St. Petersburg."[27]

Despite this rebuff, Ames tried several times over the next few months to arrange a transfer, offering to set up a special analysis group to look at all the CIA's Soviet cases from a counter intelligence perspective. Fortunately, this audacious approach to head a task force that would actually investigate the betrayals that he had carried out got nowhere.[28] He also applied to be deputy station chief in Moscow, a plum assignment for a high flier within SE and one that would have given Ames extraordinary access. That, too, was turned down.[29]

During his tenure at the Czechoslovakia Branch, however, Ames was appointed to a promotion panel for all GS-12 operations officers of the

Directorate of Operations, thus gaining access to their identities and personnel records. Although the chief of the CIC and the chief of the analysis group were aware of the security concerns related to Ames as well as his poor performance record, they were in need of a case officer from the Directorate of Operations. The head of the analysis group was told in vague terms by the deputy chief of CIC of the general suspicions regarding Ames's trustworthiness but believed Ames's assignment was "manageable."[30] In fact there appears to have been no serious attempt to "manage" him.[31] As part of this assignment, Ames once again had access to exactly the kind of material that his Russian masters wanted, including data on U.S. double-agent operations.

In October 1990, Bearden finally moved against the man he saw as a "slug" and appointed someone else chief of the Czechoslovakia Branch. Bearden later described this as a move made because of the security concerns that had been raised about Rick. Bearden also saw Ames as an ineffectual officer whom he wanted out of his way. "When I moved him out [to the Counter Intelligence Center], I was moving out a lot of people, a whole lot of people at the same time," said Bearden. "I was trying to move the old lifers out to get in some new blood. We were trying to cope with the changes in Eastern Europe and the former Soviet Union."[32] Bearden reassigned Ames to the Counter Intelligence Center Analysis Group, in a research position where he would have some access to classified information but would see much less of the top-secret traffic that had been a part of his daily routine for the past few years.

Meanwhile, the CIC probe into Ames's financial status had been making its leisurely progress. The CIA investigator responsible for examining Ames's unexplained wealth returned from his two-month training course in March 1990, but got sidetracked by a source who needed to be questioned about a possible leak in another CIA office, which required a trip overseas and a series of debriefings over the next five months. Then, with the collapse of the regime in East Germany, the files from the headquarters of the Stasi, the East German secret police, became accessible, and in June the investigator traveled to what was once East Berlin. There he coordinated a search through the files looking for confirmation that the East Germans had knowledge of CIA operations that could only have come from a mole. But there were millions of files, most of which were listed by code name. It proved a nightmare trying to match code names with known cases and then cross-reference that information with what was known or suspected back at Langley. It would be more than a year before the first intelligence began to filter back from the Stasi files that suggested there might indeed have been a mole at work in the CIA.

But with the transfer of Paul Redmond to be deputy chief of CIC, the investigation was given a new lease on life. While the lone investigator continued on his plodding path, Redmond established a group that began to look again at the whole question of a mole. He was certain one existed, but there was little support for the theory, and he was not in a position to command major assets to go after what many considered to be a personal obsession. During his career at the CIA, Redmond had gained something of a reputation as a troublemaker, somebody who did not fully understand the bureaucratic rules of the game. In the very structured world of the CIA, such behavior is not welcomed, and so he was forced to act on his own initiative.

Even so, the investigation was seriously hampered by the culture that pervaded all aspects of the DO. Redmond himself could have commanded resources outside the SE Division. There was the Office of Financial Management or the inspector general's audit staff who could have tried to make sense of Rick's finances and were qualified to do so. The Office of Security could have taken a more active role if it had been called upon to do so. But, as always within the DO, there was a very strong reluctance to take its business outside the confines of the department.

"It is a characteristic of all bureaucracies, but especially the clandestine service in CIA, that if you have a problem down in the ranks, then the inclination of lower-level managers is not to move it upward until you have no other choice in the hopes that you can solve the problem yourself," said Bob Gates. "The danger, from their standpoint, of sending a problem upward is that the more senior managers will want to help you fix it and you may not like the way they want to help you fix it. Somebody may get blamed. Somebody may get fired.

"The DCI is very much like an early medieval king of France. He is surrounded by powerful dukes, four of them in CIA, and most of the time they just want to be left alone in their own domain. The only time the king has any value to them is when they really get their ass in a crack and they have to have his help. Then they go to him and seek his help, usually late in the game. It is very difficult for the DCI, particularly if you are not a career person, to crack the domain of the dukes."[33]

The CIC was again diverted in August 1990 by a defector's report that a CIA mole had been handing intelligence over to the Russians in the mid-1980s. This sounded like a startling lead and was pursued through the fall until it eventually decided that the defector was unreliable. That inquiry turned up no more damaging evidence against Ames, but the investigator who had been poring over the Stasi files returned to Langley in September. Dusting off the old file, he sent out a routine request for a credit check on Rick and Rosario. This revealed little except that they had good credit. It did show, however, that Rick had a large number of bank accounts at several different banks, a situation that was unusual enough for the investigator to call it to Redmond's attention.

Redmond decided that there was now enough evidence to justify a new series of background checks and another polygraph. Ames had last been through the polygraph in 1986 and was not due to have another until 1991. Even as Redmond and his colleagues became more and more convinced that Ames was rotten, there remained no question of taking their suspicions outside the division. Instead, they were worried that bringing his polygraph forward might make Ames suspicious, so they decided to wait until the routine polygraph examination the following year in the hope that something might turn up.

But Ames had now become a festering sore within the CIC, and as the year drew to a close, Redmond's nagging finally persuaded his boss to write a letter to the Office of Security that was sent on December 5, 1990, requesting an investigation.

1. In connection with our investigation into the compromise of a number of SE Division operations during the mid-1980's, we request that the Office of Security open a reinvestigation of

Aldrich H. Ames and review the records of his account at Northwest Federal Credit Union. Our request is based on our receipt of information concerning Ames' lavish spending habits over the past five years. Ames is an SE Division Operations Officer currently assigned to the Counter Intelligence Center. While serving in the SE Division, he had access to a number of operations that were later compromised. He was favorably polygraphed on 2 May 1986.

2. The Counter Intelligence Center has learned the following information about Aldrich Ames and his spouse, Rosario C. Ames:

    • On 6 September, 1989, Ames and his spouse purchased a home located at 2512 N. Randolph St., Arlington, VA. The home was purchased for $540,000. There is no record of mortgage or lien filed with Arlington County. A credit check conducted in September 1990 also failed to disclose a mortgage. Ames and his spouse lived in an apartment prior to the purchase of the above home.

    • In November, 1989, [information deleted from memo] Ames was renovating the kitchen of his new home and redecorating. [information deleted from the memo], Ames was sparing no expense.

    • Upon his return from Rome (July 89), Ames purchased a maroon Jaguar, Virginia license number QH1319. The automobile is valued at approximately $49,500. Purchase price and place of purchase are unknown.

    • [information deleted from the memo] on 1 August 1989, Ames exchanged $22,107 worth of Italian Lira at First Virginia Bank, Arlington, VA (that's appoximately 28,363,281 Lira).

    • [information deleted from the memo], on 18 February 1986, Ames deposited $13,500 into a checking account number 183-40-150 at Dominion Federal Bank, Vienna, VA.

    • [information deleted from the memo], on 18 October 1985, Ames deposited $15,660 in checking account number 183-40-150 at Dominion Federal Bank, Vienna, VA.

3. While we are certainly concerned with the above information, there may be a logical explanation for Ames's spending habits. Between 1985 and 1990, Ames's mother died. We do not know if Ames received any money or property via insurance or inheritance. A review of public records in the county where his mother lived could answer the question of inheritance. Unfortunately, we do not know the location of his mother's last residence. We have been informed that Ames's mother's obituary was listed in *The Washington Post*. She was formerly employed as a teacher in Fairfax County. [information deleted from memo] she lived in North Carolina.

4. The money could also have come from his in-laws. Ames's in-laws are well connected politically in Colombia. Rosario was formerly the Protocol Officer for the Colombian Embassy in Mexico City. She was directly appointed to that position by the President of Colombia.

5. The deposits made into the Ames's checking account could be explained by loans he may have received from Northwest Federal Credit Union [information deleted from the memo]

6. There is a degree of urgency involved in our request. Since Ames has been assigned to CIC, his access has been limited to a degree. Unfortunately, we are quickly running out of things for him to do without granting him greater access. It is our hope to at least get Ames through polygraph before we are forced to take such action.

7. If you have any questions regarding this investigation, please contact [information deleted from memo]. We appreciate your assistance in this matter.

[Signature deleted from memo][34]

Finally, the CIA was focusing in on its man. And yet, despite all the bureaucratic changes that had been installed by DCI Webster, the CIA would not actually alert the FBI to the existence of this memo or indeed to the existence of Rick Ames until May 1993, twenty-nine months after their suspicions were put down on paper. Part of the reason for this may be that the FBI and the CIA were in the middle of a serious row that had further soured the already difficult relations between the two agencies.

The dispute involved Felix Bloch, a State Department employee, who in 1989 had come under suspicion of spying for the Russians. The FBI had launched a major investigation, which had failed to produce enough evidence for an arrest and conviction. The Bureau was convinced that Bloch was a traitor and had been infuriated when the case became public. Every time photographs of Bloch appeared in newspapers or on television, accompanied by questions from the media about the FBI's competence, the Bureau's men became more and more angry. By mid-1990, the Bureau believed it had tracked down a potential source living in Germany. The problem was the location of the source was not known and the only way the Bureau could think of finding him was through the unorthodox method of advertising in German newspapers.[35]

The idea to place the ad was discussed at the highest levels of both the Bureau and the CIA and approved. Then the Bureau notified Ed Pechus, the CIA station chief in Bonn, who was known as "the Poison Dwarf" to his British colleagues. Pechus considered the plan both stupid and dangerous and refused to cooperate, infuriating the FBI. Back in Washington, Robert "Bear" Bryant, who was in charge of the case, became so angry that he went to his superior and in writing asked for an obstruction-of-justice investigation to be launched against Pechus. Although the request was turned down, it caused considerable bad feeling between the FBI and the CIA.

"The FBI sometimes thought the 12-mile limit [for their activities] was passé and wanted to operate abroad like they operated in the U.S.," Milt Bearden said later. "This problem with the supposed witness for the Bloch case was discussed at very high levels at the Bureau and at the Agency. The business of placing an ad in the newspaper and the legal aspects of the obstruction-of-justice allegation was really only a piece of the long-term battle between the two organizations."[36]

When Bearden took over as Bonn Station chief in the summer of 1992, the whole case had become a running sore and was doing serious damage to the long-term relations between the Bureau and the Agency.

Nonetheless, he tried to improve the situation: "I said [to the Bureau people], Look, the station chief has responsibility for how CI and other operations are run abroad, and Germany being a sovereign country, we can't have our operations running in directions that create difficulties for our relations with the Germans. I don't want to cause any unnecessary problems for CIA–FBI relations, so let's work together on this."[37] But the rift between the two organizations continued and ensured that there was no discussion of any substance between them about the Ames case at this time.

On December 14, nine days after the memo was written requesting an Office of Security investigation, Ames had access to a secret CIA document that described a Russian intelligence official in the KGB's Second Chief Directorate, a counter intelligence group, in Moscow, recently recruited by the CIA. After using the document to write a classified CIA memorandum on a related topic, he proceeded to type a message to his Russian handlers in which he turned over the KGB counterspy three days later. "I did learn that GTPrologue is the cryptonym for the SCD officer I provided you information about earlier." Shortly thereafter, GTPrologue turned up missing, and it is now believed that he was executed.[38]

The request for an investigation of Ames initiated by Redmond finally demonstrated that someone in the Agency was sufficiently concerned to try to get something done. By this time, the short list of possible mole suspects totaled more than a hundred people and had changed very little over the past four years. There was still a failure to accept the possibility that someone like Ames, a long-term agent who had virtually destroyed the CIA's covert capability against its main target, could actually exist. Yet outside the Agency, others were not so relaxed.

Around the time when Ames was first fingered by a coworker for his extravagant spending, the Senate Intelligence Committee decided to appoint a task force to investigate the status of counter intelligence and to make recommendations for improvements. In some ways, this was simply an extension of the study done after the Howard case, which had made a series of recommendations for improvements that had been ignored. This time, the committee was determined that the investigation come up with some tough ideas that would be implemented. The task force included such luminaries as Warren Christopher, who would later be President Bill Clinton's secretary of state; Arthur Culvahouse, a Washington lawyer with extensive experience of intelligence matters; Lloyd Cutler, later to be Clinton's White House counsel; and Admiral Bobby Ray Inman, who had spent most of his naval career in intelligence.

These wise men gathered their information in the early part of 1990 and then briefed the committee on May 23 and July 12, 1990; the results of their work were published the following year. To the intelligence community, what they had to say was difficult to hear. Essentially they found that counter intelligence had lacked any real focus since the departure of Jim Angleton and that the limited effort that was made to defeat any traitor there might be took little account of the changes that had occurred in the world of spies in recent years.

During the course of the hearings, a research paper published by the Defense Personnel Security Research and Education Center (PERSEREC) was presented, providing the committee with a broad overview of the demographics of Americans who had committed espionage between 1945 and 1989.

Most American spies have been Caucasian, heterosexual males. The spies are fairly well educated, generally married, and most frequently hold technical or intelligence jobs.

In terms of volunteering and recruiting, 73% of the spies were volunteers as compared with 27% who were recruited, either by foreign intelligence agencies or by fellow Americans. Patterns of volunteering and recruiting changed over the 44-year period with the large shift toward volunteering in the past 20 years.

As for motivation, money has been the major reason for espionage, followed by ideology and disgruntlement/revenge. When we look at motivation over the past 44 years, money has increased dramatically.

There are more long-term spies, here defined as those whose espionage careers lasted more than 2 years, among those to come to espionage at a later age. In other words, spies who begin espionage young are less likely to survive a 2-year career.[39]

The research, which was the most comprehensive ever to have been carried out in the United States into the motives of traitors, was very revealing. It showed that the classic spy is motivated by money, not ideology, is a volunteer, not recruited, and is frequently disgruntled about progress at work and relations with his immediate family. Anyone who had bothered to look would have discovered that Ames fit every single one of the most important aspects of the profile.

The panel of wise men, conducting the hearings, had thirteen recommendations to improve the CI effort.

1. [Establish] by statute uniform minimum requirements for everyone granted a TOP SECRET security clearance. The proposal is applicable to all three branches of Government. There is at present no law on the books which establishes such requirements, and, indeed, the Panel found that these requirements vary from agency to agency.

   The Panel's proposal, as the Committee will note, establishes a number of requirements. Among them that persons who receive such a clearance consent to the Government's being able to access certain types of their financial records as well as travel records. Reports of foreign travel would be required of these Government employees, as would reports by them of efforts by foreign nationals to improperly solicit classified information.

2. [Amend] the Right to Financial Privacy Act to permit persons with TOP SECRET clearances to provide their consent to the appropriate governmental authorities obtaining access to certain of their financial records. It is necessary because the Right to Financial Privacy Act as it is written now permits an individual to consent to access to his financial records for a period of only 3 months.

3. All Government communicators, in whatever agency they may be employed, be subject to the possibility of a limited, counter intelligence-scope polygraph examination during the period of their employment as communicators. Basically, they

would be asked simply if they were a spy. The Panel's attempt is to reach that population of Government employees who run communications centers processing classified information, those who build coding machines, and those who devise codes.

4. The fourth proposed new statute would give the Director of the National Security Agency discretionary authority to provide assistance to employees for up to 5 years after they leave the National Security Agency to help them cope with problems. Experience shows that post-employment problems can jeopardize the classified information to which employees have become privy during the period of their employment.

5. [It would be] a crime to possess espionage devices if the intent to violate the espionage statutes can be shown. A law such as this would make it possible to prosecute someone found in the possession of such devices as burst transmitters, sophisticated concealed cameras and such, where the intent to commit espionage can be shown.

6. [It would be] a crime to sell to a person representing a foreign power documents or materials that are marked or otherwise identified as TOP SECRET without the Government having to prove as an element of the offense that the classification marking had been properly applied. The Panel's intent in recommending this is to allow the Government to prosecute such conduct without having to reveal the TOP SECRET information in question.

7. [Create] a new misdemeanor offense for any Government employee who knowingly removes TOP SECRET documents without authority and retains them at an unauthorized location. The Panel's intent here is to provide the Government with a lesser criminal sanction to deal with Government employees stockpiling highly classified documents with the thought that later they may wish to convert them to personal use.

8. [Extend] an existing statute which provides for the forfeiture of profits associated with the violation of one of the principal espionage statutes, *18 U.S.C. 794*. The proposal would extend that, the so-called "Son of Sam" law, to other kinds of espionage convictions.

9. [Permit] the Government to deny retirement pay to United States retirees in the Civil Service Retirement System who are convicted of espionage in foreign courts where the offense concerned United States national defense information.

10. [Amend] the Fair Credit Reporting Act to permit the FBI to obtain consumer credit reports on persons who are certified by the Director of the FBI as suspected of being agents of foreign powers, as that term has been defined by the Foreign Intelligence Surveillance Act of 1978.

11. [Amend] the Electronic Communications Privacy Act of 1986 in order to permit the FBI to obtain subscriber information about persons with unlisted telephone numbers who are called by foreign powers or agents of foreign powers.

12. [Amend] the existing statute which provides discretionary authority to the Attorney General to pay rewards for information concerning terrorism, to permit such rewards to be paid for information leading to an arrest or conviction for espionage or for information which had prevented the commission of espionage. The Panel would authorize payments of up to a million dollars for this purpose.

13. [Extend] the court order procedure now used for electronic surveillances, established by the Foreign Intelligence Surveillance Act, to physical searches done for national security purposes.[40]

If some of these recommendations had been implemented at the time, or even if the recommendations had been implemented after the Howard case first surfaced, there is little doubt that Ames would have been caught earlier. With the ability to subject him to more regular polygraphs, examine his financial records as a matter of routine, or scrutinize in more detail some of the credit reports that were available, the investigators would all have turned up new intelligence. But, of course, none of these recommendations existed at the beginning of the investigation into the leaks in the mid-1980s. Even after the devastation of the Howard case and the exposure of the Walker spy ring, there was little appetite to accept even further restrictions on the intelligence community. While Congress clearly understood that something was wrong down at Langley and that there was a continued real risk of a serious penetration of American intelligence by a foreign power, there was little impetus to take on the entrenched intelligence community.

In the end, both the CIA's lawyers and the White House supported some legislative action, but Congress lost its nerve, fearing a lacklash from the civil liberties lobby. And the DO continued to fight off anyone who tried to tell them that something was wrong. Just as damaging, they resisted any attempts to introduce the kind of reforms that would prevent further damage in the future. It was blind. It was stupid. And it was just what Ames and the KGB wanted.

FOURTEEN

The Noose Tightens

The Redmond-inspired memo from the Counter Intelligence Center to the Office of Security in December 1990 was finally to prod the slumbering beast into action. It was so alarming that the Office of Security immediately ordered an investigation of Ames. A check into his account at the Northwest Federal Credit Union revealed nothing unusual. Indeed, it showed that Ames had borrowed $25,000 of the purchase price for the Jaguar, making the deal appear less suspicious. The Office of Security made no other request for information from other banks or lenders that month because, they later claimed, they did not know they had the authority to do so.

But the wheels of the preliminary investigation now began to grind slowly forward. In January 1991, Ames was sent various forms to complete for the purpose of updating his background information. With his usual distaste for any kind of paperwork, Ames required a leisurely three months to return the various bits of paper, duly completed. By April 12, the Office of Security had finished what turned out to be the first comprehensive investigation of Ames since the betrayals began five years earlier. The report included the first interviews with some of his colleagues, who saw Ames as a failure and a security risk:

Ames was assigned to CIC "under a cloud." . . . One individual recalled that SE Division did not trust Ames or his Soviet agents. There
were questions about Ames's handling of a particular agent and also
concerns about his judgment.

In Rome, Ames seemed to have considerable contact with his Soviet
and Eastern Bloc assets. A colleague noted Ames received many calls
from assets at work. The person also noted that Ames routinely left his
safe open when he was leaving for the day, and had admitted he wrote
an agent contact report at home on his personal computer.

In Rome, Ames could not be expected into the office before 9 or
10 a.m. At least once per week there was evidence that Ames had been
drinking during his lunch hour.

Another of Ames's co-workers said he didn't think Ames was a spy,
but wouldn't be surprised if that someday came to light. When asked
to explain his remark, the person retracted it stating that the profile of
Ames was wrong for him to be a spy, but he didn't trust Ames as a colleague. He reportedly had seen Ames take some actions that he was
specifically instructed against, such as giving his agent a laptop computer after his superiors told him not to.

Another person interviewed commented that Ames lived at a higher
standard than most other government employees and this person believed that there was money on the spouse's side of the family. The person stressed that Ames's government salary did not explain his level of
spending.

Another co-worker reported that he understood Ames paid cash for
his house, a purchase well into the $500,000 range.

Another colleague stressed that Ames made no attempt to conceal
his wealth and observed that Ames had new cars and relied on household help.[1]

These were more than just the backbiting comments of colleagues
who did not like a coworker. In any organization the litany of laziness,
security breaches, and discrepancies in his personal spending habits
would have been enough to set the alarm bells ringing. In the CIA,
an organization that makes security an obsession and honesty a pre-
requisite for continued employment, there appeared to be grounds for

disciplinary action if not summary dismissal: here was a man whose colleagues considered him a dangerous and drunken slob.

The report landed on the desk of the same investigator who had been looking into Ames for the past year. Incredibly, he believed that the investigation told him nothing new. And "thus, he did not believe it would be necessary to conduct follow-up interviews with any of the sources, nor did he discuss that possibility with [his supervisors]."[2]

Later, when he was questioned about this apparent dereliction of duty, the investigator argued that even if he had wanted to carry out further inquiries, the questioning might have alerted Ames—a remarkably feeble defense, given that Ames never learned about the first investigation. Besides, any inquiry carries with it the risk of alerting its subject, but that is never used as a valid excuse for ignoring the threat posed by a traitor. To compound the damage, the CIA security officer who assessed the results of the reinvestigation determined that it "had no CI implications." Thus, no action was taken with respect to Ames's security clearance on the basis of the investigation.

On April 12, 1991, the results of the background investigation were in the hands of the Office of Security. At almost exactly the same time, Ames was being put through the polygraph examination that had been suggested for him the previous fall. The polygraphers knew that there was some question about Ames's unexplained wealth but they had none of the details. Neither the Office of Security nor the CIC thought to give them a copy of the December memo that had sparked the investigation in the first place. Nor did anybody think that the polygraphers might have found it useful to be given a copy of the result of the background investigation. Instead, they went into the test armed only with rumors and with no sense of the urgency of the investigation or the extent of the damaging information that was already available.

The casual way in which all this was handled almost defies belief. Later, senior CIA officials agreed that the polygraphers should have been apprised of all the information that had accumulated against Ames. But however obvious that might be with the benefit of hindsight, at the time he was given a routine polygraph with no particular emphasis on his finances.

Ames had a healthy respect for the polygraph and had been very nervous before the one he took five years earlier. Since then, he had become a millionaire from his work with the Russians. He lived in a smart house and drove a smart car. His wife wore beautiful clothes and they traveled abroad far more often than he could possibly have afforded on his Agency salary alone. He expected to be asked some awkward questions, so during the preliminary interview that precedes all polygraphs, Ames skillfully volunteered that he had some additional money from his wife's family, that he owned some property in Colombia and had made a number of successful investments.[3]

During the polygraph he was asked whether he was concealing any financial difficulties from the Agency. To this question, which was designed to find people who were having trouble paying their bills, Ames was able to answer quite truthfully that he was fine.

"Ames stated that if the Agency had interviewed him about his spending in the context of the reinvestigation, he would not have been terribly alarmed. In fact, he prepared himself for the possibility that he would be asked about his finances. Ames attempted to account for the cash purchase of his Arlington home by having a gift letter prepared and notarized making it appear to have been a gift from his mother-in-law. He states that at some point someone would learn that he had purchased the house for cash and it was reasonable to expect that someone would ask him about the source of his wealth. But no one ever did."[4]

Confirming the fallibility of the polygraph, Ames didn't react when he was asked if he was working for a foreign intelligence service. But he did indicate deception when he was asked if he was concealing contacts with foreign nationals. The question was repeated again and again by the worried polygrapher, and each time the flickering needle on the chart indicated the telltale spike of a lie. Following normal CIA procedure, the examiner declared the test "incomplete" and Ames was told to come back for another examination in four days. In his file notes, the first examiner commented, "I don't think he is a spy, but I am not 100% convinced because of the money situation."[5]

On his return, Ames was confronted by a different polygrapher. Whether this time there was an unstated wish to help him through the test or whether he was fed the same range of difficult questions but in a different form is not clear. The result was that Ames sailed through. Not only that, but he passed with even less response to all the questions than had been indicated the first time around.

FBI officials offer a slightly different account of Ames's 1991 polygraph test and claim that his answers did register deceptive responses to the questions focusing on his financial situation. These were disregarded when the polygraphers gave Ames his second chance with a series of softer questions designed to help him pass.[6]

The polygraph had clearly been shown to be a total failure. Ames had not been trained in any of the techniques that are supposed to allow a guilty person to appear innocent. He had simply tried to relax and hoped for the best. During the course of two separate polygraphs, he had been able to make it seem as though he had no unusual money sources, no contacts with foreign nationals, and was not working for a foreign intelligence organization. In every important area, the polygraphs had got it 100 percent wrong. But so much faith is placed in the lie detector within the Agency that its results were seen by most people as a testament to Ames's innocence. Within CIC there was something akin to relief when the results of this latest examination were received. Despite the fact that Ames was unpopular, people *wanted* to believe he was innocent. The alternative was too horrible to contemplate.

At the time of the polygraph, the Agency had still not bothered to check Ames's assertion that it was Rosario who provided the spare cash. In July 1991, when an officer from the CIC was scheduled to make a trip to Bogotá, there was an opportunity to finally get some answers about how rich Rosario really was. The question of Ames's finances was a side issue for the officer, and the inquiries he made seem to have been only very cursory, producing the kinds of answers that could have been picked up in a cocktail party conversation. He reported back that Rosario's family appeared to be well connected, from the middle or upper social class, and had a prosperous lifestyle. By that time, of course, much of that visible prosperity was due to the proceeds of Rick's spying, some of which he had been funneling into property and land in Bogotá.

Since this report bolstered the results of the polygraph, both the Office of Security and the CIC decided to wind down the investigation. It wasn't until August 1992 that another request was made from CIA headquarters to Bogotá for information regarding Ames's finances. Nor was there an effort either to answer any of the other questions raised in the December 1990 memo about the claimed sources for Rick and Rosario's wealth. Nobody checked the records to see if Rick had, in fact, received some money on the death of his mother from a life insurance policy; nor did anyone look into just why Rick's lifestyle had improved so dramatically between his departure for Rome and his return to Washington.

With the dispute over Felix Bloch still fresh in their minds and the long-simmering disagreements between the Agency and the Bureau, it is hardly surprising that the CIA also failed to report any of its suspicions to the FBI. The CIA's failure to take the "deceptive" polygraph rating more seriously was later deemed "careless" by FBI agents—and enhanced the mounting tension and bitterness between the two agencies.[7]

As one former intelligence official noted, the FBI's institutional judgment about such matters is "to find the guy and put him in jail," whereas the CIA's approach favors "thinking this thing through before you haul somebody off in chains."[8]

There was not only squabbling about who should hunt traitors within the CIA and FBI but also who should get access to intelligence as and when it became available. With the collapse of Communism, a huge volume of previously secret intelligence surfaced in the former Communist countries. Among them was the treasure trove of the Stasi files in the former East Germany, which resulted in yet another ongoing row between the two organizations about which one would have primary control over the files. This petty infighting was partly resolved in November 1991 when CIA director Bob Gates met with Attorney General William P. Barr in the CIA director's dining room to straighten out the question of smoothing out the thorny relationship.[9]

Despite such mediation, the hunt remained fragmented and even within the CIC, a separate channel continued to operate. Despite the apparent evidence to the contrary, Paul Redmond remained convinced that a mole was still at work in the Agency, and he simply didn't believe the results of the polygraph or the fairly scanty information that had come back from Bogotá. In April 1991, he and a colleague went down to the

FBI counter intelligence headquarters in an office building at Buzzards' Point in Southeast Washington, overlooking the Anacostia River. They explained to the Bureau's agents that, because of the flood of material now coming out of the former Eastern bloc, there was a real opportunity to solve the mystery of the 1985–86 compromises once and for all. If they worked together, the Agency men argued, they stood a real chance of cracking the case. As a result of the meeting, the FBI sent two agents to the Counter Intelligence Center at the CIA to begin working full-time with two CIA representatives to attack the case in a systematic way. While these two agents were to be vital in the investigation, they, too, failed to officially notify the FBI concerning their suspicions about Ames.[10]

That summer, the new team began the whole investigation from scratch. They gathered all the available intelligence on the sources who had been compromised, jailed, or shot. They looked at the networks that had been rolled up and the Soviet disinformation campaign that had begun to develop in the late 1980s. Every case was cross-referenced with every other, every clue entered into the database to see if any common factors emerged, and every CIA officer who had knowledge of any of the cases was also entered into the computer. By August, the unit had identified 198 CIA employees who had access to the 1985–86 compromised cases. Of these, twenty-nine, including Ames, merited priority attention. At this stage there were not enough data to refine the names much further. Instead, the CIA officers involved in the investigation, who knew nearly all those on the short list, began to winnow it down even further. It was here that the obvious elements that should have attracted attention years earlier began to come to the fore. It was the drunks, the habitual womanizers, the men and women with money problems who stayed on the list. The hard workers who appeared to have no problems outside of their appearance on the list were ignored. It was an unscientific but effective approach that at least gave the investigation some rapid forward momentum.

It was hardly surprising that Ames appeared on every single list that was prepared. He had access to all the compromised cases; he was known to have a drinking problem; his career had stalled; and there were unexplained questions about the source of his money. But there was still not nearly enough to narrow the list just to him. There were plenty of others who superficially carried the same kind of baggage, and the team needed answers on all of them before they could shorten the list even further.

Ames appeared completely unconcerned about any possible investigation into his own affairs. Between January and March 1991, he made three separate $10,000 cash deposits in his Dominion accounts.[11] Besides storing the money in bank accounts, Ames found other uses for his funds: in 1991, a seemingly "civic-minded," patriotic Ames contributed $1,500 to the Democratic National Committee.[12]

In mid-April, he filed another false tax form, listing $60,340.22 as his total income for the tax year 1990.[13] A week after filing the false form, Ames attempted to conduct an overseas meeting with his KGB handlers and flew to Vienna. In a scene reminiscent of a comedy film, Ames wandered around the city looking for the meeting point and was unable to track down Andre, his KGB controller. He returned to Washington in despair, sure that he had been betrayed by the very people he had learned to rely upon for moral and financial support. It turned out that once again he had been too drunk during the previous encounter to recall the venue for the next meeting and had simply gone to the wrong city.[14]

The summer of 1991 was a quiet and lucrative one for the Ames family. They spent lazy summer evenings in the hot tub they had recently installed on their back terrace, and afternoons collecting their payments from the Soviets. Between mid-May and August 1991, in four separate transactions, Ames deposited more than $30,000 in their Dominion account.[15] On or about November 19, 1991, a cash deposit of more than $6,000 was made at the Dominion bank. But for the first time, it was made by Rosario, not Rick. In late November, Rick made a $7,300 cash deposit in the Dominion account.[16]

About this time, Dominion bank executives developed suspicions about the Ameses' numerous cash deposits. They began filing reports with the Internal Revenue Service, suggesting that Ames was "structuring" cash deposits, attempting to keep each one below $10,000.[17] By inquiring about the possible structured deposits, the bank officials were fulfilling their obligation to comply with a federal law, adopted in the early 1970s, to report multiple cash deposits that are just below the $10,000 mark, as well as cash deposits of $10,000 or more.

Although the IRS generally distributes the information to members of its own investigative body, Patrick Heck, a currency expert on the staff of the House Ways and Means Committee, says that since the information is all computerized, if other agencies, such as the CIA or FBI, asked for information by a person's name, "they probably could get it."[18] The FBI could certainly have obtained the information from the Treasury's Financial Crimes Enforcement Network (FinCEN), which manages a number of databases connected to a main computer at the IRS's Detroit Computing Center, where banks send their currency transaction reports (CTRs).

Although FinCEN was established in April 1990,[19] it has in its data banks all the data collected since the mid-1980s, after the passage of the Bank Secrecy Act (this act principally dealt with the reporting of currency transactions over $10,000 and international transportation of currency or monetary instruments over $10,000).[20] Generally FinCEN responds to requests from law enforcement agencies in its network (including the Justice Department; Alcohol, Tobacco and Firearms; Drug Enforcement Agency; Federal Reserve; IRS; Customs; and Postal Service), though sometimes FinCEN initiates its own investigations when analysts, who are in touch with field agents of these various organizations, come across unusual or interesting currency movements they know no other agency is following. Because resources are limited at FinCEN, the vast majority of work that it does involves these other agencies, supporting their investigations and apprising them if investigations they request overlap, or seem to have a connection with, investigations other agencies have initiated (FinCEN maintains a database of all the requests it receives).[21] Because of FinCEN's limited resources, it usually focuses its efforts on large currency flows in the multi-hundred-thousand-dollar or million-dollar range, so that the relatively small deposits of individuals like Ames are not likely to attract the attention of FinCEN analysts unless a bank official or law enforcement agency directs it to look at cases such as structured deposits.[22]

Problems arose over the subsequent decade as criminals figured out how to get around the law; for example, by breaking up deposits larger than $10,000 into smaller sums. Section 5324 of the Bank Secrecy Act was passed in the late 1970s, making it illegal to structure deposits. A Supreme Court case shortly thereafter, *U.S. v. Ratglatf*, put an additional burden on the prosecution of people who structure deposits. The Court found in this case that the government had to prove that the person structuring the deposit knew that doing so was illegal. Pending new legislation will close that loophole, as it says that structuring deposits is illegal whether or not one knows it is.[23]

Banks are now required to report any deposits they perceive to be suspicious. There is obviously a certain subjectivity to what constitutes suspicion, but any single large deposit (for example, $150,000) would be suspicious, as would regular (numerous times per month) smaller deposits, including regular deposits under $10,000. The IRS relies on the banks to know their customers and their customers' banking habits, and generally banks are pretty helpful when it comes to reports of suspicious transactions. These reports, either in hard copy or on magnetic tape, are forwarded to the IRS's main computing center in Detroit.

Dominion did file at least two CTRs about Ames's transactions, both on February 18, 1986, because Ames made deposits of more than $10,000—two totaling $13,500 and two totaling $10,500. Since many of Ames's other deposits approached $10,000, Dominion should have filed numerous other times for suspicious deposits—and may well have done, but information on such filing is not yet available. The tenor of the information, though, suggests that Ames's name appeared several different times on computer databases created to detect signs of illegal activity. These occurred because on numerous different occasions over several years Ames received large wire transfers from abroad or bought large amounts of foreign currency. The FBI and the CIA do not regularly check such databases, because to do so they would have to request information from FinCEN that would identify the targets of highly sensitive investigations to an outside agency.[24]

In September 1991, despite having been effectively forced out of the SE Division a year earlier by Milton Bearden, Ames managed to obtain the approval of the same SE Division chief to become head of a KGB working group in the SE Division. While this position did not entail access to ongoing operations, it did give Ames entrée once again to SE Division personnel and records. Ames's task during his three-month tenure with this working group was to "put a stake through the KGB's heart."

"The point being that the coming dissolution of the Union and the shocks to the KGB after the coup were such that the KGB was extremely vulnerable or was at least potentially vulnerable to what we may be able to do to discredit it politically, bureaucratically, with the new Russian leadership."[25]

Of course, in the light of what followed, this appointment was little short of laughable. Ames and his colleagues were identifying potential weaknesses in the KGB and working out plans of action to exploit them. At the same time, sometimes even on the very day of a meeting, Ames would be writing up his notes of the meeting on his home computer and relaying them to the KGB so that it could take preemptive action. It is hardly surprising that this group achieved nothing.

In early December, Rick again attempted to arrange an overseas visit with his Soviet comrades. That his communications with them remained intact even at this time is rather extraordinary, since the KGB had been formally dissolved and succeeded by a new intelligence agency, the SVR. On December 2, 1991, he flew to Colombia, without arousing suspicion, and had a series of brief meetings with Russian intelligence officers. He personally filled them in on the KGB working group though it could, in fact, produce only a fraction of the intelligence his Moscow masters wanted from him.[26]

Rick's return to the SE Division was short-lived, and soon after his journey to Colombia, in December 1991, he was named a referent for Central Eurasia, International Narcotics Group, and transferred to the Counter Narcotics Center (CNC).[27] The position of referent is basically that of a contact person for requesters dealing with a particular unit. The referent serves as a liaison of the unit to these requesters, answering their questions if possible and referring them to the appropriate analyst if an answer is not readily available.[28]

His transfer to the CNC had been the first recognition that he was a security risk, although there had been no question of his top-secret security clearance being withdrawn. In theory, the move should have reduced his access to sensitive material, especially if his supervisors had been warned that he was under suspicion. But that warning was not given until almost a year after the move and well after the full-scale covert investigation had been launched.

Despite the move, Ames was still able to obtain material his handlers wanted. He remained in close touch with some of his old buddies in the SE Division. A group of five employees, including Ames, would meet outside the building at ten-thirty and two-thirty every day for a cigarette break. To the group, Ames was an old colleague, and they all happily gossiped about the latest developments in their area. This made perfect intelligence for Ames to pass on to his handlers. Between puffs, the officers would regale each other with the latest goings-on in the division, and Ames would carefully note down what he heard for later relaying through his dead drops.[29]

And, while there was a standard instruction in the DO that no computer retain a port for a floppy disk so that there would be no way any material could be copied directly onto a disk and taken out of the building, no such restrictions applied to CNC, because it was considered a lower-level operation. While access to the most secret files was not possible from CNC, Ames was able to scan all the operational messages that came into the CIA from his terminal in the CNC. He inserted a floppy disk and copied hundreds of files, including secret cables from CIA stations all over the world. Such was the material Ames was about to dump in a dead drop when he was arrested.

That December, like every December since he had returned from Mexico, Rick and Rosario hosted their annual Christmas party. It was a time for friends to get together, chat about old times, grouse about work, and exchange stories. It was a time, too, for Rick to get his colleagues drunk and pump them for the kind of fresh, raw intelligence that his masters loved.

At the CNC, Ames had been given responsibility for the Black Sea area, to take advantage of his background.[30] Interestingly, he went to Russia to take part in a joint intelligence conference on drug shipments, sponsored by Washington and Moscow. His Russian counterpart at that meeting turned out to be Vladik Enger, Fedorenko's colleague from the days at the Soviet UN Mission.[31]

For Ames, the reassignment to the CNC was an unwelcome move, but there was little he could do. He knew there was a resumed search for the mole under way but he still had no idea that it was focused on him. He remained arrogant enough to believe that whatever resources they might send against him, he was smart enough to beat them. But time was running out at last.

While some of those on the joint FBI–CIA team were convinced that Ames was the mole, there was still no hard evidence—just the instinct of the hunter for his quarry. What was needed was a way of narrowing the focus of the investigation by eliminating the coincidences of circumstances that had placed so many innocents alongside the single guilty man or woman. So it was decided to launch a detailed background investigation on every one of the 198 employees on the list. This would involve interviewing each of them to learn just how much they really knew about the compromised cases. At the same time, polygraphs would be given to those who had not had one in the past few months, their medical records would be reviewed, and the Office of Security was specifically asked to look at the personnel records of all but twenty-nine of the people on the list. Those were reserved for the CIC investigators, and heading the list of twenty-nine was Rick Ames.

Just when the investigation was getting into its stride, the CIA received some information passed via a CIA officer from a source in the SVR that suggested the Russians did indeed have a mole in the CIA. This dramatic piece of news, which was bolstered by information that appeared to confirm some of the details the team already had about cases that had been compromised, looked like an exceptionally promising lead. For an entire month the team tried to track down the information, seeking confirmation of all the facts from the SVR source. But the deeper they went, the more suspicious the information looked, and they reluctantly concluded that the SVR source did not exist. The CIA officer who had set the hare running was summoned home for questioning, and it was decided that he had made the whole story up as a way of bolstering his career. He was fired and the team got back on the case.

On November 12, 1991, the joint CIA–FBI investigative unit interviewed Ames as part of the plan to process the existing short list themselves. In order to keep the suspicions of any of the interviewees at a minimum, these meetings were essentially a "get-to-know-you" session in which the investigators could gauge the man and his answers to some fairly basic housekeeping questions: how paper flowed, who did what, and who went to which meetings. It was obvious to each person interviewed that there was an effort under way to go back and find out what went wrong in 1985–86, but the interviewers did not suggest to those being questioned that they were under suspicion.

During his meeting, Ames twice volunteered that he had received a security violation while in the SE Division for not closing and locking his safe. He stated that the safe contained case chronologies and combinations to other safes. In retrospect, it appears that Ames offered this information as an explanation for the 1985–86 compromises and to detract from any suspicions that he was the mole. It appears to have had the opposite effect.[32]

In late 1991, Ames alone was selected as a priority target and a comprehensive computer search of his DO records began. The search produced the reports Ames had written about his contacts with the Soviet official Chuvakhin during 1985 and 1986. It also unearthed a July 1986 cable that contained an FBI query about contacts with Chuvakhin that Ames had not reported. This cable represented the beginning of the FBI's frustration with the CIA over the Ames case, and as the CIA files made clear, the Bureau's requests for action had, at the time, simply been ignored.

But this was a different era, and it was clear that the Ames case was not simply about an officer who failed to file bits of paper. One of the FBI agents immediately went to headquarters to review the file of the Ames-Chuvakhin meetings. The complete file held the records of every single meeting that Ames had reported holding with Chuvakhin. But the file was incomplete and revealed very little information apart from the initial requests by the FBI to get Ames to report. It was much later, in 1992, that the FBI agent discovered the source in the Washington field office where all the Chuvakhin records were kept. Then it was discovered that the FBI had recorded far more meetings between the two men than Ames had ever reported.

In January 1992, the FBI Washington field office decided that the initial information that had been gathered on Ames and the other suspects justified the setting up of a special FBI task force to investigate Soviet penetrations of the CIA and FBI. It focused on resolving old leads, rather than duplicating the approach of the joint unit. For a change, everyone was kept informed about the progress of the different investigations.

In the spring of 1992, with the evidence against Ames mounting inexorably, Paul Redmond ordered the CIC investigator who had begun to look at Ames's finances three years earlier to complete his investigation as a priority. Using statutory powers under the Right to Financial Privacy Act, the Agency began to bring in all of Ames's available financial records. It was to be a very rich haul.

The first reports came from credit-card companies and showed that the Ameses were charging $20,000 and $30,000 per month, much of which had been spent on foreign travel that had not been cleared with Langley. This first trickle of information soon became a flood. In response to the queries from the CIA, the banks, too, began to report back on Rick's finances and it became clear that hundreds of thousands of dollars had been deposited in Ames's accounts over the previous six years, much of the cash arriving by wire transfer from abroad. None of this money could be accounted for by Ames's salary, and at first it was simply assumed this was money that had been kindly given to Ames by Rosario's "wealthy" family. This appeared less likely when it was learned that the wire transfers to Rick's accounts had come from the Crédit Suisse bank in Zurich and not from Bogotá. When the Chuvakhin link was finally made, the investigators realized there was a direct correlation between the money deposited by Ames and the unreported meetings with the Russian. Now, at last, they had some evidence that seemed to tie Ames directly to the Russians and to the betrayals.

On March 15, 1993, the joint FBI–CIA unit issued its final report, code-named "Playactor/Skylight," which did not name Ames but did examine the 1985–86 compromises in detail and for the first time linked those with the different KGB disinformation campaigns that had followed the betrayals. The report concluded that there probably was a mole within the Agency and even attempted to narrow the focus of the hunt to a short list of forty people, one of whom was Ames.

"We are virtually certain there was a KGB penetration of CIA who followed closely on the heels of CIA defector Edward Lee Howard. This subject probably began to disclose CIA/FBI operations to the KGB by July 1985, if not earlier. The KGB then proceeded to roll up our agents throughout 1985–86," said the report.

"The subject was assigned to CIAHQ in 1985 and was in a position to compromise Soviet operations virtually 'across the board.' The subject was employed in SE Division or one of a few slots in CI staff."[33]

The Playactor/Skylight report gave the FBI the ammunition it needed to launch a thorough investigation after a series of briefings from the joint team who shared the results of their own inquiries into Ames. After eight years of fruitless searches for the mole, the CIA had finally admitted what the FBI had long suspected: that it had been harboring a mole deep inside the organization.

FIFTEEN

Discovery

Sitting at his IBM PS/2 computer, in the middle of March 1992, Rick typed in "Kolokol" as the cursor blinked in front of him. His code word, Kolokol, means bell in Russian and was once used as a warning cry by the Mongols.[1] It gave him access to the secret files that he had created for his spying. While the Russians might still use old-fashioned chalk marks and dead drops to deliver and receive messages, the messages themselves had become more sophisticated. Both Rick and his SVR controllers often communicated via floppy disk with the bundles of documents Rick stole from the Agency wrapped around them and sealed in a plastic bag.

The message contained yet another demand for more cash. Rick marked the signal site SMILE, a mailbox located on the corner of Thirty-seventh and R streets in Northwest Washington that is used by American University students who live in the Burlieth neighborhood, just minutes away from the Russian diplomatic compound.[2] With a slash of the chalk he kept in the glove compartment of his Jaguar, he told the Russians there was a package waiting for them at dead drop BRIDGE.[3]

Within days of his making that drop, the Russians responded with another pile of money, and Rick began spreading it around his various bank accounts.[4] On March 19, just weeks before filing another false income-tax report, Ames made two deposits in the Dominion account, totaling more than $15,000.[5]

Throughout 1992, long after the investigation of Ames began, the money kept rolling in. In January alone, the Ameses made cash deposits totaling more than $20,000. On Valentine's Day, Rick, in two separate cash deposits, divided $12,500 between his accounts which were now spread between the Riggs and the Virginia Dominion Banks.[6] Rick and Rosario "rewarded" themselves with numerous new possessions: on January 25, 1992, Rick made check number 543 of his Dominion Bank of Virginia checking account payable to Rosenthal Jaguar, in the amount of $25,059.86, for the purchase of a maroon 1992 XJ6 Jaguar.[7] Their house was becoming a monument not to good taste but to the kind of extravagance that instant and apparently unlimited wealth can produce. Rosario, who appeared to be a compulsive shopper, now owned six 18 karat gold necklaces and four 18 karat gold bracelets as well as closets full of designer clothes; Rick sported four watches, including one each from Gucci and Raymond Weil. Their dinner guests ate off Meissen china with sterling silver cutlery and drank out of French glassware. Lladro china figures sat on tables and Chagall prints hung on the walls. Rosario had taken to shopping at Dean & Deluca, the Georgetown gourmet food store, which is the most expensive in the Washington area.[8]

This extravagant lifestyle caused the Ameses constant financial problems. Although their means were far beyond those of any reasonable human being, they were spending money compulsively. No matter how fast the cash came in, the credit-card bills always seemed to be even larger. In June, once again, Ames contacted his Russian handlers. He typed them a message in which he nervously complained about their failure to respond with the delivery of money. He told them he was desperate for more funds and that he was forced to sell stock to meet his immediate financial needs. Again, he asked them to deliver money—as much as $100,000 through the dead drop PIPE.[9] It would seem that the Russians came through with the money: after making a $2,500 contribution to the Democratic National Committee, Ames, through three separate transactions, deposited more than $15,000 in his Dominion and Riggs accounts throughout July. But before those monies arrived, Rick would have more than financial problems to deal with.

In June, Rosario had lost her purse and needed a wallet to hold the money she was going to draw from the bank that day. Searching in the top of Rick's closet for an old wallet, she found one. Looking inside, she came across a slip of paper on which were written the words "meet me in the country of your mother-in-law." There was no date, and clearly this was an old assignation.

Married in name but with a tempestuous, even violent, relationship, Rick and Rosario by this time were bound together by little more than their love for Paul and their large bank accounts. Rosario had become increasingly dissatisfied at what she perceived to be a loveless and joyless relationship. She immediately assumed that the note was from a lover, a woman—perhaps even a Colombian—who was meeting her husband during one of his many trips abroad.

That night over dinner she confronted Rick with the evidence, and he denied both an affair and anything else untoward. Rosario refused to believe him, but despite her persistent questioning, he would admit nothing. Instead, he claimed the message was simply from somebody in the Operations Directorate at work; a planned meeting that never happened. It was standard tradecraft, he claimed, never to mention the country where a meeting was due to take place. For the next two weeks, she continued to badger him, nagging at him every evening after work, consumed with the idea that he had betrayed her with another woman.

Finally, he agreed to take her out to dinner to Germaine's, an expensive local restaurant located on the second floor of a building at Wisconsin Avenue and Calvert Street. With their prosperity had come an enjoyment of fine food and Rick had taken to eating lunch at Germaine's at least three times a week as well as several evenings a month with Rosario. It has been a fashionable eatery in Washington for years, its pan-Asian cuisine matching the cosmopolitan nature of the city. It is a favored haunt of presidents, politicians, and the media, who enjoy the widely spaced tables, the huge glass window with a view of the vice president's house in the distance on Massachusetts Avenue, and the ever-changing photographic exhibits on the walls. Nowadays William Perry, the secretary of defense, and Warren Christopher, the secretary of state, are regulars. When Ames was a customer, he would often see William Webster, the former DCI and director of the FBI, at a neighboring table.[10]

Rick had chosen the evening carefully and had clearly decided that it was time to draw Rosario into his conspiracy. Until now, Rosario had been an ignorant accomplice making the occasional cash deposit for Rick and enjoying the fruits of his investments. She had never questioned the source of the ever-growing sums of money that were pouring into the household. She never thought to ask just how it was that Rick's "investments" had continued to grow at a phenomenal rate while the stock market went through the crash of 1987 and the volatile period of the early 1990s. Instead, she simply accepted the fiction of the mythical Chicago investments. Subconsciously she must have realized that questioning might produce answers that she didn't want to hear and that not asking was the line of least resistance. But now, the house of cards was tumbling down. He was fed up with her constant questioning, worn down by her insecurity and her bad temper. Afterward, she thought he had probably prepared a speech that would have softened the blow, but apparently he never got to use it. That night, when she once again pressed him for an answer about the note, he simply confessed:

"All right, I do some work for the Russians."[11]

In her wildest imaginings, Rosario claims, she had never believed that he would be a traitor to his country. For her, the fact that he was working for the CIA or for the SVR mattered little. As far as she was concerned, they were both evil and had few redeeming qualities. What did matter was that Rick had betrayed her personally; both during their courtship and throughout their marriage he had been living a lie.

"My first reaction apart from utter panic was one of denial. My first impulse was to say, well, this is obviously something that has to do with your work . . . like the CIA told you to do this, some sort of strange operation. I knew that these things happen, that people get sent over . . . and he said no . . .

"I didn't want to know what it was. I said, I don't want you to tell me anything else. He never went into details. I knew, though, that he had met them in Bogotá, that's why there was a reference to Bogotá there. . . . That's when my panic was total. . . . He had used my family. I was just so panicked, devastated, scared, speechless."[12]

Over the next few weeks she wrestled with her conscience, trying to decide what to do. Should she, in turn, betray Rick to the authorities? That would mean breaking up her family, ensuring that her son, Paul, would grow up without a father. Should she leave Rick and return to

Colombia? That, too, would mean that Paul would never see his father again. This debate was not about what was right for America, for she had little loyalty to the country and certainly cared even less for the CIA. Instead, it was a simple calculation of what would be best for herself and her family. In coming to a decision, she managed to convince herself that her husband was such a low-level operator in the spying community that he would probably never be discovered. Rosario claims she never had any real idea about the true nature of his betrayal and certainly never understood that he was, in effect, a mass murderer whose acts had resulted in the deaths of numerous men.

She decided to stay silent.

But once she became an accomplice, their life together was ruined. She was already a worrier who became frantic if Rick was late picking up Paul from school and delivering him home. Between the school and the house—a ten-minute journey—she might call him twice on the car phone to make sure they had not had an accident. The added burden of living a secret life proved almost intolerable. Their whole focus became not their future together or the future of their son, but their survival. Their lives became increasingly narrow until, instead of looking forward several years in the future, they could only project a few weeks or even days until the next meeting, the next covert action.

In August, Rosario, now involved in the conspiracy, made two deposits, totaling nearly $5,000. A week after Rosario's deposits, Ames typed another letter to the Soviets on his home computer.[13] In the letter, dated August 18, 1992, Ames informed his friends of his access to specific classified documents, upcoming dead drops, and a planned meeting with his handlers in Caracas, Venezuela. Ames also addressed another issue: he explained to the Russians that his loving wife, Rosario, knew about and supported his espionage activity. "My wife has accommodated herself to what I am doing in a very supportive way," he wrote. At what point Rosario became involved remains essentially unclear, although Rick admitted in a jailhouse interview that it was the same sloppiness that led authorities to him, that led her to discover his espionage activities.[14]

The next day, August 19, Ames attempted to deliver the message to the Russians. Early in the morning he drove to a secret meeting spot referred to in court documents as signal site ROSE, and indicated to the

Russians that he had information for them, by placing a small pencil mark at the designated area. Then, later, sometime before 4:00 p.m., Ames drove to dead drop GROUND and left the Russians his letter and classified documents. The next morning Ames returned to signal site ROSE to check that the chalk mark had been erased, indicating that the Russians had picked up his package. They had not. It was a frightening moment, the one all spies come to dread. When small lines of chalk are the only contact between source and controller, the umbilical cord linking one with the other, the marks assume an extraordinary importance. He worried that they had learned he had been discovered and even thought briefly that for some reason they might have cut him loose. But there was nothing to be done except cover his back. He retrieved all the documents from the dead drop and returned home.

For the next month, Ames did not attempt to contact the SVR. In mid-September he authored another message on his home computer, explaining to them that his previous attempt to transmit documents was not successful and that he would signal them at signal site ROSE again and attempt to transmit the documents through dead drop GROUND. The very same day, Ames marched into the CIA Office of Security and falsely reported that he intended to travel to Bogotá, Colombia, to assist his mother-in-law, when actually he was planning a secret meeting with Soviet spies in Caracas, Venezuela.[15]

In other documents obtained from the ribbon of his computer printer, Ames said:

> Given the shortness of time before our next meeting, I am putting a note on the package which I hope will cause the people here to send you a telegram confirming my intent to make our scheduled meeting on 5/6 October.
>
> Besides getting cash in Caracas, (I have mentioned how little I like this method, though it is acceptable), I still hope that you will have decided on some safer, paper transfer of some sort of a large amount.
>
> Until we meet in Caracas . . . K 18/19 August.

Little is known about Ames's trip to Caracas except that he traveled through Bogotá and met with SVR officers on October 6, 1992, and received a $150,000 cash payment. Upon returning to the United States, he began depositing his latest payments. On October 8, there were two $8,500 deposits made to his Riggs account. The same day he deposited another $17,000 in his Dominion A account. By the end of October, his additional cash deposits totaled more than $42,200—and throughout November he added nearly $20,000 more to his various accounts.

In early December 1992, the SVR again contacted Ames. The message laid out a plan describing how Ames could transmit information by a new spate of dead drops. Additionally, it described the logistics of their upcoming meeting in Bogotá scheduled at the time for the following November or December.

But time, at last, was beginning to run out. The FBI–CIA joint task force had finally made the match that should have been done at least a year earlier. One of the team visited the FBI's Washington field office at Tysons Corner and pulled the files relating to the surveillance of Sergey Chuvakhin, the Russian diplomat whom Ames had claimed to be recruiting back in 1985 when he began his spying. Those records proved to be a perfect match with the information on the deposits into Ames's bank accounts. As Ames met Chuvakhin, so he paid money into his bank accounts.

"We found the deposits perfectly matched the meetings," said Ronald "Rudy" Guerin, one of the FBI agents involved in the case.[16]

It was enough. At last there was hard evidence that could not be ignored and that everyone could agree pointed to Ames as the traitor. Now it was the FBI's turn to drive the investigation. There would be no hesitation, no delays, and no question that Ames was in the frame. He was to become the focus of one of the most concentrated spy hunts in modern history.

Bob "Bear" Bryant is a career FBI agent. Trained as a lawyer, he joined the Bureau in Salt Lake City before transferring to Washington to be in charge of the field office there. On his desk rests a simple plaque that reads: "You lied," a memento from his wife after he promised her that the job in Washington would last only three years.[17] He had risen steadily through the FBI's ranks and is considered one of the toughest and most experienced of its field men. Unlike most Bureau agents, he shows the occasional flash of independence by wearing striped shirts instead of the uniform white. Otherwise he is a traditional careful operator who prefers shadows to the limelight. He likes to tell the story that after he joined the Bureau and was on the initial training course, he was sent to the unarmed-combat class. He was matched with a prospective agent much shorter than he and was confident that he could hold his own. However, with one well-aimed blow, Bear was knocked to the ground, unconscious. It was an early lesson in matching not just brawn but brains against an opponent. It was Bryant who would now lead the hunt for evidence against Ames.

Bryant had been closely involved with the Felix Bloch investigation and had tried to initiate an obstruction-of-justice investigation, which Wayne Gilbert, then his boss, had turned down. This time, Bryant was determined that any CIA interference in this case would be kept to a minimum.

John Lewis, Bryant's deputy, was in charge of counter intelligence. He was a CI specialist who had come back to the Bureau after working in the National Security Council during Ronald Reagan's presidency. A cautious agent whom colleagues describe as "bloodless," Lewis had a reputation as a dogged investigator.[18]

The supervisor who would actually run the case was Les Wiser, a lean former lawyer from the Midwest who had joined the FBI six years earlier. Wiser was a different personality from his two older colleagues. Not only did he appear to be from a different generation—Lewis and Bryant were in their late forties and early fifties and Wiser was forty—but he had yet to have his independence honed down to an acceptable Bureau level. He had been made a supervisor on the CI squad at the young age of thirty-eight and was clearly destined for further promotion. He wears fashionable wire-rimmed spectacles, sports a bushy dark mustache, and still retains a thick head of wavy, dark hair. His dogged determination was to have a critical impact on the investigation that was to follow.

Armed with the intelligence that had matched Ames with Chuvakhin and the bank deposits, the team came together in May to put in place the complicated logistics required of such an undercover operation. First Wiser needed to gather a small team of experts who would be able to analyze the information that would swiftly start flowing into their

Buzzard's Point office. He brought in Tim Caruso, who had been involved in the original ANLACE investigation, and Rudy Guerin, another experienced counter intelligence officer. He also needed a computer expert to manage the data and perhaps decipher some of Rick's communications; an accountant to unscramble the complex financial web that Rick had spun; and two others to actually handle the vast flow of data that was to come flooding into the office.[19]

To ensure that the team's security was watertight, the group moved out of the FBI's field office in Buzzard's Point. On May 12, they set up their operation several floors below next to a Navy medical center. To anyone who asked, they were simply reinvestigating an old leak dating back to the Casey era. It was, they assured the curious, no big deal.

Wiser then brought together a special surveillance squad to monitor Ames twenty-four hours a day. These men understood the need for stealth and deception in any undercover operation. As in the movies, they had their share of gadgets—the directional microphones, the lasers to pick up conversations from windows, the miniature cameras. But the surveillance team was not just a couple of guys in a car. By the time the squad was ready, there were fifty people employed full-time with a range of cars, motorcycles, and vans at their disposal. From now on, wherever Rick went, the squad would be both behind and ahead of him.

The most important requirement now was information. What was Rick planning? Whom was he meeting and how were the meetings set up? It was evidence that the FBI wanted, evidence that would stand up in court.

"When we opened the case, no one knew that this was the man," said Wiser. "That's part of what the investigation was about, to ascertain whether he was in fact guilty of espionage. I mean, he might have been guilty of something else. He had unexplained wealth and maybe his story about the wealth from his in-laws was true. You had to consider that possibility. But everybody has instinct and a gut reaction, and two plus two usually adds up to four, and in this case it proved to be true."[20]

To try to gather that key intelligence and to establish a pattern of movement in and around the Ames house, the surveillance team borrowed a truck from a local tree-trimming firm and in the middle of the day parked it next to the trees that grew opposite the Ames house. Two

FBI agents stood nervously in the cherry picker as the driver raised them into the air. As one agent gingerly wielded a chain saw and lopped off a few branches, the second man attached a small box to the nearby telephone lines. From the outside this looked like any other telephone junction box. Inside was a miniature camera with a wide-angle lens that could record every movement in and out of the Ames house, day or night. The film would be automatically relayed to the nearby Tysons Corner branch office for analysis. Over the next few weeks, the hidden camera allowed the team to build up a detailed profile of Rick and Rosario's routine.

One of the things they learned early in the investigation was that the garbage was collected on North Randolph Street on Wednesday mornings. Bear Bryant ordered the team to set up a trash call that would intercept the Ameses' rubbish before it was hauled away. First, the team established just when neighbors walked their dogs at night and when would be the best time to make their call. Then, after midnight on Tuesday nights, an unmarked van with a specially silenced muffler would drive up to the trash barrel, a hand would reach out of the back, haul it inside, and substitute an exact replica complete with similar rubbish. For the next few hours, the agents would sift through the garbage, photographing and photocopying anything that seemed interesting, before replacing the original trash back outside the house. That way, if either Rick or Rosario got up unusually early and decided to dump some more garbage, when they lifted the lid of their barrel they would see only their usual rubbish.

A covert entry was made into the Ames house while the family was out, and bugs were placed in the kitchen, the living room, and the master bedroom, so that almost every conversation that Rick and Rosario had over the next few months could be heard and recorded by the FBI.

Finally, the team organized a bug for the telephone to the Ames home. This required no visit to the house by agents but a call to the local switching station, where an additional circuit was attached to the number. It is an undetectable system and ensured that every single call in and out of the Ames house was carefully recorded.

On March 9, 1993, Ames typed on his computer a message to his SVR controller, promising more documents. The best intelligence he could manage this time was an appreciation of the current low morale in the SE Division. Morale might have been of academic interest to Moscow Center but was of little real value. His new position in the Counter Narcotics Center had reduced his access to the kind of juicy material that Moscow had grown used to. They had been pressuring Rick to deliver more, and he in turn was worried that if he failed, they might cut his income. Given the scale of his current expenditures and the increasing demands from Rosario, this was a very unwelcome idea. So he promised them that he would soon be transmitting more classified documents.

The next month, right on schedule, Ames filed a false U.S. joint income-tax report for himself and Rosario, reporting a total income of only $67,577.90.

Then on May 26 the surveillance team got lucky. They followed Ames to work that morning and saw him deviate from his normal route to work and watched him place a small chalk mark at SMILE, the mailbox at Thirty-seventh and R streets. He then drove on and left a package at BRIDGE, the pedestrian footbridge spanning Little Falls Parkway. It was a message that he headed "urgent," asking for another delivery of cash. Just four days later, the SVR left a signal at NORTH, the telephone pole on the corner of Military Road and Thirty-sixth Street in Arlington, that Rick monitored on his way to work. That evening he picked up a bundle of cash from PIPE, the drainage pipe in Wheaton Park. Following the drop, throughout the first week of June, in four separate transactions at the Dominion and Riggs banks, Ames made deposits of nearly $30,000.

Reinvigorated by this new infusion of cash, Rick tackled his spying with a new enthusiasm. Through much of June, he tried to obtain intelligence on U.S. capabilities and methods of detecting Russian nuclear submarines. By the third week he had gathered a mass of documents and computer files in his office and was ready to pass them on.[21]

Wiser and his team knew by now that there was every chance that Ames was their man. His suspicious activity, the cash deposits, and the pattern of odd behavior established over the previous years all came together to spell one word—*spy*. But the hard evidence that would stand up in court still proved elusive. To try to find that evidence, the FBI, in concert with the CIA, organized a raid on Rick's office at the CIA. This was an easier and less risky first step than going into his house. It could be done in the middle of the night when Rick would be sure to be at home in bed, and it could be managed so secretly that the chances of discovery were minimal.

Rick's office lay on floor G in the main building at Langley, and the night of June 5, 1993, the small search team walked through a door marked VOB and passed cubicles that would normally have been filled with CIA case officers. Then, at the far side of the room, they paused in front of office GVO6. On the door was the name RICK AMES. There was a brief pause while the CIA officer accompanying them unlocked the door with a master key, and they were in.[22]

The office proved to be a testament to the lax security at the Agency. More than 144 secret documents were found, as well as ten top-secret files, some of which were among the most highly classified because they contained Sensitive Compartmented Information (SCI). Such documents are generally identified by "Top Secret" followed by a single word, such as "Byeman," for material gathered from overhead collection systems (satellites), and SITK, or "signals intelligence—talent keyhole," which includes overhead photography. In theory, access to this kind of material is very strictly controlled. It should not have been available to Rick in his position.

Many of the documents were dated after Ames was transferred to the Counter Narcotics Center and bore no relation to his current work. It was clear that he had simply been ambling through the corridors of Langley, picking up a document here and a file there, trawling for intelligence he thought might interest the Russians. Despite his job, colleagues appeared not to be concerned that he was showing undue interest in matters as diverse as counter intelligence and military intelligence about the former Soviet Union.[23]

Although the evidence found in Ames's office appeared damning, the team still needed corroboration that he was an active spy and not somebody who had committed some acts in the past and had now stopped. It was certainly apparent that he had borrowed classified documents. It was also clear that he was servicing dead-letter drops, and there seemed to be unauthorized contacts with diplomats from the Russian Embassy. On the team, suspicion had now hardened into certainty that Ames was their man. But with the memory of Felix Bloch still fresh in his mind,

Bryant wanted to make this case completely watertight. At the same time, he needed to make sure that Ames was given no opportunity to pick up on the fact that he was under surveillance and head for Moscow, as Edward Lee Howard had done. It was a fine line the team was having to walk, and it gave Ames some opportunity to exploit the loose surveillance.

There was some concern when in July, as part of his responsibilities for Counter Narcotics in the Black Sea region, Ames boarded a plane for a trip to the former Soviet republic of Georgia.[24] In August, less than a month after Ames's visit to Georgia, Fred Woodruff, an American, was murdered in Georgia, after a motorist fired a rifle into the car he was riding in. Woodruff worked at the Agency and had previously given the Georgian government information regarding secret Russian military support to Georgian ethnic separatists who were opposing the Tbilisi government.[25] Initially, the FBI concluded that Woodruff was a victim of random violence, not the target of an assassination, but after Ames's arrest, the CIA began an investigation into whether there was a connection between Ames's July visit and Woodruff's death. Prior to the original FBI investigation, some U.S. officials speculated that Woodruff was murdered by Russian GRU (military intelligence) agents. Results of the CIA inquiry indicate Woodruff was killed by a casual assassin, and no evidence has been found that his death was anything other than a random shooting or anything to do with the Ames case.[26]

In late July Ames received a message from the SVR that set out future procedures for servicing dead drops and for meetings abroad with his personal handlers. These suggestions were accompanied by more cash, and on July 20, he deposited more than $10,000 in his Dominion and Riggs accounts.[27]

Despite the tightening of the noose, nothing was done within the Agency to give Ames grounds for suspicion. In early August 1993, he was designated chief of the Europe and Central Eurasia Branch of the International Counter Narcotics Group of the Counter Narcotics Center. This move marked his final professional shift within the CIA ranks, and he held this position until his arrest in February 1994.[28]

But while Rick's job at the CIA was not a problem for him, the family's finances continued to be a source of concern. On August 22, Cecilia

Dupuy, Rosario's mother, informed her daughter of money problems, some of which related to properties owned by Rick and Rosario in Colombia. Their Colombian holdings were fairly extensive by now: it is believed that in addition to owning an oceanfront farm, known as "Guajira," they also owned two condominium apartments there. Rosario's mother and brother lived in one of the condominiums; two of its four bedrooms were filled with books and antiques sent from Washington.[29] Cecilia asked her daughter when she would send money for the "administration and telephones of [her] properties in Cartagena, Bogotá, and Guajira."[30]

The surveillance teams had been dutifully following Rick to and from work for three months, and it was becoming increasingly tough to change their patterns sufficiently to prevent him from spotting them. Proper surveillance at Langley was extremely difficult because of a shooting outside the headquarters that January. Mir Kansi, a Pakistani immigrant, had used an AK-47 automatic rifle to kill two men and wound three others who were sitting in commuter traffic waiting to turn into Langley on January 25.[31] The killings had understandably sent a shock wave through the Agency, and security at the building and the outside grounds had been tightened. So paranoid were the FBI agents that they had not alerted the CIA to their operation in case word of it leaked. This made it that much harder to keep close to Rick without looking just like the very kind of suspicious vehicle that CIA security was on the watch for.

They were also concerned because of the publication, that August, of Ronald Kessler's book *The FBI*.[32] In it he devoted a whole section to FBI counter intelligence work and hinted that the Bureau had a highly placed source within the SVR. Ames read the book and immediately focused on the relevant section that might suggest a danger for him. Ames knew that the SVR had compartmentalized all the information about him but, of course, he had no idea just who had knowledge about him. Through their own monitoring, the FBI knew that Rick had shown a keen interest in the book and that he had speculated that the FBI might have gathered information about him. Whether this was just low-level curiosity or whether he was genuinely alarmed, the FBI did not know.

Also, by the beginning of September, the FBI units had spotted some

Russian Embassy officials lurking around Langley. That in itself was not necessarily surprising, given that the Russians had an obvious interest in what the CIA was doing. But the FBI knew that the Russians were routinely picking up their shortwave-radio conversations and would also be running a series of counter espionage measures to try to detect if their top spy in the CIA had been uncovered. The mere appearance of the Russians at Langley on different days and at different times spooked the Bureau. Agents worried that somehow the Russians might have put together the coded radio traffic and the Ames case or even that Ames himself might have warned them he was being watched.

"On my instructions, I had told my surveillance, I wanted to make sure that they did not get made," said Lewis. "We still did not know how skilled he was at counter surveillance. Now he, don't forget, he's a trained CIA officer who's served overseas and he had received counter surveillance training, and we just didn't know how good he was and so they took a very cautious approach. I'd rather have them get lost than you get made."

As part of this caution, Bryant was concerned that absolutely nothing be done to alert Ames. He had ordered the trash collection suspended while the progress of the case was evaluated. He wanted to be certain that Ames still had no idea just how close they were before ordering the full-scale surveillance back into action.

The surveillance team had established that Rick was a man of almost absolute routine. He would travel to work, stay there until lunchtime, go to lunch, and then return home around 6:00 p.m. They felt safe in keeping the surveillance vehicles parked some distance away from Langley and moving them up shortly before he was expected to appear. But on Thursday, September 9, Ames broke with his routine and left home very early in the morning, half an hour before the surveillance team came on duty. As they were driving into position thirty minutes later, Ames returned to the house before leaving for work as usual.

That afternoon, the same thing happened. He left Langley around 4:00 p.m. and drove away before the FBI could get their cars into the area. The FBI believed that Ames's action could only be explained by the fact that he had gone to service a dead drop.

"He'd gone operational," said Lewis. "He was making a drop and we had missed him."

That night, Rick and Rosario went to a PTA meeting at Paul's school. This time, there was no mistake. He left the meeting early, drove from northern Virginia into the District, across Memorial Bridge and up Massachusetts Avenue, around the Naval Observatory, and then back-tracked along Garfield. He turned into Garfield Terrace, which is a cul-de-sac, turned around in a driveway, and then retraced his steps back home.

As soon as he had left Garfield Terrace, members of the surveillance team flooded the area looking for anything that might indicate a message from Ames to the Russians or from the Russians to him. There was nothing to be seen. What they did not realize at that stage was they should have expected to see nothing. That morning Rick had placed a chalk mark on the mailbox on Garfield Terrace, signal site ROSE, to tell the Russians that he had put a package in dead drop GROUND. His return trip to Garfield Terrace that evening was simply to make sure the chalk mark had been removed, telling him that the Russians had got his message and picked up the package.

Back at Buzzard's Point, Bryant was furious that the team had missed Ames at such a critical moment. He told Wiser that it could have been a turning point in the investigation and he had blown it. There was fallout, too, from further up the chain of command, where there was a real concern that, like Howard, Ames might escape.

That weekend, Wiser brooded about Thursday's failure, reflecting on just what little room he had been given to maneuver by both Lewis and Bryant. He was certain that the evidence they needed was there if only they could find a way to lay their hands on it. He began to wonder what Lewis and Bryant's order to "suspend" the searches of Ames's trash meant exactly. Clearly it was a ban, but surely a ban was temporary, and if it was temporary, that meant that Bryant intended to reinstitute the searches sometime soon. And they had always told him that as a supervisor he should show initiative. Right? Right.

On Monday morning, he called the trash experts on his team into his office and told them to go for one more search that Tuesday night.

Wiser was asleep when the telephone rang at 4:00 a.m. on Wednesday morning. It was the searchers and they had good news. Scrunched up amid the kitchen refuse and the old newspapers was a single yellow 3-M Post-It note:

I am not ready to meet at B on 1 Oct.

I cannot read North 13–19 Sept

If you *will meet* at B on 1 Oct. Pls. signal North

w [piece missing] of 20 Sept to confi[piece missing]

No message at pipe.

If you *cannot* mee[piece missing] 1 Oct, signal North after 27 Sept with

message at pipe.[33]

The message was a draft that Ames had written for his Russian controller. Unhappy with the wording, he had crumpled it up and simply thrown it in the trash. This was an extraordinarily sloppy piece of tradecraft that even a bungling amateur would not have committed. But by now, it appeared, Rick had come to believe he was almost invulnerable. His arrogance and his disdain for his colleagues at the Agency were so great that he was certain he would never be caught. *They* were just too stupid and *he* was simply too intelligent.

By four-thirty Wiser was in the office. As soon as he saw the note, he understood its significance. He raised both hands to heaven, looked up, and said, "Thank you, God."

The message was easily deciphered by the FBI. NORTH was a signal site and Ames was unable to read it because from September 13 to September 19 he planned to be in Ankara on business. He wanted to meet his controller in Bogotá on October 1 and needed a confirmation that that was okay. To confirm the trip, he told the Russians, all that was required was for them to leave a chalk mark at NORTH. There was no need to put an actual package in dead drop PIPE. If the October 1 meeting was not possible, then a message should be left at NORTH after September 27.

At last they had the first piece of confirmation that Ames was operational and that he was still spying for the Russians. That Wednesday morning, Wiser had the difficult task of explaining his insubordination to Bryant, but the expected reprimand was softened by the wonderful reward he brought with him.

"I didn't want to do the trash cover because I didn't want to heat up the neighborhood," said Bryant. "Mr. Wiser, in his infinite wisdom, decided to go ahead and run the trash cover, and that next morning, he was in front of my office. He and Mr. Lewis were very happy because we were getting beat up pretty good, and they had this note and I was delighted to see this note. It was a marvelous piece of insubordination."

Around September 19, Ames made his airline reservation to fly to Bogotá. But then he received another signal from the Russians, through NORTH.[34] He later relayed their messages to Rosario:

RICK: Yeah, well listen. There . . . there's news. No travel.

ROSARIO: Oh . . .

RICK: Yeah . . . not going.

ROSARIO: Oh . . .

RICK: So you should ah . . . guess . . . ah . . . give Ceci a call whenever you can get through to her and . . . ah . . . tell her that . . . they ah . . . My visit was canceled.

ROSARIO: Uh huh. Does that mean that you retrieve something?

RICK: Yeah. Uh huh. Yeah.

From this phone conversation, the FBI investigators concluded that Ames observed a signal at site NORTH on September 19, which the SVR placed to postpone the October 1 meeting in Bogotá. Ames was told he would next be contacted by his handlers through PIPE.[35] On September 30, Ames canceled his airline reservation.

On October 3, Ames followed the Soviets' instructions and retrieved a message from dead drop PIPE. The note, written on a blank classified-advertisement form for *The Washington Times*, described the location of a future meeting, which would be held the first week of November.[36] The note also indicated that Ames should RSVP regarding this upcoming meeting via signal site SMILE.[37] In closing, the Russians stated that their operatives "are ready to meet in a city known to you on 1 Nov." After reading the message Rick assured Rosario that "all is well." Later in the conversation she asked him, "Financially too?" He replied, "Ah Yeah, Ah. Wait 'til I get there."[38]

On October 6, yet another trash run struck gold. A note, written by Ames almost a year earlier and only just thrown away, was carefully unfolded. It read: "You have probably heard a bit about me by this time from your (and now my) colleagues in the MBRF," suggesting that Ames had easily made the transition from his KGB associates to their successors in the Russian intelligence service.[39] The MBRF, until December 1993, was the Russian Federal Ministry for Security, responsible for conducting counter intelligence investigations in Russia. In early December, the MBRF was succeeded by a new network, called MB. In January 1994, the MB was also succeeded and replaced by a reorganization of the Federal Service for Counter Intelligence, referred to as the FSK. Exactly why Ames should have been dealing with the Russian equivalent of the FBI rather than the SVR, which equated to the CIA, is not known. What is known is that the vast majority of his contacts were with the SVR and not with the MB, which is charged with counter intelligence inside Russia.

This accumulation of evidence coincided with a planned trip by the Ames family to Pensacola, Florida, for a wedding. They left on the night of Friday, October 8, and the weekend was clear for the FBI. On October 9, Rudy Guerin led the team of FBI burglars, including a computer expert and two others who specialize in searches that leave no trace, into the Ames house and set to work.

Rick's personal password was child's play for the computer specialist to crack. It took only a matter of moments to copy the entire contents of the hard drive onto the laptop computer they had brought with them. Every document in the house was photographed for later analysis and every cupboard searched, airline ticket logged, and piece of expensive jewelry noted.

Back at Buzzard's Point, it was the computer expert who had the best story to tell. Rick had kept virtually every message he had received via floppy disk from the Russians and had carefully stored every file he had ever made for them. There was a list of all the dead drops and the signal sites and details of how the communications actually worked.

In one document, dated June 8, 1992, Ames wrote the following:

My most immediate need, as I pointed out in March, is money. As I have mentioned several times, I do my best to invest a good part of the cash I received, but keep part of it out for ordinary expenses.

Now, I am faced with the need to cash in investments to meet current needs—a very tight and unpleasant situation! I have had to sell a certificate of deposit in Zurich and some stock here to help make up the gap. Therefore, I will need as much cash delivered in PIPE as you think can be accomodated [*sic*]—it seems to me that it could accomodate [*sic*] up to $100,000.

But not all the documents were about money or logistics. Another one recovered during the search is believed by the FBI investigators to have been written on or about December 17, 1990. This piece of correspondence discusses a CIA operation regarding an "SCD Officer." (The SCD was the Second Chief Directorate of the KGB, responsible for internal security.) According to CIA records, there was an SCD officer being operated then by the CIA as a human asset. She later disappeared. This was further clear evidence—if any more was needed—that Ames was the mole.

As time passed, the couple, particularly Rosario, became increasingly anxious. Not only was she "supportive," as Ames earlier described her to his Russian handlers, but she tried to impose a sense of discipline on the operation. In an October phone call, a nervous Rosario interrogated her husband about a signal he was supposed to leave on a mailbox, to indicate to his handlers that he was prepared to meet in Bogotá for an information exchange. "Why didn't you do it today, for God sakes," Rosario screamed into the phone. Her husband meekly admitted that "[he] should have, except it was raining like crazy." "Well, honey," she said, in an exasperated tone, "I hope you didn't screw up."

The day after the phone conversation, October 13, Ames heeded his wife's advice. He left his Arlington home particularly early that morning, evading the FBI surveillance, and returned by 6:44 a.m. It is believed by the FBI investigators that in that twenty-two-minute time period he visited SMILE and signaled to his SVR officers that he would meet them in Bogotá, by placing a chalk mark at the site.[40]

Near the end of October, Ames prepared for his meeting with the Soviets in Bogotá. In a tapped phone conversation, which occurred on October 25, Rosario gave her husband tradecraft tips when she ordered him to use a carry-on bag instead of a suitcase to transport the cash he expected to receive from his handlers.[41] "You always have this envelope with this big hunk [of cash], I mean really," she said to him in a condescending voice.

Several days later, a concerned and demanding Rosario offered her husband another plan for concealing the transport of the cash. It would be a good idea, she advised, if he left some of the money with her relatives in Bogotá.[42] In an October 29 phone call she explained, "I don't want you to bring back anything that will make them look in your luggage."[43]

Shortly before he departed on his trip, Rick and Rosario had chosen an alibi for his disappearance, in case anyone inquired.

Rick gave her instructions: "If anybody calls during the day—it's not going to happen, but I'm [unintelligible] . . . but if anybody happens to call, you tell them I went up to Annapolis. You don't have to explain why."[44]

Before he left, Rosario needled him about other details of the trip as well. "You get the money in dollars, right," she inquired before he left.[45]

All these precautions were futile, of course, as the FBI was not only listening to every conversation but was also planning to be in Bogotá ahead of Rick so that agents could follow his every move. On October 30, 1993, Rick flew to Bogotá and was immediately picked up by the FBI surveillance. There was some sensitivity in Washington about sending FBI agents into Colombia on an operation without informing the local government. However, it was decided that the risk of a leak from notifying the Colombian authorities was too great, and the FBI team was warned to keep a low profile and to do nothing that might attract their attention.

After landing, Rick called Rosario to tell her his garment bag had been delayed by the airline when he arrived. Rosario told her husband that she was "very, very nervous."[46] Later in the conversation, her nervousness turned to frustration and hostility. "I know you don't give a shit about the suitcase, but, I mean, okay, fine. . . . I'm just hoping you didn't have anything . . . uh . . . you didn't have anything that shouldn't have been in the bag in the bag." "No honey," he assured her.[47]

Ames was photographed meeting his SVR controller and the final piece of the jigsaw puzzle fell into place. Later that day, Rick called an obviously nervous Rosario to assure her that everything was fine. She snapped at him once more about his luggage and asked him if any other bags had been lost. The following day, Rick called her again and told her about the "short meetings" he was attending that evening and the following afternoon.[48]

The SVR delivered to Ames a communications strategy for 1994. Besides establishing new signal sites, named TAD, JOY, MAT, SAL, and RAY, which were designated for dead drops in February, March, May, August, and September, the plan also laid out the logistics for a face-to-face meeting in November 1994 and another in 1995 in either Vienna or Paris.[49]

On November 1, Ames called his wife from Bogotá and briefly described his interaction with his SVR handlers.

ROSARIO:	Why, what's up?
RICK:	How are you?
ROSARIO:	No. Honey, it's . . . what's up? Why are you there?
RICK:	No. Nothing. Nothing. I had a short meeting this evening.
ROSARIO:	Oh.
RICK:	I came back and Elisio was here and so we had a good time. [Pause]
ROSARIO:	Did you really meet?
RICK:	Uh huh.
ROSARIO:	When did you get back?
RICK:	[to someone in the background] When did I get back? [to Rosario] About nine.
ROSARIO:	Well, honey, you don't, honey, Rick . . . Why do you have to . . .
RICK:	Nine-thirty.
ROSARIO:	Why do you have to ask my mother when you got back? Don't be an asshole.

Later, the conversation continues:

ROSARIO:	. . . The only reason I was upset is that I thought that it had been all for nothing and that, you know, you hadn't . . .
RICK:	No. No. Uh uh. No.
ROSARIO:	You're sure?
RICK:	Yeah . . .

The conversation continues:

ROSARIO:	So what are you going to do tomorrow?
RICK:	I'm gonna have to do a little shopping in Unicentro, then I

have meetings in the afternoon, and then out in the evening
as well.

ROSARIO: Okay, just be careful and you swear to me that nothing
went wrong?

On November 3, Rick returned from Bogotá. Shortly after his return
he and Rosario talked about the details of his meetings with his handlers,
including the possibility of his upcoming overseas trips scheduled for the
following year.

"So, when do you go back to Bogotá? In a year or what," Rosario
asked.

"Yeah, well, not Bogotá. Either Caracas or Quito."

"Why those places?"

"Well, at least it's not Lima. I mean you could get murdered in Lima."

Rick informed her of his reasons for going to Bogotá that year:
". . . have to do four deliveries to me over the next year to build up the financial situation. They're holding . . . ah . . . one hundred and ninety
thousand dollars."[50]

The following day, just a day after his return, Ames again began stash-
ing cash in local Dominion and Riggs bank accounts. By the end of the
week, via six transactions, Ames had deposited more than $40,000—just
before making a $9,600 cash payment to Neiman Marcus in partial set-
tlement of an account in excess of $10,000.[51]

On December 1, 1993, Rosario phoned her mother in Colombia and
discussed at great length the finances of their foreign estates:

ROSARIO: I want you to go to the bank before you come up and find
something out for me. Ask the manager of the bank if I
open an account at Citibank putting you and/or Pablo
[Rosario's brother] with authorized signatures on the account, what would that allow you to do down there? The
lady up here at the bank told me that it might vary, depend-
ing on the laws of each country. I need to know what it
would imply down there. Since they restricted the changing
of dollars for Colombians, what would that imply? Are
Colombians allowed accounts in this country?

CECILIA: Of course.

ROSARIO: Well you have to ask this lady. I cannot keep writing checks like that. The money for the house is causing problems. It is not convenient to . . . You are going to have to resign yourselves, as Rick says, that you will have to change your money in the bank. You cannot keep selling checks to phantom entities in Florida, because I do not know . . . they might be legal but . . . it is making Rick very nervous. So you cannot keep doing that.

On February 9, 1994, just weeks before their arrest, Rosario began to suspect that something was not right. She called Rick and told him she suspected that their phones might have been bugged.[52] Several days later, she nervously encouraged Rick to leave a message for his Soviet friends before the weather changed. When he did not respond to her suggestion, she again reminded him the next day that he should send the message immediately.[53] On February 15, Rosario asked Rick whether he planned to send a message the following day.

Finally, with Rick expecting to leave for Ankara and Moscow, the FBI decided to bring Nightmover to a close. On the morning of February 21, 1994, FBI agents arrested Ames in his car outside his house. Rosario was arrested minutes later.

SIXTEEN

Denial

When the FBI searched the house after the arrests for evidence of wealth, they found a lithograph by Matisse, a signed print by Chagall, a jeweled Russian Orthodox icon, pre-Columbian gold, fine china, an expensive camera, watches, computer and stereo equipment. Jewelry, one report indicated, was "everywhere." Eighteen pieces were strewn around the bathroom sink, among them a diamond heart pendant, a sapphire-and-diamond ring, and a thirty-inch strand of pearls. "It looked as if Tiffany's had exploded."[1] A housekeeper was later to say that Rosario " 'brought home something new every day,' usually jewelry or clothes from a tony store."[2]

Nancy Everly, Rick's faithful sister, began to pick up the pieces. Once the FBI had picked over Rick and Rosario's possessions, she took away what the government did not want as evidence, including forty-five boxes of clothes.[3] She also had power of attorney in the settlement of their affairs, and had to get rid of some two thousand books, including *The Rosenberg Files* and *Great True Spy Stories* as well as *Critique and Crisis: Enlightenment and the Pathogenesis of Modern Society.* Included in the library were books Rick inherited from his father, such as Sherman Kent's *1949 Strategic Intelligence for American World Policy* and Allen Dulles's *The Craft of Intelligence* (inscribed "to Dad, Christmas 1963

228

from Rick"). There were also volumes such as *The International Banking Handbook* and *International Financial Management.* It was a library that was "very war-oriented, very power-oriented. And there are a lot of cookbooks."[4] There were very few personal growth or self-help titles, the exception being *Your Gut Feelings: A Complete Guide to Living Better with Intestinal Problems.* The library was bought, in its entirety, by Chet Hanson, proprietor of the Old Book Company of McLean. The money from the sale would go to support Paul.[5]

At the arraignment in the U.S. Magistrate Court in Alexandria, Virginia, on February 22, the day after the arrests, Ames appeared almost unconcerned at his changed circumstances. Speaking in a calm, clear voice, he declared that he was unable to afford an attorney, and the Judge, Claude Hilton, appointed Plato Cacheris, a prominent Washington lawyer who had represented numerous high-profile clients, including Oliver North's former secretary, Fawn Hall, during the Iran-Contra investigations. In the course of his thirty-eight-year career, Cacheris has also represented such notables as Marlene Chalmers Cooke, the wife of Washington Redskins owner Jack Kent Cooke, and Sheik Kamal Adham, a key figure in the Bank of Credit and Commerce International scandal.

Rosario, who had seen neither her husband nor her son until this court appearance, was visibly distressed by her sudden reversal of fortune. Choking back tears, she stared around the court, her dark eyes taking in the rows of reporters scribbling in their notebooks, the female guards on either side of her. The shackles around her ankles and the olive drab prison uniform were a far cry from the designer clothes and high-style living she had grown used to. She, too, requested an attorney, after signing an affidavit saying that she had no money. She was later told she would be represented by William Cummings, an Alexandria-based lawyer and former federal prosecutor who had been the U.S. attorney in Alexandria during the late 1970s.

Because the two had not retained lawyers immediately following their arrest, the court deferred ruling on Rick's pretrial detention, scheduling a hearing on the matter for Thursday, February 24, 1994. Later that day, at Cummings's request, the court again rescheduled the detention hearing for Tuesday, March 1, 1994.[6] At this hearing Assistant U.S. Attorney Mark J. Hulkower, who was handling the government's case, made a carefully calculated effort to continue the pressure on both Rick and Rosario to cooperate. He and the federal team had decided, rightly, that Rick cared about his son and would respond to any threats against him. Hulkower strenuously opposed Rosario's motion to be released on bond, despite her attorney's plea that she be reunited with her five-year-old son, Paul.[7]

The reaction to the arrests was extraordinarily swift. By the following morning, the White House had issued a statement saying that President Clinton "views [the case] as a very serious case involving our national security." It also declared that the president was taking steps to assess the situation, such as ordering National Security Adviser Anthony Lake, CIA Director R. James Woolsey, and others to examine the case's national security implications.[8]

The investigation had been so closely held that no real work on the damage caused by Ames's spying had been done prior to the time of his arrest. Immediately after the arrest became public, DCI James Woolsey set up a special CIA task force to assess the damage. It was so extensive that more than a year later, the assessment was continuing; it still has an open-ended brief.

That same day, in order to try and allay concerns in the Agency about the damage done by Ames, DCI James Woolsey addressed several hundred CIA officers in the Agency's auditorium at Langley. In his speech, which was monitored by every CIA employee via closed-circuit television, he attempted to explain not just the damage caused by Ames but the reasons why he [Woolsey] had refused to take polygraph tests, although other, recent directors had taken them. In addition to the fact that political appointees are not required to go through such testing procedures, Woolsey admitted that he remained "skeptical" about their legitimacy. The statement about the polygraph was an extraordinary one for Woolsey to make, given the reliance on the lie detector within the Agency culture. As had happened with Ames, the polygraph was seen not just as an adjunct to an investigation, which it is, but as a defining tool in its own right, which it very definitely is not. Refusing to take a polygraph and admitting it so publicly was seen within the Agency as undermining the work of the CIA's own staff in trying to protect security leaks through the use of the polygraph.

As one former CIA officer put it: "The trouble with Woolsey is that he means well but he keeps throwing mines out ahead of himself and then treading on them."[9]

Two days after the arrest, Republican senators publicly critiqued Clinton's post-Ames Russia policy, indicating the erosion of bipartisan support for financial aid to Russia. GOP senators urged that aid to Moscow be immediately limited and that Boris Yeltsin, the president, be supported only with caution. Clinton responded by emphasizing the need for denuclearization of Russia and the significance of economic privatization, critical to ensuring that the countries of the former Soviet Union become democratic. Although Clinton implied that money should continue to flow to Russia, he did tell Russian officials to withdraw diplomats who might have been involved in the Ames case. He stressed that if they did not leave on their own, they would be expelled from the United States.[10]

The following day, February 24, Clinton followed up on his threats to oust foreign dignitaries with knowledge of Ames's activities by expelling Russian diplomat Aleksandr Iosovich Lysenko from Washington. Lysenko had no direct connection to Ames, though he was the head of the SVR station in the United States. Russia followed suit by expelling U.S. Embassy counselor James Morris, identified by the Russians as the CIA station chief in Moscow.[11]

In fact, there was never any serious question of the administration's linking the spy case to foreign aid. On the contrary, from the moment President Clinton learned of the case in January, there was a determination that everything possible be done to minimize the impact of the case and to try to keep the linkage between the spying and aid as small as possible. Using a carefully rehearsed formula, the White House called on the Russians to denounce their spying activities and to punish those involved in the Ames case. "We hope if the Russians do take appropriate action we will continue, over the long term, a productive relationship, not because we are operating on charity here, but because some of our most vital interests are tied up in a relationship with Russia," a White House official said.[12] Although it was not stated whom the United States blamed for controlling the operation, White House officials said that Ivan Gromakov, the former resident SVR chief, who was on leave in Russia when the scandal surfaced, was responsible for handling Ames.

The Russians responded to all the fuss by simply denying that Ames was their man. "No matter who Ames has been," said Tatiana Samolis, the press officer for the SVR, "Ames never had any contact with Lysenko," a statement that was accurate and no doubt was designed to keep their response from being too flagrantly deceitful. "The Russian side would not like to see this conflict dragged out. Quite the contrary, we would be keen to return to the interaction already existing between the Russian and American intelligence services since there are quite a number of interests that coincide between our two states, and the areas where we could interact is pretty large.

"Talking about the Ames case, I cannot but remind you that he has never been caught red-handed.

"Intelligence operations in the modern civilized world do not serve as a barrier to maintain friendly and sometimes allied relations between states. Therefore, all this fuss over the case, attempts to transform the problem from purely professional into a high level political one, is beyond me."[13]

Two days after the arrests, the CIA had dispatched a three-member team to Moscow to discuss the case with the SVR. Clinton had told the Russians he expected them to cooperate with the CIA, but this suggestion was greeted in Moscow with the levity it deserved. In fact, in a series of meetings over the course of twenty-four hours, the Russians simply denied they knew anything about Ames. If the roles had been reversed, the CIA men would have responded in exactly the same way, so this was little more than a diplomatic dance to which all the parties knew the steps, even if they didn't lead anywhere.[14]

On February 28, Plato Cacheris filed a motion with the federal court of the Eastern District of Virginia opposing the government's motion for pretrial detainment. The defense based its argument on the improbability that Ames could flee even if he wanted to, given that his foreign and domestic assets were already frozen and that he had been discharged from his job.[15] Cacheris suggested that instead of being detained, Rick be released to the custody of his sister Nancy Everly, a resident of nearby McLean, Virginia, along with electronic monitoring and required check-ins with law enforcement authorities on a frequent basis.[16]

That day, the prosecution was focused on Rosario, filing court papers opposing her motion for pretrial release. In its plea, the government wrote that she might flee the country, pointing out that she had extensive ties to other countries, spoke several foreign languages, and perhaps had access to some of the cash that her husband had stashed abroad.[17] The prosecution also pointed out that in addition to owning property in Colombia, Rosario had also retained her *crédula,* a Colombian identification card. Not only did she have the means, they argued, she also had the motive—Paul, who at the time was being prepared to go to South America to live with her family.[18]

When on March 1 the government entered its opposition to the motion set forth by Rick's lawyers for a pretrial release, it cited the defendant's incentive to flee, his ties to other countries, his known foreign bank accounts, and the property that the Russians had purchased for him for construction of a dacha to establish clear and convincing evidence that he was a flight risk. Additionally, the government emphasized his experience as a CIA operative who had worked and traveled abroad, urging that his "CIA training must be evaluated in conjunction with the substantial resources he has available overseas."[19]

This period of early jail time in the relatively comfortable confines of the modern red-brick Alexandria Detention Center produced a contrast in styles between Rosario and Rick. For her, the arrest had been deeply traumatic, as had the period of separation from her son. After so many years of denial, first that Rick did anything of significance for the CIA and then that he did anything of significance for the Russians, Rosario was finally confronted with the reality of her own complicity in her husband's work. She now understood that Rick had killed ten men and had produced almost unimaginable misery for dozens of others who were in prisons much less comfortable than the one where she was incarcerated. She might have been expected to recognize not just her husband's guilt but her involvement in what had taken place and the fact that she had benefited materially from his spying. But it wasn't until Mark Hulkower, the federal prosecutor, raised the image of her son Paul's growing up and never seeing his mother or father again that she became a willing collaborator with the prosecutor and his team. Nonetheless, she appeared to find the reality of Rick's duplicity and her loss of control over her life and his almost impossible to handle.

"Rosario over the following months kept trying to convince people and the media that she had done nothing wrong and that she was being prosecuted for not turning in her husband," said Hulkower. "She continued to show no responsibility for her own actions. She has blamed the FBI for mischaracterizing her statements, Rick for having gotten her involved in espionage in the first place, her attorney Cummings for not representing her better and me for my role. Her lawyer said in the sentencing that she accepted responsibility for what she had done, but she herself has never really acknowledged publicly what she did."[20]

After several days when Rosario appeared to become increasingly disturbed, with hours spent crying, matched with hysterical screaming bouts during which she railed against Rick, family, and friends with equal fury, she was supplied with a psychiatrist. John Kalil, who is one of the most experienced criminal psychiatrists in the Washington area, was eventually to spend more than sixty hours with Rosario trying to get her to confront what she and Rick had done. He was to tell colleagues that she was a manipulative woman who was unwilling to accept responsibility for her actions or for those of her husband. He believed that because of her family background, she suffered from serious feelings of inadequacy combined with an intellectual arrogance that allowed her to convince herself that not only did she deserve the financial rewards Rick provided, but that she was smart enough to survive any problems that might arise. As happened with many who met and worked with Rosario, Kalil entered the relationship with an open mind and left it feeling that she was a scheming and controlling woman.

In sharp contrast to his wife, Rick appeared to be a relatively contented man in the weeks and months that followed his arrest. He seemed to relish the attention, enjoying the interviews with prosecutors and the debriefers from the CIA and the FBI. After his years of seeking the affirmation of his peers and having resorted to spying to get the recognition he wanted, now, at last, everyone was knocking at his door. He, Rick Ames, was the man they all wanted to see. He was the one who had fooled them all for so long. Sure, they had caught him but now they really needed him to tell them what they had failed to find out on their own. He might have been caught, but he was still smarter than all of them.

For his interrogators, men and women who treated loyalty as sacrosanct, his attitude caused fury. The fact that Rick was unwilling—ever—

to express a single word of regret for the men he had killed and the lives he had ruined won him few admirers. But Ames seemed not to care and genuinely looked forward to the debriefing sessions.

He particularly welcomed the courtship by the media that began as soon as he was arrested. There were repeated requests from television and print media for interviews, and he was happy to grant several to those he felt would give his views a decent airing. The competition for interviews was particularly fierce among television journalists; in the space of a few weeks, Katie Couric, Diane Sawyer, Connie Chung, and Deborah Norville all visited him in the Alexandria jail. Each reporter did her best to convince him that she was the one most suited to hear his tale. The rivalry reached a climax when Connie Chung, in her enthusiasm to win the interview, gave Ames, the spy and killer, an enthusiastic and encouraging hug before saying goodbye. This performance was not enough to sway Ames, who gave the interview to Diane Sawyer.[21]

The one regret that Rick appears to have had is over his separation from Rosario. The two were being kept in separate parts of the same prison and so Rick began a lengthy correspondence with her.[22] In long, rambling, handwritten notes, he proclaimed his love for her and asked her to understand why he had taken the course he had chosen.

I [do know] very well not only the size of my faults but also how small my successes have been. In rough order they are: impotence, drinking, my side business, procrastination and carelessness. Each of them and taken altogether make me fear that I have or am in the process of forfeiting your love, making marriage sterile and inflicting tremendous damage on you, causing you doubt, anxiety, loss of self confidence and a feeling of trapped hopelessness, even desperation. . . . And I ask myself, how can someone cause such harm without intending it. Because I don't intend it—I haven't got a shred of hatred or resentment towards you. . . . My love for you wants only your happiness and I fear you are not—unhappy mainly because I have failed. . . . Teach me to love I said! Well, I've turned out to be a poor student.[23]

If Rick hoped to woo Rosario with these letters, he failed.

"There were lots of letters telling me that he loved me," she said. "But he understands a different kind of love and it's not my kind. He seems to have been able to section off his brain; one life for me and Paul, one for the CIA, one for the Russians. Who was the real Rick? I have no idea."[24]

On April 28, dressed in a jail uniform with a crucifix dangling from her neck, which she clutched frequently throughout her address, Rosario pleaded guilty to charges of conspiracy to commit espionage and tax fraud. The same morning, before a crowded courtroom and his weeping wife, Ames pleaded guilty to giving up some of the CIA's most important secrets. He also admitted that he was guilty of conspiracy to commit espionage and tax fraud. In a fifteen-minute speech, he confessed that he had "betrayed a serious trust," although he attempted to minimize the damage of his actions.

"These spy wars are a sideshow, which have no real impact on our significant security interests over the years," he told the court. He compared himself to "a corrupt government official receiving a bribe or a stock speculator acting on inside information." "As an intelligence officer with more than 30 years experience, I do not believe that our nation's interests have been noticeably damaged by my acts, or for that matter, those of the Soviet Union or Russia noticeably aided," he said.

He then went on to develop a theme that was to recur in interviews with the media over the next few months: that spying was essentially a game between spies that achieved little of value and should, except in exceptional circumstances, be scrapped.

"I had come to believe that the espionage business, as carried out by the CIA and a few other American agencies, was and is a self-serving sham, carried out by careerist bureaucrats who have managed to deceive several generations of American policy makers and the public about both the necessity and the value of their own work.

"There is and has been no rational need for thousands of case officers and tens of thousands of agents working around the world, primarily in and against friendly countries. The information our vast espionage network acquires at considerable human and ethical costs is generally insignificant or irrelevant to our policy makers' needs.

"Our espionage establishment differs hardly at all from many other Federal bureaucracies, having transformed itself into a self-serving interest group, immeasurably aided by secrecy.

"Now that the Cold War is over and the Communist tyrannies largely done for, our country still awaits a real national debate on the means and ends—and costs—of our national security policies."[25]

As was the case throughout his interrogation, Ames showed no remorse for his actions and seemed remarkably relaxed about his role as one of the most successful mass murderers in history. But he had chosen the grounds for his defense well and his speech played perfectly into a growing sentiment in Congress and among some senior officials in the administration that it was, indeed, time for a new look at the workings of the intelligence community. Rick's speech was to have a major impact on the debate about the future of intelligence, and in the months ahead, the media and members of Congress turned to him to seek his views about what should be done. While a debate is needed, the attention devoted to Ames was extraordinary, the equivalent of consulting Jeffrey Dahmer or Ted Bundy about the merits of the criminal justice system in America.

The prosecutors, however, dismissed Ames's remarks as attempts to justify and minimize his criminal wrongdoing. "These are crimes which caused people to die, as surely as if the defendant pulled the trigger," said Assistant U.S. Attorney Mark J. Hulkower. "They died," he added, "because Rick Ames wasn't making enough money from the CIA and wanted to live in a half million dollar house and drive a Jaguar."[26]

Ames was sentenced to life in prison without the possibility of parole. Rosario's sentencing was delayed until August in order to gauge just how much Rick was cooperating with his debriefers. Full cooperation meant a sentence of five years for Rosario. Anything else and her sentence would be increased.

At the time of his sentencing, in accordance with the terms of Rick's plea bargain and as a sign of his commitment to cooperate fully, the couple turned over to the government their home, their car, and their bank accounts. They also made a deal with the authorities that would require that they turn over any money they might make in the future that was related to their spying activities.

With the sentencing out of the way, Rick was able to continue the theme of his court statement with a series of media interviews. This caused fury in the intelligence community, which hated the idea of such a man being given a platform to espouse his views in such respected publications as *The New York Times*. But there was little they could do to stop him talking, and reporters and editors appeared to believe that he had important things to say. To try to stop the steady drip of poison, the CIA went on something of a counteroffensive, with briefings provided to selected journalists that set out details of the men Ames had killed and the damage he had done.

DCI Woolsey described Ames as "a greater traitor than Benedict Arnold who was trying to reinvent himself and will doubtless soon step into the media spotlight as an objective and veteran commentator on the intelligence game."[27]

The media onslaught has contributed to Ames's increasingly unstable mental state. According to those involved in his interrogation, he has become increasingly emotionally volatile as the months have gone by. At times, he appears tearful and depressed and then, after the latest round of courting by the press, is upbeat, even euphoric. This has made it very difficult to take an accurate polygraph and there have been persistent readings suggesting that he continues to lie about the extent of his espionage.[28]

Indeed, not only have the media come to Rick, but he has also reached out to them. In one of the more bizarre episodes after his arrest and while he was still in the Alexandria jail, Ames managed to send a fax to one of his old friends in Moscow. It was addressed to Tomas Kolesnichenko, the *Pravda* correspondent he had met and shared many liquid lunches with while they were both stationed in New York. This was the same man who the CIA believes first identified Ames as a possible traitor. Now the spy asked the Russian to come and visit him in jail, and Kolesnichenko duly made his plans to come over in September. It is extraordinary that Ames was not only allowed the use of a fax in jail but that he was allowed to use that fax to communicate with a man both the Agency and the FBI suspected of being a KGB agent. Not only that, but the communication was not detected, and it was only by chance that the FBI learned of the impending visit.[29]

Today, all the FBI will say about the episode is that "they did try to contact him. We have some suspicions that there was an intelligence purpose to it, but they did not succeed."[30]

Questioning of Ames continued at the maximum-security federal penitentiary in Allenwood, Pennsylvania, where he had been moved on August 11. His questioners wanted the extra time to review areas previously covered with him and to compare his version with information they were gathering from other sources. The sentencing of Rosario Ames, initially scheduled for August 22, was delayed until September 23 at the request of attorneys on both sides.

Meanwhile, Rosario had fallen out with Bill Cummings, her lawyer. Still unable to accept her guilt, she felt that he had betrayed her and was collaborating with the prosecution to ensure that she would not get a fair hearing. There is no evidence to support her beliefs, but Rosario dismissed Cummings. Her mother found the money to hire John Hume, another prominent Washington attorney with considerable court experience. In advance of her sentencing, Hume organized an exceptionally sympathetic portrayal of Rosario, which included an interview in jail that appeared in *The Washington Post*. There was an equally sympathetic interview with Diane Sawyer on ABC's *Primetime Live*.

Neither interview made the slightest difference to the original plea bargain when the sentencing finally took place on October 21. Mark Hulkower alleged that Rosario—at least in the FBI recordings—never even broached the subject of Rick's stopping his activities, instead asking him to be careful or inquiring whether the money was there. And he asserted that increasingly during her incarceration she had taken less and less responsibility for the role she played in her husband's activities.

Hume pointed out that no tapes had been made of their conversations in the first few months after she learned of his espionage, adding that in Colombia a wife cannot be prosecuted for knowing about the crimes of her husband.[31] These points were developed further in articles in *Semana* and in *The Washington Post*, where Rosario asserts that she signed the income-tax forms and other papers without examining them because "when it comes to finances, I am useless."[32]

Judge Claude M. Hilton sentenced Rosario to sixty-three months with the eight months spent in the Alexandria Detention Center credited to her record.[33] With this credit and time off for good behavior, Rosario could be released in three years and eight months. At the hearing, she asked to be sent to the prison in Danbury, Connecticut, so that she could be near Kennedy Airport and her son could fly in to visit.[34] There is some chance that the cost of flying Paul to America from Colombia may be eased by the Russians.

Rosario spends most of her time working in the jail's education department teaching inmates Italian and Spanish and acting as a translator. Her mail is censored and she claims she has received no communication from outside and has no plans to see her son, Paul, who simply thinks that she is away for a while and will soon return to Colombia. Despite the wealth of evidence that she has read in the newspapers and the numerous interviews she has seen with Rick, Rosario remains completely convinced that she is a victim not a villain.

"The more I learn, the more I realize I was totally duped in the whole affair," she said.[35]

This inability to come to terms with her spying and Rick's betrayal of her continues to eat away at her mental stability and she is prone to bouts of acute depression and crying. She plans to write her life story, a process which perhaps might allow her to address the reality of her own role in embracing the profligate life that Rick's spying brought home. Some officials think the SVR will make good on the $1 million to $2 million they told Ames they were holding for him and use it to help his wife, but neither Rosario nor Rick has any evidence that this is likely to happen. It would be illegal for either Rick or Rosario to financially benefit from their spying, but as Paul lives outside America and is now a Colombian citizen, the Russians could pay him and there is nothing that the federal authorities in the United States could do about it. The Russians have a long history of staying loyal to their spies and traditionally work hard to get them out of jail. There are some CIA agents currently in jail in Russia, including some betrayed by Ames, and it may be that the Russians will try to exchange them for him. However, there have been no overtures from the Russians to the American government thus far.

With the Ameses jailed and the hunt for the mole over, there was just one final act to be completed before the Feds could get on to other business. The FBI believed that Ames had been paid $2.7 million by the Russians, but despite all their investigations, they managed to recover only $750,000. The FBI believes that it has gotten all the money that can be regained, and that there are no secret accounts hidden somewhere for the day when Rosario gets out of jail.[36] But in a final effort to squeeze the last cent out of the estate, in December 1994 the government put up for auction the goods they seized in the February raid on the house.

It made for a tawdry end to what had been the last great spy case of the Cold War. At the auction house in Smyrna, Georgia, the thirty-eight lots attracted the attention of spy enthusiasts and the simply curious. On offer was the mix of second-rate goods for which the Ameses had paid premium prices in blood money. Bidding was brisk, with a number of choice items—a Cartier watch, diamond earrings, and a Lalique glass fish—going to Bob Slack, the owner of Great Gatsby's, a local antiques shop. Convinced that his customers would pay a premium for Ames-related material, he went on to pay $600 for a pen, $500 for a Swiss Army knife, and $1,400 for a jewelry assortment including a bear pendant. The auction brought in a total of $36,400.[37]

"It's the greater fool theory," said Slack. "There's a greater fool than us that's going to buy it."[38]

Now the real work of assessing the damage Ames caused to American intelligence and the aftereffects of his spying could begin. While Rick Ames was a tawdry individual with few, if any, redeeming qualities, the spying he did and the time it took to uncover it exposed so many examples of gross ineptitude and bureaucratic inertia in the intelligence community that he was to act as the most important catalyst for change since World War II.

SEVENTEEN

Whitewash Wednesday

When James Woolsey became DCI in January 1993, he expected his tenure to be one of evolutionary change. He planned to continue the progress made by Bob Gates in restructuring the CIA after the Cold War, and he felt he could contribute significantly by making the Agency more open and more accountable to the first Democratic administration in twelve years. He seemed the ideal man for the job. He had chaired a panel set up by Gates that had looked at the future of space-based intelligence systems; he was a lifelong Democrat and knew many of the other members of President Clinton's cabinet; he had worked as an arms-control negotiator during the Reagan and Bush administrations and so had a good understanding of the Russians; and he was a successful lawyer who brought to Langley all his considerable analytical skills.

Before he was sworn in as DCI, Woolsey met with Gates, who had held the position since 1991. The two men discussed the most pressing issues that the newcomer was likely to find on his desk during his first few months on the job: Russia, North Korea, Iran, and the growing threat of Islamic militants around the world. There was no mention of Rick Ames. This was hardly surprising, as Gates knew almost nothing about the case. By the end of 1992, the DO had still failed to inform the DCI that the most important molehunt in the Agency's history was not only under way but had narrowed its focus to one man, Rick Ames.

What Gates knew about the case amounted to very little. At the time he left the Agency in 1989 to become deputy national security adviser, he was aware that the investigation into the 1985–86 compromises had essentially stalled. Work was still being done, he knew, but it was getting nowhere.

"If someone were to ask me in January 1989 'Where does this case stand?' I would have said 'They are working hard, they are worried, we have a handful of compromises we can't explain and people are working on it.' "[1]

When Gates returned as DCI in 1991, he asked to be briefed on the progress of the investigation and was given essentially the same answers he had heard two years earlier. There had been little progress, although the possibility that the sources had compromised themselves or that they had been betrayed by Clayton Lonetree had been dismissed. The focus now was on the hunt for a mole. But even that limited knowledge did not provide Gates with any sense of the damage that had already been done by the spy working inside his Agency. On the contrary, the DO maintained the fiction that all was well with the SE Division and that sources continued to deliver prime intelligence.

By the time the search had narrowed and begun to focus on Ames at the end of 1992, there was still no effort to inform Gates that it was likely the CIA had been harboring a man who would at the very least cause serious embarrassment to the Agency. The first Gates knew of the existence of Rick Ames was when he read about his arrest in the newspaper.

"What I can't grasp is why, by the Fall, Winter of '92, '93, no one came to tell me 'we've got the man, we don't have our court case yet, but we're pretty sure we know who it is.' "[2]

What is even more surprising is that once the extent of Ames's perfidy was revealed, the information was as fresh to Gates, a career CIA officer and former DCI, as it was to the rest of the public. Along with some other senior CIA officials, he had known of the compromises in the mid-1980s, but only in the most general terms. He had no idea that the SE Division had been virtually shut down, that every important operation in the Soviet Union had been compromised, and that the identities of many, if not most, of the covert operators in the DO had been handed over. That amounted to a wholesale rape of the CIA and was nothing like the isolated series of problems that he had believed was being investigated.

The rivalry between the Directorate of Operations and the Directorate of Intelligence is legendary, with the covert operators believing the analysts have little understanding of their work and devalue the product they bring home. Gates, of course, had made his career in the DI, and so there was some natural antipathy in the DO against him. But that alone cannot account for the clear lapse in communication, the insistence on keeping within the narrow confines of one branch of American intelligence the knowledge that would affect the lives and economic well-being of thousands in the community. The reality is that there has not been a director from the DO for twenty-five years, and there have been only two directors from the DO since 1963. The Ames scandal has almost certainly assured that in the future all DCIs will come from outside the Agency.

"Why didn't they tell me? The only thing I can think of is that, after November, when I announced that I intended to retire, that maybe they decided to wait until a new director came in. It's pretty thin gruel. They knew long before that. They also knew that I'd have been awfully tempted to fire the head of the counter intelligence staff and the DDO for their failure to tell me and keep me apprised of the investigation."[3]

It was not until late in the spring of 1993 that Woolsey was informed that the investigation might be coming to a close, and by then, his reputation as an effective DCI was already in trouble. Woolsey's standing in Washington was to be of critical importance in the debate that followed Ames's arrest, because he was the point man for all inquiries regarding the performance of the CIA during the investigations. It was he who had to explain the actions that had been taken and the lessons that had been learned. In all of these areas, Woolsey was found wanting.

From the very beginning, Woolsey fell victim to the chaos of the early days of the Clinton administration. It is the custom that the DCI has a daily audience with the president, making the early-morning drive from Langley to dangle some choice tidbits hot off the satellite or fresh from some particularly sensitive source. Politicians tend to have a fascination with some of the more arcane aspects of intelligence and are frequently seduced by the sometimes astonishing technology that the CIA has at its disposal. These meetings were a way for successive DCIs to gain access to the inner circle, and because the meetings were usually at the start of the day, have a key influence on the course of the political debate. But President Clinton's schedule was a shambles. It was difficult to get an appointment, and even when one was arranged, it was frequently broken by a harassed president who always said yes and never understood how to carve up his time.

Clinton was surrounded by young supporters who had fought a successful election campaign and now had positions of great power in the White House. To many of these children of the 1960s and 1970s, who had been brought up on the excesses of the Casey years and history lessons about Vietnam, the CIA was the enemy. The Agency was seen as one of the last bastions of the Cold War, filled with plotters, murderers, and people who broke the law. This attitude also affected the influence that Woolsey was to have in the White House.

The administration had been swept to power on a tidal wave of idealism. This time, officials were convinced that they were going to change things for the better. There was a high moral purpose to everything which brooked no opposition, and anyone who gainsaid what those involved saw as the powerful forward momentum of the administration became part of the problem and not part of the solution.

Woolsey, the careful lawyer, saw his role as the messenger of the intelligence community. It was his job to tell officials the unvarnished truth as he and his officials believed it to be, based on the best available current intelligence. This meant that when there was bad news or contrary information to impart, he did not hesitate to pass it along. And there was plenty of it about.

The administration believed that Boris Yeltsin, the president of Russia, was the single most important figure in Russia. Strobe Talbott, the deputy secretary of state and the administration's Russian expert, believed that support for Yeltsin was critical if Russia was to survive the reform process intact. The Agency disagreed, arguing that Yeltsin was a drunk who was in poor health and had only a tenuous grip on power. Clinton, a neophyte in foreign policy, sided with Talbott and came to see his soft approach to Russia to be one of his great foreign policy successes.

In 1993, Haiti emerged as a foreign policy challenge for the administration that was much closer to home. President Clinton had pledged to support the return to power of exiled President Jean Bertrand Aristide, who was widely feted in Washington as a symbol of democracy. The

Agency had a very different view of him and a CIA report was leaked to the press that portrayed him as a drug-taking murderer with a long history of mental problems—all allegations that Aristide denied. The substance of the report was undermined when it was revealed that some of the facts were wrong and came from unreliable witnesses. Woolsey was held accountable and was seen as irresponsible.[4]

Then came North Korea, where the Agency was placed squarely against the State Department and the White House in a conflict over the country's alleged secret program to make nuclear weapons. The CIA and DIA were both convinced the intelligence proved that the North Koreans had already developed one nuclear device and were well on the way to making several more. The State Department thought that this information was bogus, a complex disinformation campaign designed to lure America into negotiations that would result in trade concessions and the opening of diplomatic relations.[5] The crisis was resolved after the Clinton administration gave the North Koreans virtually everything they had been seeking. This has allowed the North Koreans to keep the nuclear weapons that Woolsey claimed they had already developed, although the Pyongyang regime has promised to cease all work on future nuclear devices.

There were other irritants, too, such as the poor intelligence available about the role of the gangs operating in Somalia, inadequate information about Japanese foreign policy, and a dispute about whether or not Gerry Adams, the leader of the Irish Republican Army, should be allowed to visit America.

The result of all this was that Woolsey became increasingly isolated within the administration. There were constant rumors that he was about to be fired, with some foreign intelligence services reporting his imminent demise to their headquarters several times during both 1993 and 1994. Administration officials took their signal from President Clinton, who saw Woolsey less and less. There were no regular briefings, and Woolsey was frequently ignored at cabinet meetings as Clinton went around the table sounding out the views of his officials.[6]

As if that were not enough, Woolsey, who had been easily confirmed as DCI by the Senate Intelligence Committee, developed a difficult and often sour relationship with Congress. In his first closed-door session with the Senate Intelligence Committee in April 1993, Woolsey surprised the lawmakers by pounding his fist on the table and accusing them of "decimating" the intelligence budget. He argued that far from needing to be cut, the budget should actually be increased.[7]

This confrontational attitude was completely out of line with the prevailing sentiment on the Hill and caused considerable animosity between Woolsey and the congressmen on the intelligence committees in the House and the Senate. In particular, Senator Dennis DeConcini, the chairman of the Senate Intelligence Committee, who had supported Woolsey's nomination, quickly turned against him.

"I thought Woolsey's reputation was good, but later on I became leery of his performance, for the Agency's good and for the nation's," he said. "Woolsey, like other political appointees, wants to be well received. He has not really cut back the budget, as promised, hoping to save or reverse the cuts the Hill has requested. Perhaps Woolsey is popular at the White House for what he has done, but I don't think so."[8]

With such a powerful enemy in place on the Hill, Woolsey was to find it impossible to manage his own agenda without there being a constant series of leaks from Congress, which undermined his stature even further. However, once Ames had been arrested, it was clear to Woolsey and to his advisers that he needed to take strong action. He ordered Frederick Hitz, the CIA's inspector general, to launch his own investigation into the handling of the Ames case and ordered a detailed damage assessment to be prepared by the Agency under the command of Richard Haver, the director of the intelligence community management staff.[9] At the same time, both the House and the Senate intelligence committees decided to launch their own inquiries.

On March 15, 1994, Woolsey laid out what have become known as "post–Ames" procedures to enhance internal security at the CIA. Among the rules implemented were new and more rigorous requirements of financial disclosure; the freezing of the promotion process until individuals could be more appropriately scrutinized; and the routine reexamination of polygraph exams.[10] All of these recommendations had been made years earlier by the Senate Intelligence Committee, but only after the magnitude of Ames's betrayal began to be known did anybody put these obvious and fairly simple safeguards in place.

On May 3, President Clinton signed Presidential Decision Directive 24, establishing a National Counter Intelligence Center under a senior FBI officer, thus taking the authority for its own CI away from the Agency for the first time. This directive didn't change any of the legal relationships between the intelligence and law enforcement communities, but it established (1) a National Counter Intelligence Policy Board to "consider, develop and recommend for implementation . . . policy and planning directives for U.S. counter intelligence"; (2) a National Counter Intelligence Operations Board to discuss and develop from an operational perspective matters to be considered or already under consideration by the Policy Board; and (3) a National Counter Intelligence Center to serve as the interagency forum for complementary activities among CI agencies.[11] Michael Waugespack, an FBI agent, took charge of the Counter Intelligence Center in August 1994.

In theory, the new bureaucracy should help remove the threat of any more Aldrich Ameses operating within the intelligence community. But Clinton and Woolsey's critics argue that by simply shuffling the desks, little of substance has yet been done. What matters now are the policies and procedures that the various new structures decide are necessary and how they are implemented.

The CIA's internal assessment swiftly revealed that Ames had indeed been the best source the Russians had ever had inside American intelligence. Just how bad the security leaks had been was revealed largely by Ames himself in a series of debriefings conducted three times a week, first at the Alexandria Detention Center and then at Allenwood Penitentiary, where Ames is serving his sentence.

"It's like turning over rocks," said Richard Haver. "Each rock has more and more crap under it."[12]

Ames admitted that his "access to information and knowledge of the Soviets was such that I could get virtually everything that I wanted."[13]

On July 15, Woolsey was sent a thirty-two-page classified study from a panel of outside experts that he had asked to give him a preliminary assessment of the Ames case. It made for gloomy reading. Because Ames was rated a "poor" recruiter, the study said, he was assigned to the CIA's Counter Intelligence Center, which at the time was considered a dumping ground for CIA underachievers.

"The directorate of [CIA] operations regarded the Counter Intelligence Center as a place that poor performers could be sent because they could not do much harm," said panel chairman Jeffery H. Smith, a former Senate Intelligence Committee staff member. "It was like a bank concluding that because one of its officers had performed poorly, he should be put in charge of the vault."[14]

Smith and his colleagues, including National Security Adviser Brent Scowcroft, former Defense Secretary Harold Brown, and former FBI Counter Intelligence chief W. Douglas Gow, had a critical effect on Woolsey's thinking about the need for reform, which he spelled out two days later in a speech in which he proposed a number of changes:

1. Managers throughout the Agency will become "responsible for the overall performance of their employees—seeing that employees who have problems get counseling and that security concerns are referred to the Office of Security and the Counter Intelligence Center.

2. "An Office of Personnel Security will be established to combine security and personnel files on individual staff that previously had been kept separate, and people in sensitive areas will undergo repeated security assessments.

3. "CIA computer security will be overhauled, and access to sensitive information, including the names of agents, will be reduced. A fundamental assessment of the entire structure and operations of the Directorate of Operations will also be conducted.

4. "Two study groups will 'strip bare and evaluate the Directorate critically' and will provide Woolsey with further recommendations."[15]

These measures were all necessary. What is surprising is that an organization whose very existence depends on watertight security should not already have such checks firmly in place. Any competent business organization faced with competition from rivals in the market would have such security controls as a matter of routine. The truth of the matter is that the Agency had become slack, convinced by the apparent inability of the KGB or SVR to penetrate its own organization that such a thing would never happen. That arrogance is exactly what every officer in the field is trained to avoid because hard experience has taught that a moment of relaxed security is the moment when sources are compromised and agents are killed. It is a pity that lessons learned in the field were not brought back and applied with equal vigor at home.

To add to Woolsey's woes, he was hit by yet another blow, this time in the form of a sexual discrimination lawsuit by Jeanine Brookner, one of his most trusted employees. The suit is important because it played into the growing impression on the Hill and among senior administration officials that Ames was just the most visible symptom of a deep malaise within the Agency.[16]

At one time, Brookner appeared to have it all. A successful case officer who had recruited a number of excellent sources in Asia and Latin America, she was appointed the CIA's first woman station chief, in Jamaica in 1989. It was a fine accolade for a career that had started in the Philippines in the 1970s when she had done the impossible by infiltrating the Communist Party and recruiting a number of sources—a feat that had not been believed possible for any American, man or woman. But when she assumed her role as station chief, she had taken on the men under her supervision, and her twenty-three-year career, which once made her a role model for thousands of women in American intelligence, was over. She was banished to a low-level clerical job at Langley, a victim of what she claims was the rampant sexual discrimination in the Agency. What made the case fascinating was that, for the first time, the court papers, although heavily censored, shed light on a world usually hidden in total darkness. What was revealed was a male-chauvinist nightmare of drunkenness, drug-taking, and wife-beating, in which the mentally unsound serve alongside the corrupt to produce a parody of the intelligence community that is far more bizarre than anything a novelist might imagine. It is difficult to believe that in this apparently lunatic world the CIA could ever spy successfully against anybody.

Brookner, who used the alias Jane Doe Thompson in her court papers, alleged that when she tried to stop the worst excesses she found among her subordinates, the men under her command turned on her and claimed that she in turn was a drunken seductress. The papers also claimed that the subsequent investigation by the CIA's inspector general, which relied *entirely* on evidence from people she had disciplined, effectively ruined her career.

The trouble began in September 1990 when "Joy," the wife of the deputy chief of station, reported to Brookner that she had been beaten by her husband in front of her three-year-old child. The man, known by the pseudonym "Harold," choked her until she collapsed. Brookner confronted the man, and he confessed that he had been beating his wife for the preceding five years. As required by Agency regulations, Brookner filed a report to Langley. And then knives were drawn. No action was taken against Harold but he moved to blunt any possible investigation by lining up some of his cronies to swear that it was Brookner and not he who was guilty.

Then there was "Arnold," a former Marine and the station intelligence assistant, who was ranked in the lowest five percent of his career category and was having an affair with the wife of another government official. At a Christmas Eve dinner party in 1989 at Brookner's home, Arnold grabbed her daughter-in-law in the kitchen, kissed her and stuck his tongue in her ear, and then fondled her at the dinner table. He had also threatened to kill the men who guarded his home and had been forced to see a psychiatrist for treatment.

"Ralph" had been using the CIA's counter narcotics Jeep for his personal business, and when he was stopped by the police for speeding, he stopped, handed over his identity card, and then drove off.

"Fred," the station liaison officer, had a consistent record of renting villas to meet his sources. Regulations required that these locations should be modest one-bedroom dwellings, and questions were asked when it turned out he had been filing for reimbursement on the rental of a three-bedroom villa. The subsequent investigation by Brookner revealed that on one occasion, instead of meeting a source, he had taken his son and various friends on a Caribbean holiday he charged to the CIA.

Finally, there was "Rachel," a committed romantic who appeared to suffer a nervous breakdown when her boyfriend returned to Florida. Even in this CIA station she caused a stir by insisting on coming to work in her slippers and having temper tantrums at her desk. She, too, had to see a psychiatrist.

This group alleged that Brookner was a heavy drinker. They alleged that she had made unwanted sexual advances to a junior CIA officer by "continuously approaching him" but never making physical contact. They alleged that in her house in Jamaica she "sometimes wore brief shorts and thin T-shirts with no perceptible underwear . . . or a long tee shirt with no perceptible or very skimpy underwear" that "made some men believe she might make a pass at them."

"These men never would have used these false allegations, which emphasize drinking and sexual provocation, against a male chief of station, because drinking and sexual prowess are not considered derogatory behavior for a man at the Agency," said Brookner.

In her defense, Brookner claims that not only did she never make a pass at anyone, but she doesn't even own the type of clothes described, not least because she had had open-heart surgery and so always wore high-necked clothes to hide the scar.

"I habitually wear underwear—a statement so obvious and consistent with my character that it is revolting to have to comment on it," she said. "Although I do not even own the type of clothing described in the report, if wearing regular shorts and a T-shirt off-duty is wrong, then most women and male officers serving there could be accused of improper conduct."

The CIA officers also accused Brookner of falsifying her overtime records by claiming an hour's overtime on Christmas Day for delivering a present to a government contact and for claiming ten hours' overtime on Thanksgiving for preparing and cooking a turkey for contacts. She was also accused of having permitted the unauthorized use of a CIA helicopter for an Agency party.

"I'm surprised these allegations could gain any credibility or momentum," said Glen Holden, the American ambassador in Jamaica at the time. "I was proud of her and I think our country should be proud of her."

In fact, the allegations themselves were so trivial that they are almost laughable. But the CIA is a huge male-dominated bureaucracy and they were taken seriously enough to be the subject of a yearlong investigation by the Agency's own inspector general. He found that she should receive counseling for alcohol abuse, that she should repay $150 in overtime, and that there had been no misuse of the helicopter.

However, the inspector general never noticed that every one of those making a complaint against Brookner had been disciplined by her. He also appeared to overlook the fact that, until the complaint, every single performance report received by Brookner had been outstanding and that after an attack of hepatitis she had always been a light drinker.

In one of the court documents, Brookner claims that she had "been the target of unwanted sexual advances from various Agency males, including, but not limited to, an ambassador assigned to the CIA Director's office, two division chiefs and various chiefs of station and operations directorate branch chiefs.

"I did not report these sexual advances because I knew I would be committing career suicide if I did."

The Brookner case is just one graphic illustration of the discrimination that appears rampant in the American intelligence community. A study in 1991 revealed that 45 percent of the women in the CIA believe they had been sexually harassed at work. They claimed that because of the secrecy that is part of the intelligence culture, the CIA had remained isolated from the social pressures that have brought changes in the workplace throughout the nation. The study, known as the "Glass Ceiling Report," recommended that managers be made aware "of the pervasive fear that employees have regarding filing grievances and making complaints without reprisal."

The CIA began by defending the suit, claiming that it had "valid nondiscriminatory reasons for all the actions it has taken." But the CIA did admit that Brookner might be able to produce "evidence of discrimination sufficient to establish" a case. Her lawyers saw this apparent contradiction as clear evidence that they were on the winning side, which indeed proved to be the case. The CIA eventually settled the suit in December 1994 by paying Brookner $410,000.

Frederick Hitz, the CIA inspector general, completed his report assessing the Ames case and the nearly nine-year-long investigation that led to Ames's capture, in late September. An unclassified version was published on October 21, 1994.[17] The report, which relied on interviews from 300 witnesses, found that institutional loyalty and indifference helped protect Ames, particularly in the Directorate of Operations, which employs approximately six thousand officers. The report identified more than a dozen active or retired officers who either ignored warnings or overlooked complaints against Ames.[18] It also noted that the Agency's security and counter intelligence operations repeatedly failed to follow up on indications that Ames might have been the mole they sought.[19]

The bungling of the investigation was increased by Agency personnel who simply refused to act. In 1989, after Ames had returned from Rome, a CIA employee reported to Ames's superiors that he was spending excessive amounts of money. The Office of Security investigation of his sudden wealth foundered when CIA officials disagreed on whether they could request his private bank and brokerage records. About the same time, the station chief in Bogotá balked at trying to track down whether Ames had inherited money through Rosario's family. The station chief said it would divert too many resources from the station's main task of going after drug dealers, and that it would require bribing someone to get her father's will.[20]

Ames is described in the IG report as "not going anywhere and no one cared." The report criticized the internal bickering, noting that in the Agency there is "ambiguity" about who is in charge in cases of suspected traitors within the CIA. It discussed the lack of "senior attention" to security and counter intelligence issues, attention that could have provided resources to investigators without taking other DO case officers away from their normal tasks. This lack of interest is ascribed in the report to the excesses of James Angleton, whose endeavors ruined the careers of numerous case officers in the 1960s and 1970s. The report also noted that counter intelligence information on Agency employees was not shared within the Agency and was not passed to the FBI, or was passed on with great reluctance.

The truth is, as the report pointed out, that with less infighting within the CIA and between the Agency and the FBI, Ames might have been stopped much sooner. As early as the mid-1980s, the FBI researched its files of photos of people going into the Soviet Embassy, finding several of Ames on occasions that he had not reported to his superiors. The FBI also found that Ames deposited large amounts of cash into his bank accounts either on the same days these unreported visits took place or shortly thereafter. (Louis Freeh, the FBI director, later ordered an investigation into the FBI handling of the Ames case, which will focus on the period in the mid-1980s when Ames's illicit contacts with the Russian Embassy were noticed but not followed up. If any FBI agents are found to have failed to follow regulations, it is likely that Freeh, who is a tough disciplinarian, will take firm action.) There was also a deficiency in the handling of personnel assignments, with a finding that Ames should have been a potential suspect by 1989, but that he still received important assignments afterward.[21] And Ames was unexpectedly given access to a computer system when he was at the CIC that gave him information on many agents the DO was running.[22]

The inspector general's report criticized the 1991 polygraph as not being well coordinated, because the polygraphers who administered the poly to Ames "did not have full and effective access to what was then known about him."[23] Furthermore, the Agency's clandestine division took more than a year to forward the concerns about Ames to its Office of Security. At that juncture, the Office of Security assigned a single investigator to the case, an inexperienced man in his twenties who put the investigation aside entirely for months to concentrate on his classes in intelligence.[24]

In testimony before the House Intelligence Committee after the IG report was released, Woolsey provided additional details of some of the problems with Ames that were left unattended over the years. Hugh E. "Ted" Price, counter intelligence chief from March 1990 to December 1990, failed to "jump on the ball" [sic] and pursue leads indicating that Ames was the key suspect by not devoting more people or resources. Although ranked 197th out of 200 officers at his grade, Ames was placed on a CIA promotion panel, a position that allowed him to do "substantial damage" because he had access to sensitive files.[25] Despite the alcohol abuse, sloppy operational and financial accounting, undisciplined behavior and poor judgment, Ames never received a single letter of reprimand during his thirty-two years with the Agency. And the only note in Ames's record about his alcoholism was from the station chief in Mexico City. Moreover, Ames was not transferred out of counter intelligence after marrying Rosario, as recommended by the operations directorate.[26] "Nobody wanted to take on the task of seeing what the problem was," said Woolsey.

About the same time Woolsey presented the IG report, the inspector general, Frederick Hitz, told a closed session of the Senate Intelligence Committee that Ames "had a long history of 'no enthusiasm, little regard for rules and requirements, little self-discipline, little security consciousness, little respect for management or the mission, few good work habits, few friends and a bad reputation in terms of integrity, dependability and discretion. Yet his managers were content to tolerate his low productivity, clean up after him when he failed, find well-chosen words to praise him and pass him on with accolades to the next manager.' "[27]

After the release of the 400-page classified IG report, Woolsey took a number of disciplinary steps. Although the IG had recommended disciplinary action against twenty-six CIA officers, he sent "severe" letters of reprimand to only four DO officials and "light" reprimands to seven others. Only one of the first group is a current Agency employee; the rest are retired. All of these officials except for one (an Office of Security official who coordinated Ames's 1991 re-poly) are DO employees. Retired officials will be barred from contract work; current officials will not be promoted or given performance awards for periods of two to five years.[28]

Other than Ted Price, the current DDO, who received a mild reprimand, none of the names of those disciplined were revealed. Unnamed CIA sources said the other names included the former DDO, Thomas Tweeten, the current CIA station chief in London; Milton Bearden, the station chief in Germany, who was about to retire; Alan Wolfe, Ames's supervisor in Rome; Burton Lee Gerber, the deputy IG and a former Soviet Division manager; Gardner Hathaway, a retired chief of the Agency's CI division; and Clair E. George, the DDO when Ames began spying.[29]

Bearden's case had been complicated by a fax that had been sent to the Senate Intelligence Committee in April in which it had been alleged that he had been Ames's mentor and that he had warned Ames that he was under suspicion of being a KGB mole. The "poison fax," as it came to be known, caused the launching of a major new inquiry. Eventually it was concluded that the fax had been a hoax.[30]

Other reprimands went to Richard Stolz, a former DDO; Alan Wolfe, a retired station chief in Rome; Jack Gower, a deputy station chief in Rome; and William Phillips, a Washington field office chief during the period when Ames contacted Soviet Embassy officials.[31] Most of these reprimands were given because the individuals did not give enough time or attention to the investigation under way to find the mole or because as Ames's superiors they had treated him too leniently. "Ames was, by all accounts, a mediocre case officer who failed as a recruiter but who worked well in an office, partly because of his writing skills."[32]

Woolsey had forbidden awards or promotions for two to five years for people involved in the Ames case, but Frank Anderson, head of the CIA's Near East Division, and John MacGaffin, the second in command of the DO, gave Milton Bearden an award on September 29, the day after Woolsey's order was announced. Woolsey demoted the two officials, both of whom retired rather than take the demotions.[33] Jack Devine, another of Ames's supervisors in Rome, was appointed MacGaffin's successor and was thus in line to succeed Ted Price, who was expected to take early retirement in 1995. Devine was not given a reprimand, as was his predecessor in Rome, Alan Wolfe, because he had tightened up administrative procedures over case officers while in Rome.[34]

Woolsey also cited numerous people he thought deserved praise. These were "the principal investigator—dogged and determined for seven hard years; the officer who moved the task from the analytical to the investigative stage and whom the IG report credits with revitalizing the CIA investigation; the researcher who established the links between Ames and the missions that were compromised; the two FBI officers who worked tirelessly to maintain the link between the CIA's and the FBI's parallel efforts; the financial analyst who uncovered the flow of funds; the investigator who conducted a thorough background check of Ames that helped put the pieces of the Ames puzzle together; the officer who continued to raise questions about Ames's unwillingness to file reports of the contacts he had with Soviet officials; and the individual who came forth and expressed her concern about Ames's unexplained wealth."[35] Paul Redmond, who for so long had been leading the campaign for a thorough molehunt, was promoted to be special assistant to the director for counter intelligence. He is now responsible for implementing many of the post-Ames reforms.

Woolsey's lenient reprimands caused outrage on Capitol Hill and in the media. Senator DeConcini commented that Woolsey's "is a very inadequate response to negligence in the biggest espionage case in the CIA's history. To me there's a huge problem here that you're not going to get at by leaving some of these people in place. It'll take dramatic reorganization to change the culture, the good old boys' club that protected this guy, promoted him and gave him sensitive positions."[36] To other critics on the Hill, Woolsey's action seemed too "judicial"—too evenhanded and not like the kind of action a CEO would take whose firm had just lost "half its production." Senator Howard Metzenbaum called for Woolsey's resignation.[37]

In response to the criticism that more people should lose their jobs, Woolsey responded that "some have clamored for heads to roll in order that we could say that heads have rolled. Sorry. That's not my way. And in my judgment, that's not the American way, and it's not the CIA way."[38]

The minimal rebukes of those responsible for the Ames debacle had the reverse effect of that intended by Woolsey. Far from improving morale within the Agency, at Langley the announcement was dubbed Whitewash Wednesday.[39] Everyone recognized that the Ames case was a watershed and that if firm action was not taken, there would simply be more ammunition for the intelligence community's critics who had long argued that intelligence should either be abolished or reduced in size and budget.

Even within the Agency, there was a great deal of unhappiness that Woolsey did not take stronger action. There was a recognition that for the greater good it was necessary to set fairness aside and in effect have a purge, not so much to placate external critics but to begin to instill the notion of accountability and responsibility in lower-level officers.

"In my own view, I think a new DO should have been appointed from outside and probably two or three other senior-level changes made. You cannot have a catastrophe of this magnitude . . . it isn't enough to just kind of rewrite some procedures and rules and say 'We'll do it differently next time.' One of the consequences of the Howard case is that I don't think anyone was fired. At some point you just have to say enough is enough."[40]

Even the victims felt that Woolsey's punishment was unfair.

"Look, I don't think there's anything more boring than self-pity," said Milton Bearden. "The Ames case was botched from the beginning. I mean, Christ, when you have the president in the Rose Garden complaining about major intelligence leaks to the Russians and the failures in the CIA because of one of its own employees, that shows a total breakdown of communications between the DCI and the White House. Whoever was responsible for that briefing did not serve the president well. Woolsey let the situation become a cannibal feast as it got rolling.

"If Fred Hitz and his gang could have keelhauled somebody, they would have, but the fact that the IG report didn't mention anyone or two or three people in particular who were responsible shows that there wasn't just one or a few specific people who had messed up. I mean, hell, it doesn't take a genius to see that of three severe reprimands, two went to people already retired, one went to me, who was about to retire, and the seven light reprimands all went to currently serving employees; there clearly wasn't any single person—or a few people—they could blame. What really pisses me off is Woolsey's comment—referring to me—that 'If he were still around, I certainly would have fired him.' That was kind of cheap. It was a schoolyard stunt—like saying 'Yea, just come over and cross this line and I'll do thus and so,' but knowing that he wouldn't have to make good on his threat.

"Woolsey was just a weak director. This image that he stood up for the Agency—that he, like, had the buttons ripped off his uniform as he sacrificed his job is just ridiculous.

"Sure, there were a lot of things along the way that could have been done better, like the '91 re-poly. But you know, we knew about the house and the Jaguar, and the house, well, the fact that it didn't have a mortgage was unusual, but not all that unusual. The argument that the money could have come from a well-to-do South American family was also possible. There're any number of people down there who would like to get married and green-carded and come to the U.S. The argument that the money had come from Rick's wife as part of the dowry was not at all unusual. What people haven't stopped to say is 'Congratulations that you caught Rick.' "[41]

In the same speech that announced the reprimands, Woolsey said that he was pursuing five key initiatives in the light of the Ames case, similar to the ones he had announced earlier in the year. These included establishing the position of special assistant and ombudsman for counter intelligence and security to oversee all aspects of CI, including revisions in the polygraph program and coordination between security and CI; requiring training for all senior CIA officers, making sure senior management and those being considered for management have training in CI; establishing the Office of Personnel Security; and changing the procedures for advancement and promotion in the DO.[42]

Both the House and the Senate committee reports were equally damning, with the Senate laying more blame on the CIA and the House putting greater emphasis on the FBI while still putting most of the responsibility on the Agency. Both had a long list of recommendations for reform, and both argued that Woolsey had failed to adequately address either the reforms required of the intelligence community or the punishment for those guilty of allowing Ames the freedom to operate with such devastating effect for so long.

Finally, on December 29, 1994, Woolsey resigned, beaten down by the months of anguish over Ames and almost entirely isolated within the administration. In the ritual exchange of letters, there was no attempt by Clinton to persuade Woolsey to stay.

"Jim Woolsey has been a staunch advocate of maintaining an intelligence capability that is second to none," Clinton said in his statement. "Jim Woolsey deserves the gratitude of all Americans."[43]

It was a sad end to what had been a humiliating experience for a man who had come into office filled with good intentions. Instead, he had become yet another victim of Rick Ames, the man who now saw himself as the conductor of the orchestra that was demanding the wholesale reform of the American intelligence community.

EIGHTEEN

Reform or Die

As Rick and Rosario Ames faded from the public's consciousness, the impact of the case was still being felt in the corridors of Washington. First there were the jokes. One, which circulated through the intelligence community toward the end of 1994, went like this:

"Who is the Enemy?"

STATE: "There are no enemies."

CIA OPERATIONS DIRECTORATE: "We know who the enemy is, but telling you would endanger the source."

CIA INTELLIGENCE DIRECTORATE: "We wrote about who the enemy is and what they might do, but management politicized the conclusions."

DEFENSE INTELLIGENCE AGENCY: "We wrote the same thing CIA–DI did, but by the time it got through the review, the enemy had come and gone."

THE NATIONAL SECURITY AGENCY: "We know who the enemy is and what they choose to do, but you aren't cleared for that code word."

MARINES: "Doesn't matter. Mess with the best, die like the rest. Do you like John Wayne movies?"

FBI: "The CIA."

The Ames case has bred a new cynicism about the roles and missions of American intelligence that is very different from the prevailing view that existed at the end of the Cold War. Then there was a sense that any change to the roles and missions of the intelligence community should be evolutionary. Now revolution is in the air.

"The CIA is in peril," said Bob Gates. "And if the Agency doesn't take radical action, some of which may not be 'fair,' the whole thing could be in very serious trouble, and the same thing is true of the clandestine service. I think the clandestine service is a unique asset for the American government, but it has been totally discredited at this point in terms of Congress, in terms of the White House, in terms of the American people. Something has to be done to restore confidence in the institution."[1]

These are very strong words indeed from the same man who set the American intelligence community on an evolutionary course of reform immediately after he was sworn in as DCI in November 1991. That month, President George Bush signed National Security Review Directive 29, which called for a comprehensive review by the executive branch of its future requirements for the intelligence community. At the time, the intention was that the results of the executive branch survey would provide a framework for the reorganization of the intelligence community to meet new challenges up to the year 2005.[2]

For the first time, twenty different government agencies ranging from the Department of the Environment to Commerce, State, and the Department of Defense were required to give their priority requirements from the intelligence community into the next century. They were asked to look at the problem not simply from the perspective of what they had traditionally received from the CIA or any other intelligence agency but from the point of view of what they would like to receive in the future. Each government agency was asked to list its priority needs, which would then be matched against the available resources. As long as the Threat, in the shape of the Soviet Union, still existed, there was no difficulty in working out the requirements, which each year were simply an evolution of those of the year before. Now, however, new enemies needed to be identified and priorities assigned to them. It was here that the consumer of intelligence could play a part. The purpose of this review was not only to embrace the different government departments in the reform process but also to help convince the CIA's enemies in and out of government that there was real reform going on; that the Agency was going to respond to the needs of the consumer rather than remain isolated at Langley, providing information that the CIA in its infinite wisdom felt the policymakers should see or might like to see.

At the beginning of 1992, as the task forces went to work, Gates defined the problem this way: "I think that 'enemy' might not be the right word in all cases, but clearly we're interested in the activities of countries that don't abide by international agreements, whether they have to do with economic affairs, or the surreptitious sale of nuclear reactors, or ballistic missiles. We're clearly interested in the activities of drug kingpins and the governments that allow them to operate, or in the activities of governments that are resisting them, to see where we can help. I think the regime of Saddam Hussein is an enemy. I think that the government of a country and its leader that will brutally and ruthlessly destroy a passenger airline in flight is an enemy of civilized nations. So I think that there are certain categories of behavior on the part of certain governments that certainly make them the focus of attention—those who support terrorism and the terrorist groups themselves, for example. On the other hand, there are other areas in which there is a collective sense of the need to know more. I think the Congress is interested in our doing more on some issues like the social and economic implications of things like pandemics like AIDS or in doing more on the environment."[3]

With policymakers charged with identifying their needs, Gates also set up fourteen task forces to examine the community's capabilities. They were charged with investigating these areas: imagery; human intelligence, known as HUMINT; management; coordination overseas; openness; real-time electronic intelligence; support for military operations; publications; coordination with law enforcement agencies; politicized intelligence; and internal communications.

Of the reports the task forces submitted to Gates, the group focusing on imagery was particularly critical of the way satellite imagery is gathered and dispersed. "A major shortfall is the piecemeal planning, separate organizations . . . concentrating on specific segments . . . no single entity in charge of overall process . . . no firm mechanism to coordinate between them . . . relatively limited knowledge of many operational military users of what capabilities are available . . . lack of effective access by operational commanders . . . limited ability to disseminate imagery to field echelon commanders . . . need for a single architect. . . ."

This damning report recommended establishing a National Imagery Agency, which would absorb the Defense Mapping Agency, the National Photographic Interpretation Center, and the National Reconnaissance Office. This recommendation was vehemently opposed by the Pentagon, which did not want to see one of its most valuable and resource-rich assets taken away. But as a result of tough negotiations between the CIA and the Pentagon, the Central Imagery Office (CIO) was created to control all U.S. satellite operations. Under the deal, the CIA got the major responsibility for designing satellites that use images, including both photography and radar satellites, while the Air Force retained the lead responsibility for electronic eavesdropping systems. All other agencies with an interest in overhead acquisition systems, including the DIA and the NSA, have now ceded control in these areas to the CIO. However, existing agencies such as the Defense Mapping Agency, survived the changes.[4] Although these changes looked fine on paper, little has actually happened since they were announced. The Pentagon management has been able to fend off most of the attempts to interfere with its control over any of the satellite systems under its command.

In response to the findings of the task forces, Gates outlined a series of sweeping changes for the CIA, which were put in place while he was DCI. He focused on numerous areas: attitude, organization, and work product.

1. To increase the value of intelligence provided to policymakers, Gates called for greater discussion of alternative scenarios in assessments, greater autonomy for parts of the Directorate of Intelligence to respond directly to policymakers' requests, and systems put in place to try to improve the contact between analysts and outside agencies so that the intelligence product was relevant to their needs.

2. To address the sensitive concerns about the politicization of intelligence, he approved a study of management practices in the

Intelligence Directorate, measures to reduce the seemingly infinite layers of the review process, an allowance for alternative views in the product, the appointment of an ombudsman to deal with complaints of politicization, and the erection of barriers between the analysts in the DDI and the covert-action people in DDO.

3. To improve communications between the community and policymakers, a computer- and video-based information system was altered so that it would allow those with clearance to access information without the need to generate volumes of paper.

4. Gates established the National Human Intelligence Tasking Center, managed by the DDO, to coordinate all human intelligence requirements across every intelligence agency. With representatives from the Department of Defense and the State Department, the center is charged with deciding which agency is best suited to achieve a particular task at the minimum risk.

5. Agency employees had complained for years about the stifling nature of the intelligence bureaucracy that seemed to suppress initiative. Gates mandated that annual evaluations should take into account how much effort each manager had made to encourage employees to speak out about ways to improve the collection and management of intelligence.

6. To strengthen centralized coordination and management, he established a new management staff directly responsible to the DCI and headed by an executive director of community affairs. This new position carries with it broad responsibility for managing both programs and budgets on a community-wide basis to establish clear divisions of labor, cut out duplication, and improve coordination. The consequence of this was to bring under the DCI responsibility for the funding of *different agencies*, and this was approved in the 1993 Intelligence Authorization Act.

Until these reforms were put in place, the National Intelligence Council (NIC) had been the department within the Agency responsible for

carrying out long-range assessments for the CIA. While its function remained essentially unchanged, Gates moved the NIC outside the CIA,
along with all the national intelligence officers responsible for producing
the national intelligence estimates (NIE). This meant its brief was
broader, helping to form the foundation of American foreign policy. To
further enhance the independence and status of the NIC, other agencies
responsible for producing analysis, such as the Joint Atomic Energy Intelligence Committee, the Weapons and Space Intelligence Committee,
and the Science and Technology Intelligence Committee, were also
transferred out of the CIA to the NIC. The Intelligence Producers Council, which formerly reported to the National Intelligence Production
Board, was renamed the National Intelligence Production Board and
also placed under the NIC.

The NIC's chairman became a member of the National Foreign Intelligence Council, which is responsible for allocating resources within the
intelligence community. A new position of vice chairman for evaluation
was established to act as an overseer of the assessment and NIE process.
His job is similar to that of the chairman of the Joint Intelligence Committee in Britain, which is to oversee the final product, look at past assessments, and make sure that lessons are learned and improvements
made.

In addition, a second vice chairman for estimates was created to take
charge of the estimating process and to implement the changes in the analytical process that the other task forces had recommended. In particular, he or she ensures that different points of view are canvassed and
incorporated into every assessment so that a clear distinction is made between estimates and fact and the known and the unknown. The idea
behind these changes was to reduce criticism of the intelligence community for being too bold in its analysis when the factual information does
not support the conclusion and to reduce politicization of its recommendations. Through these changes, Gates had addressed many of the
needs of the policymakers who use intelligence data. Nonetheless, refin-
ing the product did not guarantee that it would result in offering the
kinds of certainties that each administration and members of the Congress wanted. In truth, these certainties, as Bill Webster explains, are not
what intelligence was designed for:

"We in the intelligence community often talk about the difference between mysteries and secrets. Secrets are knowable, if you're good, you can find out what the secret is. The mystery is a little more difficult if not impossible. You can't know what someone is going to do before they know what they are going to do. And that's a mystery. The mysteries are part of the area of limitation. The users of intelligence should not look to us for the kinds of things we don't do as well. We are not a 'not for prophet' agency."[5]

During this period, the community also recognized, for the first time, the critical role that open-source material plays in intelligence gathering. Gates appointed an open-source coordinator whose job is to catalogue all open-source holdings within the community and to design a system that will allow everyone across the community to have access to the open-source database.

The Gulf War had raised a number of concerns about the lack of tactical intelligence delivered by the CIA. As a result, the Agency established the new post of associate deputy director for operations for military affairs and an associated Office of Military Affairs. This office was designed to coordinate the work between the CIA and the Pentagon down to an operational level to ensure that the intelligence community has a better understanding of the military's needs while the military also knows more about the Agency's capabilities. The newly created Central Imagery Office also established a comprehensive operational image architecture, which would integrate satellite and other imagery to allow battlefield commanders to keep up-to-date with developments on the ground.

All these moves presupposed that the mood of the country and in Congress remained in favor of a steady approach to reform; that the intelligence community was basically not broken and so there was no real need to fix it. But despite the reforms of the Gates era, the intelligence community remains structurally little different. While the budget for intelligence will steadily decline from its current level of $28 billion (of which the Agency absorbs around $3 billion) to around $22.5 billion by 1997, the organizations remain the same. Although the precise figures have never been published, one estimate for the size of the intelligence community is that the CIA employs around 20,000 people, with 6,000 in the DO, and fewer than 2,300 in the DI. The DIA numbers 5,000 employees, the Air Force 16,000, the Army 14,000, the Navy around 10,000; Intelligence and Research within the State Department 300, counter intelligence within the FBI, 2,500, and the NSA 40,000. Including a large number of contract employees, the total number of people working in American intelligence is around 110,800.[6]

This enormous figure seems increasingly inappropriate for the scale of intelligence operations required by the country in the aftermath of the Cold War. After all, even before Ames, Congress had been critical of waste and duplication in the intelligence community. In a report accompanying the Fiscal Year 1991 Intelligence Authorization Bill, for example, the Senate Intelligence Committee stated that "the tactical and national intelligence communities appear to be excessively isolated from one another, leaving each free to pursue self-sufficiency in their particular realms. Military commanders seek self-sufficiency through organic systems and organizations on the argument that national systems cannot be relied upon for support. The national community, likewise, emphasizes its peacetime missions and pays scant attention to the commander's needs."[7]

Senator Dennis DeConcini had been on the Intelligence Committee for eight years and was its chairman until January 1995. His views reflect those of many people in the federal government: "In the 1980s, I found a culture that was not productive and didn't advance the gathering of intelligence. There was a perception that the intelligence community would get a generally large appropriation for its work and assumptions that this money would generally keep flowing and that the Agency didn't need to explain why it needed the money it did."[8]

He, too, noted the duplication of intelligence functions, not only in the areas they covered, but also in using the exact same sources to generate information. DeConcini also argued that the politicization of intelligence was largely created by William Casey, and resulted in decisions that had been extremely costly to the nation. During the early 1980s, for example, the Agency portrayed the Soviet Union as "an immense economic power," a judgment that was used by the Reagan administration to sell Star Wars and the military buildup of that period. The Iran-Contra debacle, several years later, was yet another instance of Casey and the Agency's overstepping its intelligence-gathering function and the need for reform.

That view is largely mirrored by others with DeConcini's extensive knowledge of the intelligence world. "The community is too large," said Brent Scowcroft, the former national security adviser and a member of Woolsey's commission investigating the Ames case. "It needs some fairly extensive squeezing. The DIA, for example, was designed to replace the service staffs but it didn't and the service staffs have grown along with the DIA. Some even think we should have a separate clandestine service responsible for HUMINT and the functions currently of the NRO but that doesn't seem like a good idea.

"As we look at the restructuring of the intelligence community, one of the lessons at the end of the Cold War is that there needs to be a shift in the balance between technical and human intelligence."[9] This single issue has bedeviled the intelligence community since the first satellite went into space.

But it is the nature of wider reform that is the question now facing both the intelligence community and the Clinton administration. The most critical question that needs to be answered is: Is the CIA necessary? During most of the period while Ames was doing his damage, the CIA was operating without eyes and ears on the ground inside first the Soviet Union and then Russia. Despite the fact that Ames had destroyed their networks, business continued pretty much as usual within the CIA. Neither Bill Webster nor Bob Gates noticed any particular fall-off in intelligence coming out of the DO to the DI for analysis. In effect, the DO was able to disguise the lack of intelligence from human sources so that the gaps were invisible.

All of this was happening at one of the most important points in modern history: Communism in the Soviet Union and the Warsaw Pact countries was collapsing and the Soviet Union itself was about to implode. It was a time of great excitement but also a period when policymakers all over the world were very nervous. Out of the chaos, a new dictator—a Hitler or a Stalin, perhaps—might emerge to launch World War III; or economic instability might become so great that the whole world's economic order might be threatened. It was a time when human intelligence could have been critical.

The fact that almost nothing of significance emerged from the SE Division for a lengthy period raises the question whether it serves any purpose at all. For successive DCIs, the product from the DO has always been only one part of the complex puzzle that goes into creating a whole intelligence picture. There are other agencies and other sources of intelligence, from satellite imagery to intercepted conversations. It has always been recognized that the DO had trouble recruiting quality sources, in part because the American culture militates against such activity and in part because the promotion process at the Agency has never been designed to cope with the vagaries of agent running.

The emphasis in American intelligence in recent times has been on gathering information by technical means rather than from human sources, and as a result, the amount of money devoted to human intelligence has declined in relation to that given to electronic and signals intelligence. The technical capability of the Americans is the envy of every other intelligence service, but it has been achieved at the expense of HUMINT. The ambitious career intelligence officer is hardly likely to focus on recruiting and running agents if he or she knows that progress up that particular promotion ladder is strictly limited. The HUMINT issue is also affected by the fact that the CIA, along with every other part of the American government, is afflicted with "short-termism"—a sense of urgency that drives attention from one crisis to the next. Targeting agents, recruiting them, and running them is not just a very hit-or-miss business; it can take years to develop a single effective source. In Oleg Gordievsky's case, it was six years after he had been spotted as a likely recruit by MI6 before the first approach was made. One of the striking things about the level of emphasis placed on HUMINT at the Agency was that it was so low. Or, rather, that whereas there were constant demands for HUMINT, there was little expectation that the demands would be met, with the exception of the occasional spectacular coup such as Top Hat.

The imbalance between human and technical intelligence-gathering is a long-standing one within the Agency and was institutionalized during the Carter administration. During the critical period of Ames's spying and the dissolution of the Soviet Union, the lack of ears and eyes on the ground resulted in a skewed view of the events occurring there. "The reality is that the only good clandestine reporting that we got out of the Soviet Union had to do with weapons systems and military planning," said Gates. "There was relatively little political reporting.

"There were a lot of Soviet political things that we now know that we didn't really appreciate at the time. And the reality is that a number of the sources we had appear to have been doubles, and by the time Ames really got going, our best military agents had been compromised by Howard. The difficult part is how you say, yeah, this reporting was worth doing, the effort was worth taking.

"I'll tell you, the biggest surprise to me in all of this is how many Soviet operations we had. We had a hell of a lot more than I thought we did."[10]

There is some irony to this statement. After all, Gates, who was DCI during part of Ames's career with the Russians, seems less shocked by the weaknesses in the Agency he ran than by the strengths he never even knew it had. Gates's view also underscores the shortcomings of the SE Division. In fact, it had long been accepted within the CIA that the material produced by the SE Division was marked by occasional flashes of brilliance but was mostly low-grade intelligence. Even those within the Agency seemed to believe that it could survive without the SE's intelligence—as it did during a lengthy period while Ames was spying.

It is that kind of culture that Gates tried to develop in June 1992, when he created the National Human Intelligence Tasking Center, which had the specific brief of improving the CIA's HUMINT capability. It is still far too early to say whether or not that initiative will be a success. However, for it to work, there will need to be a significant change in long-held attitudes. Both Congress and the CIA will have to focus on HUMINT as a priority. Thus far, they have failed to do so. In the July 1994 Intelligence Authorization Act, for example, the House voted to cut the allocation for human intelligence because the Agency did not present a comprehensive plan for it for the next century.

Nonetheless, there is a general recognition, not just in America but in every developed nation, that human intelligence is going to be more important in the years ahead than at any other time in the recent past. The priorities that all intelligence agencies have—terrorism, proliferation of nuclear weapons, and drug trafficking—can be fully met only if there are sources on the ground providing the kind of information that can stop an attack or prevent a shipment.[11]

So far, only Gates has set out a coherent plan for the future, which he spelled out at a conference at the beginning of December 1994 and later made public in an article in *The Washington Post*.[12] His agenda has eleven main points:

1. The CIA should be cut and focus only on interests that are vital to national security—the former Soviet Union, China, regional powers and conflicts, terrorism, and nuclear proliferation. The Agency should no longer waste valuable resources on such marginal issues as the environment or population issues.

2. The DO should be re-formed to take account of the obvious failures that arose in the Ames case, including improving diversity of personnel, cutting bureaucracy, and encouraging initiative and responsibility.

3. Congressional oversight should be strengthened and term limits for members of the intelligence committees abolished. This would avoid the constant necessity of educating committee members about intelligence matters and avoid repeating the mistakes of the Ames case, where Congress was not informed of the damage done to the CIA in the 1980s.

4. The duplication of military intelligence should be eliminated, and almost all competitive analysis among the DIA, the CIA, and other agencies should be stopped. The only exceptions to this would be situations involving foreign military threats and the proliferation of weapons of mass destruction. The CIA would stop maintaining a database on foreign armed forces and weapons, whereas the DIA would provide only tactical military intelligence.

5. The national and tactical intelligence programs should be consolidated to serve both the policymakers and the Defense Department.

6. The director of the DIA should be given a fourth star, made director of military intelligence, and given authority to create one intelligence organization to serve the armed forces.

7. The CIA would abandon all its paramilitary capabilities and pass them over to the Pentagon. The Agency should not be involved in military work that the armed services can do as well or better.

8. A National Imagery Agency should be created to place one person in charge of setting priorities for the full range of U.S. imagery-collection capabilities.

9. A system needs to be put in place to manage the wealth of unclassified information that is available. This would help the intelligence community gain access to information it now wastes time gathering and would also make available information to other interested groups such as universities and think tanks.

In explaining the system he envisions, Gates observed that "the funny thing is that my daughter, who is a student at Indiana University, has more access to more libraries from her college dorm than does an analyst at the CIA. What I envision is first of all a stand-alone unclassified computer network that ties together the overt collection of open-source material. And then I would tie the whole thing to Internet and then tie it into the National Library system. When a new requirement comes in from the policymaker, the analyst would first go to the open sources and then decide precisely what else is needed from covert collection."[13]

10. Policymakers must be forced to take a more active role in deciding the priorities for the intelligence community. This would help direct the tasks of every agency and ensure they remained focused on what was actually required rather than what the community thought it should provide.

11. The trend toward greater openness should continue so that the public and politicians have a growing and continuing understanding of the intelligence community, what it does, and how it does it.

These radical ideas, which have not been welcomed in the intelligence community, are the first articulation of what is certain to be a revolution that will unfold over the next five years. The architect of that revolution is likely to be Les Aspin, the former secretary of defense, who was appointed by President Clinton to head the President's Foreign Intelligence Advisory Board. In August 1994, as the full extent of the damage caused by Ames began to be appreciated, the president and Congress agreed to appoint a special commission, headed by Aspin, that would look into the future role and missions of the intelligence community. The seventeen-member commission will have the broadest possible mandate, despite active opposition from the CIA and other intelligence agencies. Nine members of the commission will be named by the president and eight by Congress, and it is due to report in March 1996.[14]

The commission will look at every agency and make recommendations for a wholesale restructuring of the intelligence community. It is likely that Aspin, a consummate Washington insider who has made no secret of his ambition to leave his mark on the city where he has spent much of his adult life, will look for radical solutions.[15]

The ideas that Gates has already discussed with Aspin provide a reasonable initial blueprint for action, but they do not go far enough to attack the underlying malaise that has infected the whole American intelligence community. What the Ames case has done is shine a bright light on the musty corridors of American intelligence—corridors that have been walked only by the privileged few over the last twenty-five years. What has been revealed is a stagnant bureaucracy and a duplication of effort that result in an astonishing waste of taxpayers' money.

During the Cold War, the focus of the intelligence community in America and among her allies was to understand the thinking of the political and military leadership in the Soviet Union and to gain deep insight into its military capability. The North Atlantic Treaty Organization required very early warning of any intention by the Warsaw Pact nations to attack NATO forces and also needed to know enough about the enemy's capabilities to be reasonably confident of winning a conventional or nuclear war. Back then, the allies believed that the Soviets could mount an attack with as little as ten days' warning; ensuring that there were enough intelligence assets in place to give that warning in time was very costly in terms of manpower and technology. Now not even the most pessimistic analyst in the Pentagon believes that the Russians could begin to launch a conventional war without their plans being detected at least a year—and, more probably, five years—before an attack could start. At the same time, the Warsaw Pact has disintegrated and there is no prospect of its re-forming, so the threat to NATO and to America has diminished by several orders of magnitude.

This is not to say that there are no economic, military, or political threats confronting the United States or the other developed nations. On the contrary, the ending of the certitude and stability produced by the superpower confrontation during the Cold War has allowed many new threats to emerge. There are a growing number of countries that either have or will shortly get a ballistic missile capability; a growing number of countries, such as Iran and Libya, that are developing very sophisticated chemical weapons; and others that are trying to develop a new genera-tion of biological weapons. Nuclear proliferation remains a problem, and such movements as the spread of Islamic militancy and the growth of ethnic tensions are certain to produce serious political and military problems in the years to come.

For all these threats, there is a strong requirement for timely and accu-rate intelligence to keep policymakers apprised of developments as they unfold. But these are different problems that require very different solu-tions from those that existed during the Cold War. There are no massed armies, no massive nuclear arsenals, and no serious prospects of global conflagration. Instead, there are a number of small, often very precise problems that require fairly precise solutions.

The intelligence organizations within each of the armed forces should be abolished and their work subsumed under the DIA, which should concern itself only with the production of military intelligence that is rel-evant to the tactics that the Pentagon will use in the deployment of peo-ple and weapons on the field. Individual commands would have DIA personnel attached to them and could employ some of their own per-sonnel, for purely tactical intelligence gatherings.

The existing institutions will, of course, argue that such a radical change would severely degrade the intelligence capability of the United States—an argument that is more about turf and budgets than about na-tional security. Today, those serving in different branches of the Penta-gon's intelligence services joke about the time spent working issues or pushing paper that has no relevance at all to the current requirements. For example, one elite naval intelligence unit is assigned to the National Military Command Center in the Pentagon to monitor Russian naval deployments. As the Russian navy has not been to sea in any significant numbers for more than four years and is today completely incapable of fighting any kind of surface war, the unit is wasting its time and its talent. But the numbers have to be kept up, and nobody wants to suffer cuts in personnel or funding.

In Britain, the Defense Intelligence Staff has already absorbed most of the military and naval intelligence capabilities. Cuts of more than 50 percent have recently been imposed in funding without a significant degradation of capability. There is no reason to suppose that what can work in Britain cannot work in America.

Much of the reduction in the Pentagon's intelligence staff could be made by eliminating the need for the collection of material that is readily available from open sources, and for the analysis of information that is frequently duplicated in other parts of the government. At the moment, the DIA, the CIA, and the State Department each has an analytical capability that frequently produces similar material. The government should establish a National Research Agency, which could act as a clearinghouse for all open-source material. The researchers would receive requests from the policymakers, gather the information that was available from open sources, and then assign the relevant parts of the intelligence community the task of delivering the clandestine components.

This would allow for the elimination of the DI at CIA, so that the Agency could focus only on the gathering of secret intelligence. It is striking to note that in Britain, MI6 operates its DO equivalent with around 360 people and the service does almost no analysis. Instead, that is carried out by a group called the Joint Intelligence Committee, which has twenty members who are able to call on information and intelligence from all branches of government in preparing their reports. Of course, Britain is not a superpower and has fewer overseas interests than America, but its intelligence analysis is routinely shared with America and is widely respected. So there is a model that has worked effectively for many years that could work in America as well.

These changes would eliminate the wasteful duplication of effort among the different government departments and intelligence agencies and allow for a single agency to act as a clearinghouse for requirements from policymakers. That in turn would help make the intelligence community more responsive to the needs of their consumers rather than simply deciding for themselves what they think would be best for the government.

The new National Research Agency would have the added benefit of becoming a national resource by producing information based on open-source material that would be available to companies, think tanks, and other interested parties who wished to get information that could help them in their work. That information could be provided free, or there could be a charge to help defray costs.

There are those who will argue that reducing the influence of the CIA and thus of the DCI and the intelligence community as a whole would be bad for the country. That need not necessarily be so. Clearly it makes no sense to have intelligence if it does not reach the highest levels of government. Under the new structure, the DCI should retain overall control of the CIA, the National Research Agency, and the DIA, as well as retaining his place in the cabinet and his access to the president.

This new structure would produce billions of dollars in savings and deliver an intelligence community that is designed to effectively meet the challenges of precision and speed that will be required in the next century. At the same time, much of the information that has been unnecessarily classified by the intelligence community would become available to business and the public. This would do a great deal to restore public confidence in the intelligence services while at the same time doing nothing to degrade a vital component of the national security umbrella that keeps America and her allies secure.

Any changes are likely to be fiercely resisted by those inside the community. But when the time comes for President Clinton to take on those vested interests, he should remember the experiences of Casey, Webster, Gates, and Woolsey, all DCIs whose plans to reform the CIA were frustrated by entrenched vested interests. The result of that intransigence was Rick Ames, a drunken loser who managed to destroy and kill everything he touched within the CIA. In the months and years to come, anyone who doubts the need for reform will have only to look at Allenwood Penitentiary, where Rick Ames will remain as a living lesson and a reminder of those who died because of his treachery.

APPENDIX 1

The Findings of the Investigation by the Inspector General of the CIA

The effort to find the source of the losses, which we have referred to as the mole-hunt, began in 1986. However, that effort was plagued after 1987 by senior management inattention and failure to apply an appropriate level of resources to the effort until 1991. For an extensive period of time between 1988 and 1990, the molehunt virtually ceased, despite information obtained from several Agency components in 1989 that should have focused attention directly on Ames. Factors that contributed to this delay included the Agency's reluctance to believe that one of its own could betray it and a continuing general distaste for the counterespionage function of investigating Agency employees. In 1991, the molehunt effort was rejuvenated, the FBI offered to participate, and the investigation gradually began to show results.

SOVIET CONTACTS

Ames was authorized to engage in contacts with Soviet Embassy officials in Washington in 1984, 1985, and 1986. Agency management failed to monitor his contacts with these officials more closely in 1985 and failed to pursue them adequately after they were requested by the FBI in 1986. This provided Ames with the opportunity to consummate the espionage he contemplated based upon his financial situation and the influence on his thinking that resulted from his prior contacts with Soviet officials in New York. If his failure to submit timely contact reports had been questioned vigorously at the time, Ames might have been told to break off the contacts or been caught in a lie regarding their nature and extent. Ames, albeit not the most trustworthy of witnesses, has said that he would have had a hard time explaining these contacts had questions been raised. If the contacts had been pursued as they should have, appropriate attention might have been drawn to Ames in 1985 or 1986 rather than years later. As it was, Ames ignored the request to report on the contacts and it was soon forgotten.

FINANCIAL INQUIRIES

The inquiry into the Ameses' finances should have been completed much sooner by CIC than the more than three and one-half years that the inquiry consumed. After it was discovered in 1989 by CIC that Ames had paid for his house in cash and moved large sums of money from abroad to domestic bank accounts, a full financial inquiry should have been undertaken by CIC and the Office of Security on a priority basis. This effort languished despite a December 1990 memorandum from CIC to the Office of Security requesting a reinvestigation of Ames on the basis of his finances and noting his potential link to the 1985–86 compromises. In addition, other available information was not correlated with the financial information.

POLYGRAPHS

The 1986 polygraph of Ames was deficient because the examiner failed to establish the proper relationship with Ames and did not detect Ames's reactions even though Ames says he had great apprehension at the time that he would be found out. The 1991 polygraph sessions were not properly coordinated by CIC with the Office of Security after they were requested. The polygraph examiners in 1991 were not given complete access to the information that had been provided to the Office of Security by CIC in December 1990 regarding Ames's finances and they did not have the benefit of the thorough background investigation that had been completed on Ames on the very day of the first examination session.

Once they had developed suspicions about Ames, the responsible CIC officers, especially with their Office of Security backgrounds, should have participated more aggressively and directly in Ames's polygraph. Since the polygraph was handled in a routine fashion, no CI emphasis was placed on formulating the questions or selecting examiners with the appropriate levels of experience. There was no strategy for the questioning and no planning how to handle any admissions he might have made. The result of the 1991 polygraph was to divert attention from him for a time.

PERSONNEL RESOURCES

In view of the number of Soviet sources that were compromised, insufficient personnel resources were devoted to the molehunt effort virtually from the beginning. The failure to request additional resources has been acknowledged by several of the key officials involved. Additional resources could have been used to systematically develop and narrow a list of potential suspects based upon employee access to the compromised cases. Prior to 1991, no formal lists of suspects based on access were created or reviewed. This was partly because access or "bigot" lists for the individual cases did not exist or were inaccurate. Although the investigation clearly had to be conducted with discretion, concerns about compartmentation must be balanced at some point against the overriding need to resolve the serious problems the compromises created. There clearly were more than three trustworthy and capable officers available in the Agency with the necessary expertise to assist in the molehunt effort. With more focused involvement by senior Agency management, additional personnel could have been added to pursue the financial inquiries and create a better mix of analytical and investigative skills.

DIVISION OF RESPONSIBILITY FOR
COUNTER INTELLIGENCE

The ambiguous division of responsibility for counter intelligence between CIC and the Office of Security and excessive compartmentation contributed to a breakdown in communication between the two offices, despite the fact that CIC was created in part to overcome such coordination problems. This breakdown in communication had a highly adverse impact on the Ames counterespionage investigation. There was a general absence of collaboration and sharing of information by CIC with the Office of Security at critical points in the reinvestigation of Ames in 1991. Office of Security officers who were assigned to CIC minimized the contribution that could be expected to be received from the Office of Security and their resulting failure to collaborate in fact produced the minimal contribution they expected. These problems and others persisted despite the fact that prior Inspector General inspection reports on Counterintelligence, the Office of Security, and Command and Control in the Agency pointed out the jurisdiction and communication ambiguities in counter intelligence matters.

SECURITY REINVESTIGATIONS

The lack of an effective and timely reinvestigation polygraph program in 1985, when Ames began his espionage activities, enhanced the breakdown of inhibitions that Ames had experienced and led him to believe that he would not be required to undergo a reinvestigation polygraph before his contemplated retirement in 1990. By 1985 the Office of Security reinvestigation polygraph program had fallen seriously behind its targeted five-year schedule and Ames had not been polygraphed for almost ten years. Although the Agency gave the program increased attention in 1985 and made a commitment to provide the resources necessary to maintain a five-year reinvestigation schedule, the hiring of new polygraph examiners created other problems, such as the need for increased management and supervision of inexperienced examiners. These problems were compounded by an exaggerated concern about the reaction of Agency officers and managers to adverse results from polygraph examinations. Employee, management, and congressional concerns regarding the intrusiveness of the polygraph led Office of Security management to soften the polygraph program and cater to "customer satisfaction," which seems to have meant not offending employees. These developments reduced the effectiveness and reliability of the polygraph program, which must be based upon an apprehension of the consequences of untruths, and encouraged employees and managers to resist the program.

DEFICIENCIES IN PERSONNEL MANAGEMENT

No evidence has been found that any Agency manager or employee knowingly and willfully aided Ames in his espionage activities. Allegations in the so-called poison fax, sent to the SSCI earlier this year, that the Chief of CE Division from

1989 to 1992 warned Ames regarding Agency suspicions about him appear to be without foundation. Many of the other statements made in the fax also appear to have been unfounded. That said, it is clear from comparing Ames's personnel file with the knowledge about him that was shared orally by employees and managers that Agency managers consistently failed after 1981 to come to grips with a marginal performer who had substantial flaws both personally and professionally. His few contributions to the work of the Agency were exaggerated while his deficiencies and cost to the organization were minimized and not officially documented or formally addressed. He had little focus, few recruitments, no enthusiasm, little regard for rules and requirements, little self-discipline, little security consciousness, little respect for management or the mission, few good work habits, few friends, and a bad reputation in terms of integrity, dependability, and discretion. Yet his managers were content to tolerate his nonproductivity, clean up after him when he failed, find well-chosen words to praise him, and pass him on with accolades to the next manager.

SUITABILITY FOR ASSIGNMENTS

Despite his deficiencies in performance, Ames continued to be selected for positions that gave him considerable access to highly sensitive information. In the face of the strong and persistent evidence of performance and suitability problems that was available, this access is difficult to justify. Our Report reviews most of these assignments in detail. While Ames's poor performance would probably not have led to termination of his employment, it did not justify permitting him to fill positions where he was perfectly placed to betray almost all of CIA's sensitive Soviet assets. Despite doubts about his performance and suitability among officials who previously supervised him, he was placed in positions that gave him access to the most sensitive Soviet sources. After a disastrous tour in Mexico, Ames was placed in charge of a counter intelligence unit that was responsible for Soviet operations, and it was there that he acquired much of the information he turned over to the KGB in 1985.

Ames was selected to participate in debriefings of Vitaliy Yurchenko, described by the Associate Deputy Director for Operations at the time as the most important defector in CIA's history. Little in his previous performance merited that selection and the task should have been reserved for the very best SE Division had to offer. His assignment to a sensitive position in SE Division after his return to Headquarters in the Fall of 1989 from Rome is inexplicable in light of the reservations about him that were held by the departing Chief of SE Division, who had considered Ames's Rome assignment as a means of getting rid of a problem employee.

Ames's selection in October 1990 to serve in CIC is hard to explain given the knowledge that was then available to SE Division's management and CIC regarding the 1985–86 compromises, Ames's work habits, his unexplained affluence, and the nature and scope of the access to information that he would have. His CIC managers had been warned that there was reason to watch him closely and certainly could have sought more specific information from their superiors in CIC. Once suspicions concerning Ames had crystallized in August 1992, when his bank deposits and contacts with the Soviets had been correlated and Agency management had been advised, he should have been placed in a position where his access would have been limited and his activities closely managed. No evidence was found that senior Agency managers were fully advised or that such alternatives were ever discussed by Agency management, and neither CIC nor the Office of Security played any role in decisions regarding his assignments until after the FBI investigation began in the spring of 1993.

APPENDIX 2

Recommendations of the Senate Intelligence Committee

Recommendation 1: The Director of Central Intelligence should revise the CIA's strategy for carrying out the counter intelligence function. The Director should institute measures to improve the effectiveness of counter intelligence to include (1) establishing as a requirement for promotion among officers of the Directorate of Operations, service in a counter intelligence or counter intelligence–related position during their careers; (2) establishing incentives for service in a counter intelligence position; (3) instituting effective and comprehensive counter intelligence training for all officers of the Directorate of Operations and for appropriate officers assigned elsewhere in the CIA; and (4) ensuring adequate access to ongoing foreign intelligence operations by those charged with the counter intelligence function. The Committee will make this a "special interest area" for purposes of oversight until it is satisfied the weaknesses noted above have been adequately addressed.

Recommendation 2: The Director of Central Intelligence should ensure that where evidence of suitability problems comes to the attention of supervisors, it is made a matter of official record and factored into the consideration of assignments, promotions, and bonus awards; that efforts are made to counsel and provide assistance to the employee where indicated, and, if the problem persists over time, the employment of the individual is terminated. The Committee will make this a "special interest area" for purposes of oversight until it is satisfied these policies have been instituted and are being observed within the Directorate of Operations.

Recommendation 3: The Director of Central Intelligence should, in particular, take prompt and effective action to deal with what appears to be a widespread problem of alcohol abuse by ensuring that CIA employees experiencing such problems are identified and are put into effective counseling and/or treatment. During this period, these employees should be suspended from their duties until they have demonstrated to a qualified professional their fitness to return to service. Should their problems continue, their employment should be terminated.

Recommendation 4: The Director of Central Intelligence should institute, consistent with existing legal authority, an "up or out" policy for employees of the CIA, similar to that of the Foreign Service, without waiting for the report required by section 305 of the Intelligence Authorization Act for Fiscal Year 1995, pertaining to the Intelligence Community as a whole. Chronically poor performance should be grounds for dismissal from the Agency. If the Director decides not to institute such a policy and does not provide a persuasive rationale to the Committee for his decision, the Congress should enact legislation requiring such a policy during the next Congress.

Recommendation 5: The Director of Central Intelligence should review and revise the performance appraisal reporting system of the CIA, to include a review of the factors upon which employees are rated and the grading system which now exists, to institute a system which reflects more accurately job performance. Where supervisors are concerned, their rating should include an assessment of how well they have supervised the performance and development of their subordinates.

Recommendation 6: The Director of Central Intelligence should revise the policies and procedures governing the operational activities of CIA officers to ensure that these activities are better supervised, controlled, coordinated, and documented.

Recommendation 7: The Director of Central Intelligence should establish procedures for dealing with intelligence compromises. At a minimum, these procedures should entail a systematic analysis of all employees with access to the relevant information and, if suspects are identified, provide an investigative methodology to determine whether there is evidence of unexplained affluence, unreported travel, unreported contacts, or other indicators of possible espionage. This type of systematic analysis should begin when a known compromise occurs, not after CIA has eliminated the possibility of a technical penetration, or after CIA has narrowed the range of possible suspects to one or two employees.

Analysis and investigation should be undertaken on the basis of access and opportunity, and should not be delayed waiting for evidence of culpability.

Recommendation 8: Pursuant to section 811 of the Intelligence Authorization Act for Fiscal Year 1995, the FBI should be notified immediately of any case where it is learned that an intelligence source has been compromised to a foreign government, regardless of whether the CIA believes at the time that there is a basis for an FBI counter intelligence or criminal investigation of a particular employee or employees. The CIA should also coordinate with the FBI subsequent investigative actions involving employees potentially involved in the case in order not to prejudice later criminal or counter intelligence activities of the FBI and in order to benefit from the investigative assistance and expertise of the FBI.

Recommendation 9: The Director of Central Intelligence should require that all employees assigned as counter intelligence investigators have appropriate training, experience, and supervision which ensures, at a minimum, such investigators will be familiar with, and know how to utilize, the investigative authorities available to the CIA and the FBI.

Recommendation 10: CIA management must ensure that adequate analytical and investigative resources are assigned to counter intelligence cases, and that other kinds of staff assistance (e.g., legal support, administrative support) are made available. In turn, those involved in these cases must ensure that their needs are communicated to their supervisors. The Inspector General of the CIA should periodically assess the counter intelligence cases of the CIA to ensure that adequate resources are being afforded to particular cases.

Recommendation 11: The status of significant counter intelligence investigations must be regularly briefed to senior Agency officials, including the Director of Central Intelligence. Such briefings should include an explanation of the resources and expertise being brought to bear upon a particular case.

Recommendation 12: The Director of the FBI should ensure that adequate resources are applied to counter intelligence cases involving the CIA and other federal agencies, and that FBI headquarters is apprised immediately of significant case developments which could form the basis for the FBI's opening an intensive counter intelligence investigation.

Recommendation 13: The Attorney General and the Director of the FBI should review the FBI's guidelines for the conduct of counter intelligence investigations to determine whether clearer guidance is needed in determining whether a subject of a counter intelligence inquiry is acting as an agent of a foreign power.

Recommendation 14: The Director of Central Intelligence should establish procedures to inform current and prospective supervisors about employees under suspicion in counter intelligence cases. While the need to protect the secrecy of the investigation is essential, as well as the need to protect the employees themselves from unfair personnel actions, the assignment of employees under suspicion without frank consultations at the supervisory level increases the likelihood of serious compromises and leads to conflict between CIA elements.

Recommendation 15: The Director of Central Intelligence should issue procedures to require, in any case in which an employee is under suspicion for espionage or related activities, that a systematic evaluation be made of the employee's access to classified information, and that appropriate and timely actions be taken to limit such access. While care must obviously be taken to ensure that such actions do not tip off the employee that he or she is under suspicion, the failure to evaluate the access of an employee in these circumstances may eventually result in damage that might have been prevented.

Recommendation 16: The Director of Central Intelligence should establish more stringent criteria for CIA employees serving on promotion and assignment boards, which, among other things, prevent the appointment to such panels of employees with poor performance records or records of suitability problems.

Recommendation 17: The Director of Central Intelligence should tighten polygraph procedures to make the polygraph more useful. Such procedures should include random examinations instead of exams at regular intervals, with little or no prior notice, and variations in the polygraph technique. These procedures should also ensure that polygraph examinations involving employees under suspicion are carefully planned and constructed, and that appropriate prior notification is made to the Federal Bureau of Investigation if such cases have potential criminal implications. In addition, the Director should review the policies applicable to the training, supervision, and performance appraisal of polygraph examiners to ensure that polygraph examinations are conducted in a professional manner and produce optimum results.

Recommendation 18: The Director of Central Intelligence should institute a fundamental reevaluation of the polygraph as a part of CIA's security program. As the Ames case demonstrates, the polygraph cannot be relied upon with certainty to detect deception. This necessarily puts far more reliance on other aspects of the security process, e.g., background investigations, supervisory reporting, psychological testing, financial reporting, etc. The DCI's review should also include a reevaluation of the use of inconclusive polygraph test results. Even where the polygraph does indicate deception, such information is often useless unless damaging admissions are also obtained from the subject. The Committee believes that if an employee with access to particularly sensitive information does not make such admissions but continues to show deception to relevant questions after adequate testing, there should be additional investigation of the issues in question to attempt to resolve them. Should such investigation fail to do so, the CIA should have the latitude, without prejudice to the employee, to reassign him or her to less sensitive duty.

Recommendation 19: The Director of Central Intelligence should reinstate the policy making persons leaving CIA facilities subject to random searches of their person and possessions, and require that such searches be conducted unannounced and periodically at selected locations. Such searches should be conducted frequently enough to serve as a deterrent without unduly hampering the operation of the facilities involved.

Recommendation 20: The Director of Central Intelligence should institute computer security measures to prevent employees from being able to "download" classified information onto computer diskettes and remove them from CIA facilities. In addition, existing policies for the introduction, accountability, dissemination, removal, and destruction of all forms of electronic media should be reevaluated. The ability of the CIA's security managers to "audit" specific computer-related functions in order to detect and monitor the actions of suspected offenders should be upgraded.

Recommendation 21: The Director of Central Intelligence should institute a policy requiring employees to report to their supervisor any instance in which a CIA employee attempts to obtain classified information which the CIA employee had no apparent reason to know. In turn, supervisors should be required to report to the CIA Counter Intelligence Center any such case where a plausible explanation for such a request cannot be ascertained by the supervisor.

Recommendation 22: The Director of Central Intelligence should institute new policies to improve the control of classified documents and materials within the CIA. In particular, the Directorate of Operations should undertake an immediate and comprehensive review of its practices and procedures for compartmenting information relating to clandestine operations to ensure that only those officers who absolutely need access can obtain such information. Further, the Directorate should establish and maintain a detailed, automated record of the access granted to each of its employees.

Recommendation 23: The Director of Central Intelligence should reexamine the decision to combine the Office of Security with the other elements of the CIA's new personnel center, and should ensure sufficient funding is provided to the personnel security function in Fiscal Year 1995 and in future years. The Director should also clarify the relationship between security and counter intelligence, specifying their respective functions and providing for effective coordination and cooperation between them.

APPENDIX 3

Recommendations of the House Intelligence Committee

Recommendation 1: The Committee recommends that hearings be held during the next Congress to monitor the implementation of all matters related to the security and counter intelligence initiatives that have been proposed in the aftermath of the Ames case and that the President's National Foreign Intelligence Program budget submission for fiscal year 1996 adequately fund these new initiatives.

Recommendation 2: The Committee recommends that the CIA's Inspector General should, within one year, undertake an inspection of the Counter Intelligence Center and the Office of Personnel Security. The Inspector General should place special emphasis on examining how the Agency has modified its procedures on the use of the polygraph to ensure that there is full coordination among the components involved in security and counter intelligence. The Director of Central Intelligence and the Director of the Federal Bureau of Investigation should also review the efforts of the National Counter Intelligence Center to ensure that these organizations are working cooperatively and that mechanisms exist to resolve problems promptly.

Recommendation 3: The Committee recommends that the Inspector General of the Department of Justice conduct an independent inquiry, similar to that conducted by the CIA's Inspector General, into its investigation of the loss of its assets in 1985–86, and its role in the cooperative effort later undertaken to explain the compromised CIA and FBI cases of that period.

Recommendation 4:   The test of the new organizational structures to deal with improving counter intelligence and personnel security will be whether they rectify recurrent problems in this area, especially the failure to resolve in a timely fashion allegations against government employees that raise security and counter intelligence concerns. The investigative process has often taken an inordinate period during which the individual may continue to have access to classified information. Such delay can no longer be tolerated. The Committee recommends that the Director of Central Intelligence establish procedures and guidelines for the timely resolution of these matters, including as necessary a procedure for forwarding certain cases to the National Counter Intelligence Board for disposition.

Recommendation 5:   The Committee recommends that the Director of Central Intelligence and the Director of the FBI jointly apprise, in writing, the intelligence committees, on a semiannual basis, of all open counter intelligence and counter espionage investigations each agency of the intelligence community has under way. In the 104th Congress, the Committee intends to develop legislation which will make this report a statutory requirement. The Committee also intends to consider legislation which will require notification to the Committee whenever assets are compromised and an investigation is begun.

Recommendation 6:   The Committee recommends that the Directorate of Operations (DO) retain responsibility for counter intelligence activities designed to penetrate foreign intelligence services. However, the counter espionage group at the Counter Intelligence Center needs to establish a cadre of trained investigators who could initially gather information in response to reports of possible espionage activities by CIA personnel and later work with agents of the Federal Bureau of Investigation in the conduct of cases arising from those leads.

Recommendation 7:   The Committee recommends that counter intelligence training at the CIA be improved. In particular, officers selected to participate in counter espionage investigations need to be well versed in modern investigative techniques, particularly those relating to the examination of financial data. To maximize the ability of CIA and FBI investigators to work together, CIA security personnel specializing in espionage cases should complete the FBI's counter intelligence training courses.

Recommendation 8:   The Committee recommends that the intelligence community develop an aggressive system for identifying problem employees for counseling and, if necessary, terminating their employment.

Recommendation 9:   The Committee recommends that the intelligence community's personnel evaluation and promotion systems be revised to ensure that marginal performers will be subject, at any point in their career, to a process which results in the termination of their employment.

SOURCES

On September 23, 1992, when the net was finally beginning to close on Rick Ames, I was sitting in Moscow having a congenial conversation with Yevgeniy Primakov, the head of the SVR, the Russian intelligence organization that had replaced the First Chief Directorate of the KGB. For his first interview since his appointment, we were sitting in a house not far from Red Square, which used to be a secret base for Lavrenti Beria, Stalin's confidant and one of the most ruthless leaders of the Russian secret service. The house is now a mixture of beautiful old wood paneling, baroque gilt scrollwork, and modern red plush velour couches.

For nearly ten years I had tried to get a visa to visit the Soviet Union and had always been turned down because I wrote about national security issues and in the eyes of the KGB that made me a spy. Now, with the collapse of the Soviet Union and the defeat of Communism, the doors had opened. Primakov said that he wanted to tell me just how the SVR was different from the KGB.

"First of all, we have repudiated the old ideological model we had before, which predetermined that there are permanent enemies and permanent friends. The old model predetermined confrontations and pushed to the background our country's national interests, which were sometimes sacrificed in order to give ideological support to our allies. Now we are not working against someone. We are working in defense of our national interest."

He went on to make an impassioned plea for cooperation with British and American intelligence on areas of common interest such as drugs and nuclear proliferation. After all, he said, America and Russia were no longer enemies and there was no longer any need to steal secrets from each other.

Of course, Rick Ames was continuing to spy for Primakov in exactly the same way as he had for Primakov's predecessors in the KGB. On the day Ames was arrested, I remembered that conversation and recalled, too, the skepticism with which Primakov's words had been greeted in London, Paris, and Washington. I wanted to learn more about Ames, to discover just why the Russians considered one man so valuable that they would risk their developing relations with their single most important supporter, the president of the United States.

After fourteen years reporting on national security issues for *The Sunday Times* and writing several books about terrorism, intelligence, and covert warfare, I had developed some understanding of the usually closed world of spies. When I first began trying to report on intelligence, I found it an impossible task. Sources were scarce, and often those that were prepared to talk proved unreliable.

Then I wrote *The Financing of Terror*, a book that looked at the money that helped finance the campaigns that were threatening democracies around the world. That book provoked some interest in the intelligence community, and a number of invitations to meet officials and talk about my findings followed. From there, a network of sources developed, sources that I was careful to nurture without compromising intelligence sources and methods.

Three years ago, by the time I came to write *The New Spies*, a book on the future of intelligence after the Cold War, many doors had opened. In the course of one six-month period in 1992 I interviewed not only Primakov but Bob Gates, then the director of central intelligence; William Sessions, then director of the FBI; Stella Rimington, the head of MI5; and Sir Colin McColl, the head of MI6. Such access would have been unthinkable just a few years earlier. No journalist had ever interviewed Rimington or McColl, and no foreign journalist had interviewed the serving heads of the CIA and the FBI.

As the end of the Cold War brought these intelligence officials out of the shadows to justify their existence, so the Ames case acted as a catalyst for the American intelligence community. Its critics saw Ames as a symbol of the need for reform, whereas the defenders of the status quo wanted to fight to preserve what was left of the intelligence community after the changes imposed at the end of the Cold War.

Finally, the people who had been involved in the hunt for the mole within the CIA had their story of frustration, failure, and ultimate triumph. Understandably, those who had finally brought Ames to justice wanted to see an accurate account reach a wide audience.

This background helped open many doors. In researching this book, I have been able to talk to past heads of the CIA and to previous FBI directors. I have also been able to speak with many current and retired CIA officers and FBI agents, all of whom were generous with their time and their memories.

To my surprise I found that some of the actors in this drama were actually old friends, such as Oleg Gordievsky—who was lucky to survive being betrayed by Ames—and Bob Gates. There are others, too, who walk through these pages who might perhaps not welcome being associated with me so publicly, but they all know who they are.

To prepare the basic story I was greatly helped by the outstanding work done by the Senate and House intelligence committees, which both launched comprehensive investigations into the Ames case. In addition, the inspector general of the CIA published an unclassified version of his report on the case. These three documents proved to be stunning resources, both detailed and accurate, and I have drawn on them extensively. It is worth mentioning, perhaps, that these three studies were read avidly by foreign intelligence agencies and are generally cited as models of how oversight of intelligence can work both effectively and publicly. This willingness to address failure and learn lessons for the future is one of America's great strengths.

In dealing with the covert world it is often difficult to check sources—frequently, getting the information in the first place is a miracle, let alone finding a second source to confirm it. In this case, I have been as careful as possible to sift through the wealth of material to check and then check again that the information included here is accurate.

I have supplied footnotes to allow those sufficiently interested to go back to published sources or to people I have interviewed to get additional information. This should also help put some of the information into context.

I have only rarely used direct speech. I do not like reporting speech unless it is recorded or it is corroborated by the person who is alleged to have made the statement quoted. Where there is direct speech I have either spoken to the person concerned or to at least two others who heard the words I have reported.

As a final check, the manuscript has been read by seven different people and agencies, and I have made every factual change that has been pointed out.

NOTES

CHAPTER 1 "THINK. THINK. THINK."

1. Unless otherwise specified, the information for this chapter comes from interviews conducted with FBI and CIA sources; interviews with Rosario Ames conducted between September 1994 and February 1995; An Assessment of the Aldrich H. Ames Espionage Case and Its Implications for U.S. Intelligence, Report of the U.S. Senate Select Committee on Intelligence, November 1, 1994; Criminal Complaint, United States District Court of Eastern Virginia, United States of America vs. Aldrich Hazen Ames and Maria del Rosario Casas Ames, February 21, 1994.
2. Interview with Mark Hulkower and Robert Chesnut, December 2, 1994.
3. Interview with Les Wiser, January 26, 1995.
4. Ibid.
5. Ibid.
6. Interview with William Rhoads, June 10, 1994.
7. Statement in U.S. District Court, Alexandria, Virginia, March 1, 1994.
8. Interview with Rosario Ames, September 21, 1994.
9. *Washington Post*, February 24, 1994.
10. Interview with a source who requested anonymity, November 9, 1994.
11. Interview with a source who requested anonymity, August 30, 1994.

CHAPTER 2 SOWING THE SEEDS

1. Interview with Professor Walker Wyman and Helen Wyman, August 15, 1994. Wyman knew both Jesse and Carleton Ames.
2. On May 23, 1955, Jesse Ames wrote his memoirs, which are essentially an account of his years as a teacher. It is unclear whether they were ever published, but a copy remains in the university library at River Falls.
3. Information from the University of Wisconsin–River Falls, Office of Public Affairs, August 1994; *Washington Post*, May 24, 1986.

4. Information supplied by the University of Wisconsin–River Falls.
5. Interview with Professor Silverstein.
6. Interview with Bennie Kettelkamp, August 25, 1994.
7. *Vanity Fair*, July 1994, p. 123.
8. *New York Times*, February 23, 1994.
9. Interview with Helen Wyman, August 15, 1994.
10. *River Falls Journal*, March 3, 1994.
11. *Chicago Tribune*, March 3, 1994.
12. Interview with Analu Jurgens, August 24, 1994.
13. *Chicago Tribune*, March 3, 1994.
14. *Vanity Fair*, July 1994, p. 123.
15. Ibid.
16. Ibid.
17. For detailed accounts of CIA operations of the period and particularly in Burma see John Ranelagh, *The Agency: The Rise and Decline of the CIA* (New York: Simon & Schuster, 1986), pp. 220–23; and John Prados, *Presidents' Secret Wars: CIA and Pentagon Covert Operations Since World War II* (New York: William Morrow, 1991), pp. 73–78.
18. Chippewa Falls News Bureau, February 24, 1994; interview with Professor Wyman, August 15, 1994.
19. Interview with Jane Wilhelm, August 18, 1994.
20. *Washington Post*, February 27, 1994.
21. An Assessment of the Aldrich H. Ames Espionage Case and Its Implications for U.S. Intelligence, Report of the U.S. Senate Select Committee on Intelligence, November 1, 1994, p. 6 (hereafter Senate Intelligence Committee Report).
22. Interview with Margaret Mims Hamilton, August 17, 1994.
23. Ibid.
24. Interview with Emily Horne Ray, October 30, 1994.
25. Interviews with Bob Enstad, August 24, 1994; Mark Wyman, August 15, 1994; Ann Guthrie, October 20, 1994; Margaret Hamilton, August 17, 1994; Kathy Strock Hartzler, October 30, 1994.
26. *Washington Post*, February 27, 1994.

CHAPTER 3 BEHIND THE SCENES

1. Interview with Robert Strang, October 6, 1994.
2. Interview with Mike Hrinda, October 25, 1994.
3. Interview with classmate who requested anonymity, October 17, 1994.
4. Interview with James Best, October 6, 1994.
5. Interview with Michael Einisman, October 5, 1994.
6. Interview with Robert Strang, October 6, 1994.
7. Senate Intelligence Committee Report, p. 7.
8. Ibid., p. 8.

9. Interview with Stephanie Zeeman, University of Wisconsin–River Falls archivist, October 25, 1994.
10. Interview with Hazel Eckard, August 26, 1994.
11. *Time*, March 7, 1994, p. 31.
12. Ibid.
13. *Chicago Tribune*, February 27, 1994.
14. *U.S. News & World Report*, July 4, 1994, p. 47.
15. Unclassified Abstract of the CIA Inspector General's Report of the Aldrich H. Ames Case, October 21, 1994, p. 18 (hereafter CIA IG Report).
16. Senate Intelligence Committee Report, p. 10.
17. An enormous amount has been written about Angleton's career. I have chosen to rely on three principal sources: Tom Mangold, *Cold Warrior* (London: Simon & Schuster, 1991); David Wise, *Molehunt* (New York: Random House, 1992); Anthony Cave Brown, *Treason in the Blood* (Boston: Houghton Mifflin, 1994).
18. Interview with Bob Gates, January 8, 1995.

CHAPTER 4   THE SEEDS OF DESTRUCTION

1. Unless otherwise specified, the information on the Fedorenko case comes from individuals intimately associated with the case who do not wish to be identified.
2. *Chicago Tribune*, February 27, 1994.
3. The best insight into Shevchenko's career comes in his own autobiography: Arkady N. Shevchenko, *Breaking with Moscow* (New York: Alfred A. Knopf, 1985).
4. *New York Times*, May 21, 1978; June 27, 1978; October 14, 1978.
5. *New York Times*, April 28, 1979; April 29, 1979.
6. *Washington Post*, April 29, 1994.
7. *New York Times Magazine*, July 31, 1994, p. 18.
8. Senate Intelligence Committee Report, p. 10; CIA IG Report, p. 19.

CHAPTER 5   COURTSHIPS

1. *Time*, March 7, 1994; *Chicago Tribune*, February 27, 1994; *Washington Post*, July 15, 1994.
2. Senate Intelligence Committee Report, p. 13.
3. Interview by Senator Dennis DeConcini, August 5, 1994, pp. 75–76 (hereafter DeConcini interview).
4. Senate Intelligence Committee Report, p. 13.
5. The best account of Courtship's work appears in Ronald Kessler, *Inside the CIA* (New York: Pocket Books, 1992), pp. 20–25; other accounts appear in Kessler, *The FBI* (New York: Pocket Books, 1993), pp. 68–69; and Mark Riebling, *Wedge* (New York: Alfred A. Knopf, 1994), pp. 349–50.
6. *Washington Post*, October, 19, 1994.
7. Interview with Rosario Ames, September 21, 1994.

8. Interview with Professor Ignacio Abello, September 15, 1994.
9. *People*, March 21, 1994.
10. *Los Angeles Times*, February 24, 1994.
11. *People*, March 21, 1994.
12. *Washington Post*, March 8, 1994; *Vanity Fair*, July 1994, pp. 120–28.
13. Interview with Professor Ignacio Abello, September 15, 1994.
14. Interview with Professor Carlos Gutiérrez, September 15, 1994; *Washington Post*, March 8, 1994.
15. *Vanity Fair*, July 1994, pp. 120–28.
16. Interview with Professor Greta Wernher, November 5, 1994.
17. Associated Press, April 20, 1994.
18. Ibid.
19. Ibid.
20. Interview with William Rhoads, June 10, 1994.
21. *Vanity Fair*, July 1994, pp. 120–28.
22. Associated Press, April 20, 1994.
23. Interview with Professor Carlos Gutiérrez, September 15, 1994; interview with Professor Greta Wernher, November 5, 1994; *Vanity Fair*, July 1994, pp. 120–28.
24. Interview with Professor Greta Wernher, November 5, 1994; interview with Professor Iqnacio Abello, September 15, 1994; *Washington Post*, March 8, 1994.
25. Interview with Professor Greta Wernher, November 5, 1994.
26. Interview with Professor Iqnacio Abello, September 15, 1994.
27. Interview with Professor Carlos Gutiérrez, September 15, 1994.
28. *Time*, March 7, 1994.
29. *Vanity Fair*, July 1994, pp. 120–28.
30. *Time*, March 7, 1994.
31. *Washington Post*, March 8, 1994.
32. Interview with Professor Carlos Gutiérrez, September 15, 1994.
33. Interview with Professor Ignacio Abello, September 15, 1994.
34. Interview with Professor Piedad Ponnet, November 1, 1994.
35. Interview with Rosario Ames, September 21, 1994; interview with Professor Ignacio Abello, September 15, 1994.
36. Interview with Rosario Ames, September 21, 1994.
37. Interview with Professor Carlos Gutiérrez, September 15, 1994.
38. Associated Press, February 23, 1994.
39. Interview with Rosario Ames, September 21, 1994.
40. Ibid.
41. Ibid.
42. *Vanity Fair*, July 1994, pp. 120–28.
43. *Washington Post*, September 24, 1994; Radiozurnal (Prague), August 25, 1994, in BBC Summary of World Broadcasts, August 27, 1994.

CHAPTER 6   SLEEPWALKING TO HELL

1. Interview with Rosario Ames, September 21, 1994.
2. Ibid.
3. CIA IG Report, p. 13; Senate Intelligence Committee Report, pp. 13–14.
4. DeConcini interview, p. 71.
5. Affidavit in Support of Warrants for Arrest and Search and Seizure Warrants, February 21, 1994 (hereafter Affidavit).
6. Senate Intelligence Committee Report, p. 16.
7. *Time*, March 7, 1994, pp. 28–34.
8. Senate Intelligence Committee Report, p. 17.
9. *Jane Doe Thompson vs. R. James Woolsey et al.*, October 25, 1994, p. 20.
10. *Newsweek*, September 26, 1994, p. 43; *Washington Post*, October 7, 1994.
11. James Woolsey, Statement to the Press, U.S. House of Representatives, September 28, 1994.
12. DeConcini interview, August 5, 1994.
13. Ibid.
14. Ibid.
15. Ibid.
16. *Sunday Times of London*, March 13, 1988.
17. *Washington Post*, January 29, 1995.
18. The details of Ames's early contact with his Soviet cutout, Sergey Chuvakhin, are taken from numerous sources. Except where otherwise cited, they are the DeConcini interview; *New York Times Magazine*, July 31, 1994, pp. 16–19; and the CIA IG Report.
19. DeConcini interview, p. 19.
20. Interview by Congressman Dan Glickman and Congressman Larry Combest, August 7, 1994, p. 7 (hereafter Glickman interview).
21. Statement of Fact in Support of the Indictment of Aldrich H. Ames (hereafter Indictment).

CHAPTER 7   THE FIRST CASUALTY

1. Gordievsky has written about his own life in Christopher Andrew and Oleg Gordievsky, *KGB, The Inside Story* (London: Hodder and Stoughton, 1990); and *Instructions from the Centre* (Hodder and Stoughton, 1991). Others have written about him in some detail, with a particularly accurate account appearing in Gordon Brook-Shepherd, *The Storm Birds* (London: Weidenfeld and Nicolson, 1988), pp. 266–79. In addition, the author interviewed Gordievsky a number of times between July 1994 and January 1995.
2. *The Listener*, March 1, 1990, p. 16.
3. *Sunday Times of London*, October 21, 1990.
4. Interviews with Oleg Gordievsky between July 1994 and January 1995.
5. Ibid.

6. *Ekstra Bladet,* June 24, 1994.
7. *Spectator,* March 5, 1994, p. 15.
8. Ibid.
9. Ibid.
10. Interview with Oleg Gordievsky, September 2, 1994. In fact, a number of those betrayed by Ames are still alive. But of the high-level sources betrayed by Ames, Gordievsky was indeed the only one to survive.

CHAPTER 8 "A COMMON, UNMARKED GRAVE"

1. *Time,* August 8, 1994, p. 32.
2. *Los Angeles Times,* February 4, 1990.
3. *Washington Times,* May 10, 1994; *New York Times,* January 23, 1994.
4. *Time,* August 8, 1994, p. 32.
5. *Los Angeles Times,* January 15, 1990; *New York Times,* January 23, 1990; *Washington Times,* January 15, 1990.
6. *Los Angeles Times,* February 4, 1990.
7. *Newsday,* January 28, 1990.
8. Peter Wright, *Spycatcher* (New York: Viking, 1987), pp. 272–73.
9. *Time,* August 8, 1994, p. 32.
10. Ibid.
11. Ibid.
12. Interview with James Nolan, October 12, 1994.
13. *Washington Times,* May 10, 1994.
14. *Washington Post,* March 6, 1994; *Washington Post,* April 29, 1994; *Daily Telegraph,* August 1, 1994.
15. *Fresno Bee,* August 1, 1994.

CHAPTER 9 THE YEAR OF THE SPY

1. Glickman interview, p. 62.
2. *Washington Post,* September 25, 1994.
3. Details on the Yurchenko defection can be found in David Wise, *The Spy Who Got Away* (London: Fontana, 1988); Ronald Kessler, *The FBI* (New York: Pocket Books, 1993); Mark Riebling, *Wedge* (New York: Alfred A. Knopf, 1994).
4. *Moscow News,* November 25–December 1, 1994.
5. Associated Press, May 8, 1994.
6. *Newsweek,* March 7, 1994, p. 30.
7. Interview with Bob Gates, January 8, 1995.
8. *Moscow News,* November 25–December 1, 1994.
9. *Washington Post,* February 27, 1994.
10. *Time,* March 7, 1994, p. 28.
11. Interview with Rosario Ames, September 21, 1994.

12. DeConcini interview, p. 19.
13. *Washington Post*, March 6, 1994; *Times* (London), July 10, 1990.
14. *New York Times*, February 24, 1994; *Minneapolis Star Tribune*, February 24, 1994.
15. *Washington Post*, December 17, 1994.
16. DeConcini interview, pp. 38–39.

CHAPTER 10 DEFENDING THE FAITH

1. Senate Intelligence Committee Report, p. 29.
2. Ibid.
3. Interview with John Lewis, January 26, 1995.
4. Interview with Oleg Gordievsky, September 2, 1994.
5. *New York Times*, July 28, 1994.
6. Interview with Bob Gates, January 8, 1995.
7. Ibid.
8. Ibid.
9. Interview with Milton Bearden, January 26, 1995.
10. Senate Intelligence Committee Report, pp. 27–28.
11. Ibid.
12. Interview with Bob Gates, January 8, 1995.
13. Interview with Myra Myers, August 25, 1994; *Washington Post*, May 24, 1986.
14. Ibid.
15. Rachel Ames, Last Will and Testament, September 13, 1971.
16. Interview with Charles Dixon, August 31, 1994.
17. *Chicago Tribune*, March 7, 1994.
18. Ibid.
19. Ibid.
20. *Los Angeles Times*, February 12, 1992; United Press International, February 7, 1992.
21. *St. Petersburg Times*, February 8, 1992.
22. *Chicago Tribune*, March 7, 1994.
23. *New York Times*, February 12, 1992; United Press International, February 7, 1992.
24. *Chicago Tribune*, March 7, 1994.
25. Ibid.
26. *Commentary*, May 1, 1994.
27. Interviews with CIA and FBI sources who asked not to be named.
28. Ibid.
29. *Washington Post*, April 27, 1994.
30. Ibid.
31. Interviews with CIA and FBI sources who asked not to be named.
32. Senate Intelligence Committee Report, p. 32.
33. James K. Murphy, "The Polygraph Technique Past and Present," *FBI Law Enforcement Bulletin*, June 1980, pp. 1–5.
34. *Minneapolis Star Tribune*, April 5, 1994.

35. Interview with Professor William Iacono, December, 7, 1994.
36. Murphy, "The Polygraph Technique," op. cit.
37. Interview with Professor William Iacono, December 7, 1994.
38. *New York Times,* February 24, 1994.
39. *U.S. News & World Report,* July 4, 1994.
40. Murphy, "The Polygraph Technique," op. cit.
41. Interview with Professor William Iacono, December 7, 1994.

CHAPTER 11   LA DOLCE VITA

1. Senate Intelligence Committee Report, p. 35.
2. DeConcini interview, pp. 78–79.
3. *New York Times,* July 28, 1994.
4. Unless otherwise specified, details of the Lonetree case come from *Time,* February 20, 1989, p. 50; *Washington Post,* February 7, 1988. The *Time* article was drawn from Ronald Kessler's book *Moscow Station* (New York: Scribners, 1989).
5. *Los Angeles Times,* October 22, 1987.
6. *Minneapolis Star Tribune,* October 1, 1994.
7. *Washington Times,* September 28, 1994.
8. CIA IG Report, p. 4.
9. Ibid.
10. Ibid.
11. Senate Intelligence Committee Report, p. 45.
12. *Los Angeles Times,* January 27, 1995.
13. CIA IG Report, p. 45.
14. Interview with FBI source, January 25, 1995.
15. Senate Intelligence Committee Report, p. 46.
16. Ibid.
17. Ibid.
18. Interview with William Webster, November 7, 1994.
19. Ibid.
20. Ibid.
21. Interview with William Webster, February 7, 1995.
22. Senate Intelligence Committee Report, p. 50.

CHAPTER 12   FRUSTRATING MARRIAGES

1. *Washington Post,* September 24, 1994.
2. Senate Intelligence Committee Report, p. 37.
3. Senate Intelligence Committee Report, p. 37.
4. DeConcini interview, p. 31.
5. *Minneapolis Star Tribune,* March 2, 1994.
6. *U.S. News & World Report,* March 14, 1994.

7. Senate Intelligence Committee Report, p. 36.
8. Ibid.
9. *U.S. News & World Report*, August 15, 1994.
10. Interview with Mark Mansfield of the CIA, December 18, 1994.
11. Indictment, p. 23.
12. Senate Intelligence Committee Report, pp. 39–40.
13. Senate Intelligence Committee Report, p. 39.
14. Interview with Vincent Cannistraro, June 27, 1994.
15. *Time*, March 7, 1994.
16. Indictment, p. 18.
17. Ibid.
18. Ibid.
19. Indictment, pp. 18–19.
20. Senate Intelligence Committee Report, p. 39.
21. Ibid.
22. CIA IG Report.
23. Senate Intelligence Committee Report, p. 40.
24. Ibid.
25. DeConcini interview, pp. 77–78.
26. *Washington Post*, September 24, 1994.
27. *Washington Post*, October 19, 1994.
28. Ibid.
29. Interview with Vincent Cannistraro, June 27, 1994.
30. Interview with Rosario Ames, September 21, 1994.
31. Interview with Dr. Ronald Moglia, December 13, 1994.
32. Interview with Dr. Bonnie Anthony, December 12, 1994.
33. Indictment, p. 19.
34. Indictment, pp. 19–20.
35. Interview with Mark Hulkower, December 2, 1994; *Minneapolis Star Tribune*, March 2, 1994.

CHAPTER 13 RETURN TO BASE

1. *Washington Post*, September 24, 1994.
2. Interview with Milton Bearden, January 26, 1995.
3. Senate Intelligence Committee Report, p. 54.
4. Interview with William Rhoads, June 10, 1994.
5. Ibid.
6. Ibid.
7. Ibid.
8. Interview with Tommye Morton, June 14, 1994.
9. *Washington Post*, March 8, 1994.
10. Interview with William Rhoads, June 10, 1994; interview with Tommye Morton, June 14, 1994.

11. *Washington Post*, February 25, 1994.
12. *Time*, March 7, 1994.
13. Ibid.
14. Ibid.
15. Ibid.
16. Interview with Jacqueline Clark, December 16, 1994; *Time*, March 7, 1994.
17. *New York Times*, March 8, 1994.
18. Senate Intelligence Committee Report, p. 65.
19. Ibid.
20. Interview with Bob Gates, January 8, 1995.
21. Senate Intelligence Committee Report, p. 65.
22. Interview with Milton Bearden, January 26, 1995.
23. Senate Intelligence Committee Report, p. 66.
24. CIA IG Report, p. 10.
25. Interview with Dave Christian, Office of Public Affairs, CIA, August 17, 1994.
26. Senate Intelligence Committee Report, p. 55.
27. Interview with Milton Bearden, January 26, 1995.
28 Senate Intelligence Committee Report, p. 55.
29. Senate Intelligence Committee Report, pp. 55–56.
30. Senate Intelligence Committee Report, pp. 55–56.
31. Senate Intelligence Committee Report, p. 56.
32. Interview with Milton Bearden, January 26, 1995.
33. Interview with Bob Gates, January 8, 1995.
34. Senate Intelligence Committee Report, p. 120.
35. *U.S. News & World Report*, March 14, 1994.
36. Interview with Milton Bearden, January 26, 1995.
37. Ibid.
38. Indictment, p. 21.
39. S.2726 to Improve U.S. Counter Intelligence Measures, Select Committee on Intelligence of the United States Senate, U.S. Government Printing Office, 1991, pp. 84–85.
40. Ibid.

CHAPTER 14 THE NOOSE TIGHTENS

1. Senate Intelligence Committee Report, p. 70.
2. Ibid., p. 71.
3. *Washington Post*, March 11, 1994.
4. Senate Intelligence Committee Report, p. 72.
5. *New York Times*, March 8, 1994.
6. Ibid.
7. Ibid.
8. *Washington Post*, March 6, 1994.
9. Ibid.

10. Senate Intelligence Committee Report, p. 75.
11. Ibid.
12. Indictment, p. 21.
13. *Washington Post*, February 25, 1994.
14. Indictment, p. 21.
15. Interview with Mark Hulkower, December 2, 1994.
16. Indictment, p. 22.
17. Ibid.
18. *Los Angeles Times*, March 12, 1994.
19. Ibid.
20. Annual Report of the Financial Crimes Enforcement Network, September 1993.
21. Interview with Anna Fotias, Financial Crimes Enforcement Network, August 31, 1994.
22. Ibid.
23. Ibid.
24. Interview with Jerry Rowe, Internal Revenue Service, September 14, 1994.
25. Glickman interview, pp. 76–77.
26. Indictment, p. 22.
27. Indictment, p. 2.
28. Interview with Dave Christian, August 17, 1994.
29. Interview with CIA source, May 5, 1994.
30. *Washington Post*, April 27, 1994.
31. Ibid.
32. Senate Intelligence Committee Report, p. 78.
33. Ibid., p. 81.

CHAPTER 15 DISCOVERY

1. Interview with Les Wiser, January 26, 1995.
2. Interview with FBI sources, January 26, 1995; *Washington Post*, February 24, 1994.
3. Interview with FBI sources, January 26, 1995.
4. Indictment, pp. 23–24.
5. Indictment, p. 24.
6. Indictment, p. 23.
7. Affidavit, p. 31.
8. Affidavit, Attachment C.
9. Indictment, pp. 24–25.
10. Interview with Dick Swanson, co-owner of Germaine's, January 27, 1995.
11. Interview with Rosario Ames, October 14, 1994.
12. *Washington Post*, October 19, 1994.
13. Indictment, p. 25.
14. Indictment, p. 26; *Washington Post*, April 29, 1994.
15. Indictment, p. 27.

16. *Los Angeles Times*, January 26, 1995.

17. Ronald Kessler, *The FBI* (New York: Pocket Books, 1993), p. 292.

18. Interview with FBI source, January 25, 1995.

19. Information on the hunt comes from interviews with Bob Bryant, John Lewis, and Les Wiser on January 26, 1995; *Los Angeles Times*, February 24, 1994, and January 27, 1995; *New York Times*, October 2, 1994; and FBI sources interviewed January 25, 1995.

20. Interview with Les Wiser, January 26, 1995.

21. Indictment, p. 31.

22. *Washington Post*, April 27, 1994.

23. CIA IG Report, p. 18.

24. *Washington Times*, March 15, 1994.

25. Ibid.

26. Ibid.

27. Indictment, p. 32.

28. Associated Press, April 20, 1994; Affidavit, p. 32.

29. Ibid.

30. Ibid.

31. *Washington Post*, February 26, 1993; May 17, 1993.

32. Ronald Kessler, *The FBI*, op. cit.

33. Document supplied by FBI, January 26, 1995.

34. Indictment, p. 32.

35. Indictment, p. 33.

36. Indictment, p. 33.

37. Indictment, p. 33.

38. Affidavit, February 21, 1994.

39. *Time*, March 3, 1994.

40. Interview with FBI sources, January 26, 1995.

41. Indictment, p. 34.

42. Affidavit, p. 14.

43. Affidavit, p. 14.

44. Affidavit, p. 13.

45. *Time*, March 7, 1994.

46. Affidavit, February 21, 1994, p. 13.

47. Ibid.

48. Indictment, p. 35.

49. Indictment, p. 35.

50. Affidavit, pp. 13–14.

51. Indictment, p. 36.

52. Indictment, pp. 36–37.

53. Indictment, pp. 36–37.

CHAPTER 16 DENIAL

1. *Cleveland Plain Dealer*, March 3, 1994.
2. *Washington Post*, March 8, 1994.
3. Interview with Nancy Everly, August 25, 1994.
4. *Washington Post*, May 7, 1994.
5. Ibid.
6. Associated Press, April 26, 1994; *Washington Post*, March 4, 1994.
7. Government Opposition to Defendant's [Rosario] Motion for Pre-trial Release.
8. *Washington Post*, February 23, 1994.
9. Interview with CIA source, November 1994.
10. *Wall Street Journal*, February 23, 1994.
11. Associated Press, March 10, 1994.
12. Ibid.
13. *Washington Times*, February 23, 1994.
14. UPI, March 6, 1994.
15. Defendant Aldrich Hazen Ames Opposition to the Government's Motion for Defendant's Pretrial Detention.
16. Ibid.
17. Government's Opposition to Defendant's [Rosario's] Motion for Pretrial Release.
18. Ibid.
19. Government's Opposition to Defendant's [Rick's] Motion for Pretrial Release.
20. Interview with Mark Hulkower, December 2, 1994.
21. *Washington Post*, July 7, 1994.
22. *Washington Post*, October 19, 1994.
23. Ibid.
24. Interview with Rosario Ames, September 14, 1994.
25. *Washington Post*, April 29, 1994.
26. Ibid.
27. *Washington Post*, July 26, 1994.
28. Interview with Senior Intelligence Officer, February 3, 1995.
29. Interview with CIA source, February 2, 1995.
30. Interview with FBI sources, January 26, 1995.
31. Ibid.; John Hume, "Sentencing Memorandum," October 20, 1994.
32. *Semana*, September 13, 1994; *Washington Post*, October 19, 1994.
33. *Washington Times*, October 22, 1994.
34. *New York Times*, October 22, 1994; *Washington Post*, October 22, 1994.
35. Interview with Rosario Ames, February 9, 1995.
36. Interview with Les Wiser, January 26, 1995.
37. Associated Press, December 1, 1994; *New York Times*, December 2, 1994.
38. Associated Press, December 1, 1994.

CHAPTER 17 WHITEWASH WEDNESDAY

1. Interview with Bob Gates, January 8, 1995.
2. Ibid.
3. Ibid.
4. *Washington Post,* October 22, 1993.
5. *Sunday Times of London,* October 24, 1993.
6. Interview with CIA source, September 22, 1994.
7. *Washington Times,* April 21, 1993; *New York Times,* April 15, 1993; *Los Angeles Times,* March 3, 1993; *Time,* January 9, 1995, p. 36.
8. Interview with Senator Dennis DeConcini, October 19, 1994.
9. *Washington Times,* January 21, 1995.
10. *New York Times,* March 11, 1994.
11. White House press release on Counter Intelligence Center, May 3, 1994.
12. *Washington Times,* January 21, 1995.
13. *Washington Post,* April 29, 1994.
14. *Washington Post,* July 24, 1994; *Washington Post,* July 19, 1994.
15. *Chicago Tribune,* July 19, 1994; *New York Times,* July 19, 1994; *Washington Post,* July 19, 1994; James Woolsey, "National Security and the Future Direction of the Central Intelligence Agency," address at the Center for Strategic and International Studies, July 18, 1994.
16. The details of Janine Brookner's case come from the following sources: *Jane Doe Thompson v. R. James Woolsey et. al.,* court papers filed at U.S. District Court for the Eastern District of Virginia, October 25, 1994; *Newsweek,* September 26, 1994, p. 43; *Facts on File,* September 22, 1994; *Washington Post,* September 7, 1994, September 9, 1994; *New York Times,* September 14, 1994.
17. CIA IG Report.
18. CIA IG Report; *Washington Post,* September 24, 1994; *Washington Post,* September 18, 1994.
19. CIA IG Report; *Washington Post,* September 14, 1994.
20. *Washington Post,* September 14, 1994.
21. Ibid.
22. CIA IG Report; *Washington Post,* October 22, 1994.
23. CIA IG Report; *Washington Post,* September 29, 1994.
24. *New York Times,* September 25, 1994.
25. *Washington Times,* September 29, 1994.
26. James Woolsey, statement to the press, U.S. House of Representatives, September 28, 1994.
27. *New York Times,* September 30, 1994.
28. *Washington Times,* September 29, 1994.
29. Ibid.; *New York Times,* September 29, 1994; *Washington Post,* September 25, 1994.
30. CIA IG Report, p. 18.
31. *Washington Times,* October 1, 1994.

32. *Washington Post,* September 29, 1994.
33. Associated Press, October 13, 1994; *New York Times,* October 13, 1994; *Washington Post,* October 14, 1994.
34. *Washington Post,* October 27, 1994.
35. James Woolsey, statement to the press, U.S. House of Representatives, September 28, 1994.
36. *New York Times,* September 29, 1994; Associated Press, November 1, 1994.
37. Associated Press, September 30, 1994.
38. *Washington Times,* September 29, 1994.
39. *Time,* January 9, 1995, p. 36.
40. Interview with Bob Gates, January 8, 1995.
41. Interview with Milton Bearden, January 26, 1995.
42. James Woolsey, statement to the press, U.S. House of Representatives, September 28, 1994.
43. Associated Press, December 28, 1994.

CHAPTER 18 REFORM OR DIE

1. Interview with Bob Gates, January 8, 1995.
2. James Adams, *The New Spies* (London: Hutchinson, 1994), pp. 52–54.
3. Interview with Bob Gates, January 14, 1992.
4. *Defense News,* June 15, 1992; *Aviation Week and Space Technology,* June 8, 1992; *Los Angeles Times,* October 16, 1992.
5. Interview with Bill Webster, January 17, 1992.
6. Interview with John Pike, Federation of American Scientists, January 24, 1994.
7. Hearing on Intelligence Reorganization, Senate Select Committee on Intelligence, March 21, 1991.
8. Interview with Senator Dennis DeConcini, October 19, 1994.
9. Interview with Brent Scowcroft, November 23, 1994.
10. Interview with Bob Gates, January 8, 1995.
11. *Washington Post,* July 21, 1994; *Wall Street Journal,* August 10, 1994.
12. *Washington Post,* December 10, 1994, and January 30, 1995.
13. Interview with Bob Gates, December 22, 1994.
14. *New York Times,* September 28, 1994; *Washington Post,* August 5, 1994.
15. *Washington Post,* August 5, 1994; *Wall Street Journal,* September 26, 1994; *Washington Post,* November 1, 1994; *Washington Post,* July 17, 1994.

BIBLIOGRAPHY

Adams, James. *The New Spies*. London: Hutchinson, 1994.

Allen, Thomas B., and Norman Polmar. *Merchants of Treason: America's Secrets for Sale*. New York: Delacorte, 1988.

Andrew, Christopher, and Oleg Gordievsky. *Instructions from the Centre: Top Secret Files on KGB Foreign Operations 1975–1985*. London: Hodder and Stoughton, 1991.

———. *KGB: The Inside Story*. New York: HarperCollins, 1990.

Ball, Desmond. *Soviet Signals Intelligence (SIGINT)*. Canberra, Australia: Strategic and Defence Studies Centre Research School of Pacific Studies, 1989.

Bamford, James. *The Puzzle Palace: Inside the National Security Agency, America's Most Secret Intelligence Organization*. New York: Penguin Books, 1983.

Barron, John. *KGB Today: The Hidden Hand*. New York: Reader's Digest Press, 1983.

Beschloss, Michael R., and Strobe Talbott. *At the Highest Levels: The Inside Story of the End of the Cold War*. Boston: Little, Brown, 1993.

Bethell, Nicholas. *Spies and Other Secrets: Memoirs from the Second Cold War*. London: Viking, 1994.

Bittman, Ladislav. *The KGB and Soviet Disinformation*. Washington, D.C.: Pergamon-Brassey's, 1985.

Blake, George. *No Other Choice*. London: Jonathan Cape, 1990.

Blum, Howard. *I Pledge Allegiance . . . The True Story of the Walkers: An American Spy Family*. New York: Simon & Schuster, 1987.

Bower, Tom. *The Red Web: MI6 and the KGB Master Coup*. London: Aurum Press, 1989.

Boyle, Andrew. *The Climate of Treason*. London: Hodder and Stoughton, 1979.

Breckinridge, Scott D. *The CIA and the U.S. Intelligence System*. Boulder, Colo.: Westview Press, 1986.

Brook-Shepherd, Gordon. *The Storm Birds: Soviet Post-War Defectors.* London: Weidenfeld and Nicolson, 1988.

Cavendish, Anthony. *Inside Intelligence.* London: Collins, 1990.

Corson, William B., Susan B. Trento, and Joseph J. Trento. *Widows: Four American Spies, the Wives They Left Behind and the KGB's Crippling of Western Intelligence.* New York: Crown, 1989.

Costello, John, and Oleg Tsarev. *Deadly Illusions.* New York: Crown, 1993.

Dailey, Brian D., and Patrick J. Parker, eds. *Soviet Strategic Deception.* Lexington, Mass.: Lexington Books, 1987.

Deriabin, Peter, and T. H. Bagley. *The KGB: Masters of the Soviet Union.* London: Robson Books, 1990.

Earley, Peter. *Family of Spies: Inside the John Walker Spy Ring.* New York: Bantam, 1988.

Epstein, Edward Jay. *Deception: The Invisible War Between the KGB and the CIA.* London: W. H. Allen, 1989.

Freemantle, Brian. *KGB.* New York: Henry Holt, 1984.

Gelb, Norman. *The Berlin Wall.* London: Michael Joseph, 1986.

Godson, Roy, ed. *Intelligence Requirements for the 1980's: Covert Action.* Washington, D.C.: National Strategy Information Center, 1981.

———. *Intelligence Requirements for the 1980's: Clandestine Collection.* Washington, D.C.: National Strategy Information Center, 1982.

———. *Intelligence Requirements for the 1990's: Collection, Analysis, Counterintelligence, and Covert Action.* Lexington, Mass.: Lexington Books, 1989.

Higgins, Trumbull. *The Perfect Failure: Kennedy, Eisenhower, and the CIA at the Bay of Pigs.* New York: W. W. Norton, 1987.

Hyde, H. Montgomery. *George Blake, Superspy.* London: Constable, 1987.

Jeffreys-Jones, Rhodri. *The CIA and American Democracy.* New Haven: Yale University Press, 1989.

Johnson, Loch K. *America's Secret Power: The CIA in a Democratic Society.* New York: Oxford University Press, 1989.

Kalugin, Oleg. *The First Directorate.* New York: St. Martin's Press, 1994.

Kessler, Ronald. *Inside the CIA: Revealing the Secrets of the World's Most Powerful Spy Agency.* New York: Pocket Books, 1992.

———. *The Spy in the Russian Club.* New York: Scribner, 1990.

Leigh, David. *The Wilson Plot: The Intelligence Services and the Discrediting of a Prime Minister, 1945–1976.* London: Heinemann, 1988.

McClintock, Michael. *Instruments of Statecraft: U.S. Guerrilla Warfare, Counterinsurgency, and Counterterrorism, 1940–1990.* New York: Pantheon, 1992.

McGehee, Ralph W. *Deadly Deceits: My 25 Years in the CIA.* New York: Sheridan Square Publications, 1983.

Mangold, Tom. *Cold Warrior, James Jesus Angleton: The CIA's Master Spy Hunter.* London: Simon & Schuster, 1991.

Marchetti, Victor, and John D. Marks. *The CIA and the Cult of Intelligence.* New York: Dell Publishing, 1974.

O'Toole, G. J. A. *Honorable Treachery: A History of U.S. Intelligence, Espionage, and Covert Action from the American Revolution to the CIA.* New York: Atlantic Monthly Press, 1991.

Perry, Mark. *Eclipse: The Last Days of the CIA.* New York: William Morrow, 1992.

Persico, Joseph E. *Casey: From the OSS to the CIA.* New York: Penguin, 1990.

Philby, Kim. *My Silent War: The Autobiography of Kim Philby.* London: Grafton, 1989.

Pincher, Chapman. *The Secret Offensive, Active Measures: A Saga of Deception, Disinformation, Subversion, Terrorism, Sabotage and Assassination.* London: Sidgwick & Jackson, 1985.

Power, Thomas. *The Man Who Kept the Secrets: Richard Helms and the CIA.* New York: Alfred A. Knopf, 1979.

Prados, John. *Keepers of the Keys: A History of the National Security Council from Truman to Bush.* New York: William Morrow, 1991.

―――. *Presidents' Secret Wars: CIA and Pentagon Covert Operations Since World War II.* New York: William Morrow, 1986.

Ranelagh, John. *The Agency: The Rise and Decline of the CIA, from Wild Bill Donovan to William Casey.* New York: Simon & Schuster, 1986.

Raviv, Dan, and Yossi Melman. *Every Spy a Prince: The Complete History of Israel's Intelligence Community.* Boston: Houghton Mifflin Company, 1990.

Richelson, Jeffrey T. *American Espionage and the Soviet Target.* New York: William Morrow, 1987.

―――. *Foreign Intelligence Organizations.* Cambridge, Mass.: Ballinger, 1988.

―――. *Sword and Shield: Soviet Intelligence and Security Apparatus.* Cambridge, Mass.: Ballinger, 1986.

―――. *The U.S. Intelligence Community.* Cambridge, Mass.: Ballinger, 1985.

―――. *The U.S. Intelligence Community.* 2nd ed. Cambridge, Mass.: Ballinger, 1989.

Riebling, Mark. *Wedge: The Secret War Between the FBI and CIA.* New York: Alfred A. Knopf, 1994.

Robertson, K. G. *British and American Approaches to Intelligence.* London: Macmillan, 1987.

Romerstein, Herbert, and Stanislav Lavchenko. *The KGB Against the "Main Enemy": How the Soviet Intelligence Service Operates Against the United States.* Lexington, Mass.: Lexington Books, 1989.

Rositzke, Harry. *The CIA's Secret Operations: Espionage, Counterespionage, and Covert Action.* Boulder, Colo.: Westview Press, 1977.

―――. *The KGB: The Eyes of Russia.* London: Sidgwick & Jackson, 1981.

Runde, Carl Peter, and Greg Voss, eds. *Intelligence and the New World Order: Former Cold War Adversaries Look Toward the 21st Century.* Buxtehude, Germany: International Freedom Foundation, 1992.

Schecter, Jerrold L., and Peter S. Deriabin. *The Spy Who Saved the World: How a Soviet Colonel Changed the Course of the Cold War.* New York: Scribner, 1992.

Shulsky, Abram N. *Silent Warfare: Understanding the World of Intelligence.* Washington, D.C.: Brassey's, 1991.

Stockwell, John. *In Search of Enemies: A CIA Story.* New York: W. W. Norton, 1978.

Treverton, Gregory F. *Covert Action: The Limits of Intervention in the Postwar World.* London: I. B. Tauris, 1989.

Tuck, Jay. *High Tech Espionage: How the KGB Smuggles NATO's Strategic Secrets to Moscow.* London: Sidgwick & Jackson, 1986.

Turner, Stansfield. *Secrecy and Democracy: The CIA in Transition.* Boston: Houghton Mifflin, 1985.

Watson, Bruce W., Susan M. Watson, and Gerald W. Hopple, eds. *United States Intelligence: An Encyclopedia.* New York: Garland, 1990.

Wise, David. *Molehunt: The Secret Search for Traitors That Shattered the CIA.* New York: Random House, 1992.

————. *The Spy Who Got Away.* New York: Avon, 1989.

Woodward, Bob. *Veil: The Secret Wars of the CIA, 1981–1987.* New York: Pocket Books, 1988.

Wright, Peter. *Spycatcher: The Candid Autobiography of a Senior Intelligence Officer.* New York: Viking, 1987.

INDEX